A Common Country

A Common Country

Solidarity and the Making of American Democracy

Nathan Pippenger

OXFORD
UNIVERSITY PRESS

Oxford University Press is a department of the University of Oxford.
It furthers the University's objective of excellence in research, scholarship,
and education by publishing worldwide. Oxford is a registered trade mark of
Oxford University Press in the UK and in certain other countries.

Published in the United States of America by Oxford University Press
198 Madison Avenue, New York, NY 10016, United States of America.

© Oxford University Press 2025

All rights reserved. No part of this publication may be reproduced, stored in a retrieval system,
transmitted, used for text and data mining, or used for training artificial intelligence, in any form or
by any means, without the prior permission in writing of Oxford University Press, or as expressly
permitted by law, by license or under terms agreed with the appropriate reprographics rights
organization. Inquiries concerning reproduction outside the scope of the above should be sent
to the Rights Department, Oxford University Press, at the address above.

You must not circulate this work in any other form
and you must impose this same condition on any acquirer.

CIP data is on file at the Library of Congress

ISBN 9780197811740

ISBN 9780197811733 (hbk.)

DOI: 10.1093/9780197811771.001.0001

Paperback printed by Marquis, Canada

Hardback printed by Bridgeport National Bindery, Inc., United States of America

Contents

Acknowledgments vi

    Introduction 1

PART I. THEORY AND HISTORY

1. Identification and the Psychology of Democratic Citizenship 13
2. American Democracy Between the First and Second Reconstructions 37

PART II. APPLICATIONS

3. Migration, Membership, and Democracy 59
4. Racial Integration and the Project of National Definition 82
5. Inequality, Citizenship, and the Permanent Tax Revolt 113
    Conclusion: Reconstruction Revisited 138

Notes 144
Bibliography 181
Index 197

Acknowledgments

This book originated as a dissertation at UC Berkeley, and thanks are owed, first of all, to the members of my dissertation committee: Sarah Song, Mark Bevir, Shannon Stimson, and Chris Kutz. They guided this project with patience and trust, improved my arguments with unfailing acuity and careful engagement, and made prescient suggestions that improved and clarified my work. It was a privilege to learn from them.

Berkeley is home to an amazing community of political theorists, intellectual historians, philosophers, and other scholars whose work is a daily example of what great public institutions can achieve. I am fortunate to have had so many talented graduate colleagues who shared their time and expertise: Nabil Ansari, Richard Ashcroft, Rachel Bernhard, Ali Bond, Andrius Gališanka, Jake Grumbach, Nina Hagel, Julian Jonker, Brian Judge, Michaeljit Sandhu, Geoff Upton, Rosie Wagner, and participants in the Graduate Political Theory Workshop convened by Kristin Zuhone and Thomas Lee. I also want to express my gratitude to several faculty members who took the time to discuss ideas and offer feedback, including Terri Bimes, Wendy Brown, Joshua Cohen, Kinch Hoekstra, David Hollinger, Daniel Lee, Eric Schickler, and Steve Vogel. Many other brilliant scholars helped me develop the ideas in this book. For this, thanks are owed to Peter Breiner, Jedediah Britton-Purdy, Daniela Cammack, Prithvi Dhatta, Kevin Duong, Becca Goldstein, David Grewal, Luke Mayville, Tim McCarty, Kevin Pham, Pierce Randall, Mitt Regan, Melissa Schwartzberg, Rogers Smith, Simon Stow, and Ronald Sundstrom. A section of this book was presented at the Georgetown University Political Theory Speaker Series; thanks to Mark Fisher and Stefan Eich for inviting me and to the attendees for their helpful comments. Thanks as well to conveners of the annual meetings of the American Political Science Association, the Association for Political Theory, and the Western Political Science Association, and to the chairs and discussants of the many panels where I received feedback on parts of the manuscript. At Oxford University Press, I am grateful to Dave McBride for shepherding the book through the review and publication process.

At the U.S. Naval Academy, I have benefited from a collegial and supportive department, and from generous support provided by the Naval

Academy Research Council, the Volgenau Fellowship, and the Miller Fellowship. For their guidance along the way, thanks are owed especially to Brendan Doherty, Howard Ernst, Mike Kellermann, Reza Malek-Madani, John Polga-Hecimovich, Dave Richardson, and Stephen Wrage. While I benefited from the support of the USNA, I want to note that all the views expressed in this book are mine, and do not reflect the official position of the U.S. Naval Academy, Department of Defense, or the U.S. government.

Some friends—especially E. J. Dionne, Jonathan Gould, Sean Hughes, and Conor Williams—deserve special thanks for years of intellectual support and friendship, which at many points sustained my writing process.

In a few places, this book features short passages that were previously published elsewhere, in somewhat different form. Parts of Chapter 1 and the Conclusion also appear in Nathan Pippenger, "Listening to Strangers, or: Three Arguments for Bounded Solidarity," *American Journal of Political Science* 67, no. 3 (July 2023): 764–775, https://doi.org/10.1111/ajps.12671; part of Chapter 3 appears in Nathan Pippenger, "From Openness to Inclusion: Toward a Democratic Approach to Migration Policy," *Perspectives on Politics* 22, no. 4 (Dec. 2024): 975-988, https://doi.org/10.1017/S153759272400001X; and part of Chapter 4, in Nathan Pippenger, "Agnosticism on Racial Integration: Liberal-Democratic or Libertarian?," *Political Research Quarterly* 76, no. 3 (Sep. 2023): 1196–1208, https://doi.org/10.1177/10659129221130296.

Finally, thanks are owed to my parents and sister, to my in-laws and to the Cordes and Selbin families, and to Jesse Cordes Selbin, who read the whole manuscript in nearly all of its iterations over the years, and whose brilliance, warmth, and generosity never waver. Along with so many others, she did much to improve this book; whatever errors it contains are mine alone. If Arthur and Zadie ever read it, I'm sure they won't hesitate to point them out to me.

Introduction

On November 19, 1867, Senator Charles Sumner of Massachusetts delivered a speech with an uneasy title: "Are We a Nation?" Without some measure of good fortune, he would not have been able to stand before an audience to pose the question at all. Eleven years earlier, the venerable abolitionist had been left bleeding and unconscious when Representative Preston Brooks of South Carolina—in furious retaliation for an antislavery speech Sumner had recently delivered—trapped him at his desk on the Senate floor and rained dozens of blows on his head with a metal-tipped cane.[1] Sumner spent three years in recovery. The violence of this incident, and the public's polarized reaction to it, reflected the sectional tensions that would soon explode into war: outraged Northerners arranged protest meetings in city after city, while grateful Southerners supplied Brooks with new canes, some bearing inscriptions such as "Hit him again."[2]

The war came. Now, Sumner was engaged in a new struggle over its meaning and legacy. Union victory had transformed the country utterly. The 13th Amendment, banning slavery, had been ratified in December 1865; in summer 1866, Congress passed the 14th Amendment, which was currently in the process of ratification in the states. Yet Sumner believed these measures did not go far enough, and his speech evinced little sense that the victorious Unionists could rest satisfied with their accomplishments. Rather, he implored his audience to "complete the good work" and achieve "final victory":

> Here I borrow a word from Locke, who, in his Essay on the Human Understanding says that, in dealing with propositions, we must always find on what they "bottom." Now, in dealing with the Rebellion, we find that though in the name of State Rights, it "bottomed" on opposition to the law of nature and an open denial of the self-evident truths declared by our Fathers, especially of that central truth of all, which Abraham Lincoln, at Gettysburg, in the most touching speech of all history thus announces: "Fourscore and seven years ago our fathers brought forth on this continent a New Nation, conceived in Liberty, and dedicated to the proposition that *all men are created equal.*" Slavery was "bottomed" on the direct opposite; and so was

A Common Country. Nathan Pippenger, Oxford University Press. © Oxford University Press (2025).
DOI: 10.1093/9780197811771.003.0001

the Rebellion, from beginning to end. Therefore you must encounter this denial. You do not extinguish Slavery; you do not trample out the Rebellion, until the vital truth declared by our Fathers is established and nature in her law is obeyed... Here must we plant the National standard.[3]

Sumner's words, which read almost as if the cannons were still firing, demonstrate how some of the victorious Unionists understood the deeper significance of their cause. Just as the cause of secession and rebellion did not actually "bottom" on dedication to states' rights as such, the cause of the Union did not bottom on devotion to federal supremacy as such. It was true that the Union's straightforward reason for war had been to maintain the supremacy of the federal government over the states: as Sumner explained, "The late Rebellion against the Nation was in the name of State Rights; therefore State Rights in their denationalizing pretensions must be overthrown."[4] But to explain the imperative of maintaining the Union, Sumner felt it necessary to draw a contrast between the rival visions of American peoplehood invoked by each side.

Like Lincoln, Sumner understood the American people to have been created by the Declaration of 1776. Throughout his career, Sumner's invocations of the Declaration consistently identified "two fundamental truths therein contained: first, that all men are equal in rights; and, secondly, that all just government stands only on the consent of the governed."[5] These two truths about equality and consent were no mere "idle words."[6] They had far-reaching implications, and they operated in tandem. In contrast to "the whole wretched pretension of oligarchy and monopoly by which citizens are deprived of equal rights,"[7] the Declaration announced a *republic*, and "the true idea of a Republic . . . is none other than a government where all citizens have an *equal voice*."[8] The denial of equal voice subjected citizens to laws in which they had no say, hollowing out the promise of a "free government" rooted in consent and replacing it with one imposed by mere force. Where "the *equal right of representation* . . . does not exist," Sumner concluded, "Liberty does not exist."[9]

If the government created by the Declaration owed its very legitimacy to the principle of equality, then the states could have no right to override that principle. Insofar as any state asserted such a right—to "disregard the universal rights of the citizen, and apply a discrimination according to its own local prejudices; thus within its borders nullifying the primal truths of the Declaration of Independence"[10]—it effectively announced that it was either superior to or separate from the political community that had been brought into being in 1776. For as Sumner explained, it was the Declaration through which "we were made 'one people,' solemnly dedicated to Human Rights."[11] When "the sovereignty of the mother country was forever renounced" in the name of equality, it was replaced with "the undivided sovereignty" of the newly formed American people, whose collective authority "embraced all the states as the other sovereignty had embraced all the colonies."[12] Properly understood, then, every state was bound to the egalitarian principle to which the revolutionaries had appealed for justification when they founded the new sovereign entity known as the United States. In this way, ultimate sovereignty belonged to the American people *collectively* rather than to each state *separately*.

As Sumner was eager to demonstrate, Reconstruction had finally afforded the opportunity to belatedly realize the egalitarian promise of 1776 by redrawing the boundaries of the American demos along the national lines that the Declaration implied, demolishing the shelters of oppression that had long been defended by appeals to the inviolable sovereignty of the states. The realization of equality was inextricably intertwined with the pursuit of "a common country": an ideal of American peoplehood that absorbed "local jealousies and geographical distinctions," in which there would be "no North, no South, no East, no West ... No single point of the compass, but the whole horizon will receive our regard."[13] "For better or worse we are all bound together in one indissoluble bond," Sumner asserted.[14] It is this conviction that explains Sumner's choice to title his remarks "Are We a Nation?" "Such is the question which I now propose," he announced to his audience, "believing as I do that the whole case is involved in the answer."[15]

It is difficult to overstate the importance of this transformation in Americans' understanding of their democracy. Americans had long debated the proper balance of national and state powers, and the political life of the early republic was deeply influenced by a Jeffersonian perspective that associated democracy with local self-rule. But the events of the Civil War era changed the democratic connotations of this debate. At the war's end, egalitarians attempted to use Union victory to transform democratic citizenship by subordinating America's influential localist tradition to a principled ideal of equality backed by a national constitution.[16] Sumner praised local self-government as an "incalculable advantage" to the American system, but he was insistent: "No local claim of self-government can for a moment interfere with the supremacy of the Nation, in the maintenance of Human Rights."[17] This unified sovereignty, he continued, "finds its counterpart and complement in the unity of citizenship, and the two together are the tokens of a united people. Thus are the essential conditions of national life all resolved into three; *One Sovereignty, One Citizenship, One People*."[18]

In short, Sumner believed that the United States would not democratize unless its people began to think of themselves as members of a common demos, reimagining their political association along the boundaries of the national state that was emerging from Reconstruction. This combination of commitments may appear strange to the contemporary eye, since the vocabulary of belonging in American politics today is dominated by self-identified nationalists who insist that Americans need to share a strong sense of common membership, but who demonstrate little commitment to either egalitarianism or democracy. In turn, and partly in response to this development, many egalitarians have grown suspicious of appeals to shared belonging—seeing them as outmoded, intolerant, and even potentially dangerous. Yet as Sumner's example suggests, this supposed tension between democratic ideals and a robust vision of shared membership reflects a limited historical perspective. If we adopt this limited perspective, we risk overlooking important aspects of the history of American democracy, misunderstanding its present crisis, and unwittingly limiting its possible futures. What this history shows is that we cannot begin to answer the basic political question of "how should we live together?" until we address an even more fundamental issue: Who, in the first place, is the "we" that is deciding what to do? Does an American demos exist (or did it ever)? Where do its boundaries lie? What is, or could be, its nature? Is it even a desirable object of aspiration?

It is little wonder that in late 1867, Sumner thought it essential to pose these questions in such explicit terms. Only the previous year, Congress had enacted (over President Johnson's veto) the Civil Rights Act of 1866, which established birthright citizenship—overturning the Supreme Court's ruling, in *Dred Scott v. Sandford*, that black people were ineligible for membership in the polity, and inaugurating a principle of inclusion that would soon be enshrined in the 14th Amendment. Then, in 1867, Congress went further, establishing (again over the president's veto) voting rights for black men in the former Confederacy, also later to be incorporated into the Constitution. As a leader of this radical phase of Reconstruction, Sumner stood at the forefront of an effort not only to dismantle a racist model of American citizenship but also to replace it with a viable form of belonging that would bring a genuine demos into being. Many of the figures who joined this broad effort to build American democracy over the next century realized that the legal and constitutional changes they sought would succeed only if they were paired with a far-reaching effort to expand the meaning of "We the People" so that it would include, for the first time, all (or nearly all) the people living in the United States. They hoped that promoting this robust and inclusive sense of peoplehood would lead Americans to see each other as fellow-members in a common demos and orient their political deliberations toward the needs and perspectives of all their compatriots. This struggle took place not only on the terrain of the nation's laws but also in its conceptions of common identity; its dominant historical narratives; its interpretations of foundational texts; and its oratory, poetry, art, and literature. Wherever exclusionary and hierarchical visions of membership in American society found expression, they sought to promote more democratic alternatives. Their distinctive vision was mobilized during every great expansion of American democracy: Reconstruction, the Progressive era and the New Deal, and the civil rights movement and Great Society.

This book aims to demonstrate the key role of this tradition in propelling America's fitful democratization in the century between Reconstruction and the civil rights movement, to reconstruct its basic philosophical framework, and to show that it still offers intellectual resources for reviving American democracy in its present moment of crisis.

The longer historical view taken here shows that the crisis now confronting American democracy did not appear suddenly; it is the culmination of decades of democratic unraveling. Today, nativism is again ascendant in the United States, where political rhetoric frequently echoes the anti-immigrant demagogues of the 1850s and 1920s. Ongoing social convulsions testify to an unfinished agenda of racial justice, while many of the spaces that activists risked their bodies to integrate have slowly become resegregated. Oligarchs wield immense power; meanwhile, profound inequality has been perversely sacralized as a sign of freedom. White supremacist ideology has returned from the margins to the mainstream.

All of these developments followed a reshaping of the American polity along more democratic, as well as more nationalized, lines in the 1960s—an era that has become known as the "Second Reconstruction." But like the First Reconstruction, whose end was hastened by the "Redeemers" of the defeated Confederacy, this latter-day attempt to democratize the United States was met with a backlash driven by racialized resentment and antipathy toward national power. Almost as soon as the Second Reconstruction had achieved its most important gains, the intellectual tradition that inspired it began to fall apart, the forces of reaction organized an effective countermovement, and the federal government—a crucial (if often cross-pressured and captured) organ of democratization since Lincoln—was on the verge of devastating losses in resources, credibility, and trust. The revolt against the Second Reconstruction has proven so durable that its apotheosis was not reached until well into the twenty-first century. (In a surfeit of symbolism, the Confederate battle flag, which never reached the U.S. Capitol during the Civil War, was flown inside the building on January 6, 2021—by an insurrectionist who carried it past a portrait of Charles Sumner and used it to attack a black Capitol police officer.)[19]

Now, armed with their own vision and vocabulary of membership, the anti-egalitarians who reshaped the American political landscape after the 1960s dominate public understandings of what it means to "belong" to the United States. This is particularly ironic since these contemporary champions of Americanism are openly contemptuous of most actually-existing Americans. As one writer affiliated with the contemporary nationalist right candidly declared: "Most people living in the United States today—certainly more than half—are not Americans in any meaningful sense of the term ... It is not obvious what we should call these citizen-aliens, these non-American Americans; but they are something else."[20]

In part, this reactionary appropriation was made possible by the fact that the democratic unraveling following the Second Reconstruction was met with a conspicuous absence where an alternative account of membership should have been. For nineteenth-century egalitarians like Sumner, the ideal of equality seemed to entail embracing American peoplehood over states' rights, but to many in the twentieth century, that same ideal seemed to entail embracing cosmopolitanism. This global scope was always part of the moral logic of egalitarianism: as Sumner had put it, "the rights which [the Declaration] promised and covenanted were the equal rights of all; not the rights of Englishmen, but the rights of man."[21] Yet it was not until well into the twentieth century that economic, political, and technological changes made it possible to imagine democratic politics liberated from the boundaries of states. In combination with reactionaries' seemingly successful effort to seize and redefine the meaning of membership in the United States, such developments led many egalitarians, in frustration and disillusionment, to cede the conceptual territory of membership. By the latter half of the twentieth century, the notion that democrats should dedicate special concern to the question of their membership in a broad American demos began to strike many thinkers as quaint, oppressive, chauvinistic, exclusionary, or simply ridiculous.

These skeptics ask a reasonable question: If our fundamental moral commitment to human equality is cosmopolitan in scope, does there remain any value in cultivating *particularistic* senses of political membership—especially given the global nature of so many contemporary problems? The answer, I think, is yes. It is not only possible but also necessary to affirm both cosmopolitan moral commitments and the value of particularistic forms of democratic belonging. A belief in the moral equality of persons finds political expression as support for democracy, since democracy is the form of government that enables people to live together in freedom and equality. In turn, if democracy is "government by discussion among equals," as Elizabeth Anderson has characterized it,[22] then it requires a form of bounded solidarity among all members of the demos, since the common political order to which they are all subject can only be governed democratically if they seek out each other's perspectives and give them special weight in the process of reaching collective decisions. Because the knowledge that informs a collective, democratic decision is not already in the world, awaiting discovery, citizens must cultivate a disposition to converse, listen, empathize, imagine, read, and so on, in ways that intersubjectively generate the perspective of a democratic "We." In this way, bounded solidarity is required to realize democracy's epistemic conditions and sustain the basic processes of collective self-rule. Endorsing this kind of solidarity does not require us to assign absolute moral priority to compatriots above foreigners or to deny that solidarity may, in some cases, transcend state boundaries. But it does entail the view that shared membership in a democratic state is a source of distinctive and significant obligations.[23]

Understood in this way, solidarity need not rest on any particular common trait among members of the demos, such as the various forms of shared identity (cultural, linguistic, ethnic, religious, etc.) proposed by a range of nationalist writers. Rather, democratic solidarity finds expression as shared *identification* among members of the demos. Identification is the common consciousness and mutual acknowledgment of belonging that enables a demos to collectively rule itself on terms of equality. It refers to dynamic processes that members commonly engage in but not to any specific characteristic that they all possess. Members of a demos can cultivate rich forms of identification even when they do not share any single characteristic in common.

Identification is not a purely subjective phenomenon: an individual does not become a member in the relevant sense simply by identifying as one. Nor is it an objective quality of membership generated by the possession of certain characteristics or legislated into existence by the state. It is an intersubjective phenomenon, arising if and only if the relevant parties identify one another as fellow-members. It is therefore part of the psychology of democratic citizenship: the way citizens imagine themselves and the other members of their political association. Because it is psychological, not legal, identification can be present even among people who are officially excluded from citizenship status, and it can be absent among people who all share the official status of citizenship. Democracy requires inclusion in both senses; it cannot be realized solely through formal institutions. The universal extension of citizenship throughout the state must be complemented by the universal extension of identification among all citizens.

As long as states exist, then, neither the force of cosmopolitan moral claims nor the reality of globalization obviate the need for visions of shared peoplehood. A cosmopolitan affirmation of human equality generates universal obligations that supplement, but do not supplant, the particularistic demands of democratic citizenship. And while globalization has transformed and expanded the connections of people across national borders, it has not altered the basic fact that fellow citizens of a democratic state remain linked in an especially significant kind of association—a vast web of institutional and social ties through which they shape their common life and exercise considerable power over one another. It remains urgent, then, to articulate visions of shared peoplehood that might bring these associations into alignment with democratic ideals. (Not only that; in some cases, even problems global in scope may in certain respects require the cultivation of more particularistic forms of solidarity. For example, while climate change obviously requires concerted global action, it is likely to drive migration flows that will increase the need for citizens in destination states to foster expansive forms of solidarity capable of incorporating new residents as equal citizens, not merely as denizens who are relegated, formally or informally, to subordinate status.)

For these reasons, the democratic tradition inaugurated during Reconstruction remains vital today, no matter how much it has receded from political imagination. Its proponents understood that to give an account of membership's *scope* was also to suggest an account of its *substance*. Citizenship meant one thing where the demos was defined by wealth, sex, race, or some other characteristic; quite another when the scope of membership extended to every individual residing within the country's borders. In attempting to convince Americans to adopt this expansive notion of shared peoplehood, the figures in this tradition were forced to engage in a project of interpretation and meaning-making. They could not claim that the American demos was an ancient national community, an unbroken lineage tracing back to heroic roots. Nor, even as they attempted to narrate a usable history that would serve their political ends, could they claim that the country's core identity had always been inclusive and democratic. There is no single, monolithic tradition of American peoplehood to revive; the more complicated reality is that dramatically different and incompatible definitions of the American demos have long contended for primacy in the United States. This fact required democratic reformers to candidly acknowledge that the

United States was an inheritance of both genuine liberatory promise and terrible oppression. As Frederick Douglass described the slave's portion of that inheritance to a white audience in 1852: "The sunlight that brought light and healing to you, has brought stripes and death to me."[24] For figures like Douglass, the achievement of a genuine American demos was not a feat to take pride in, but rather an ongoing effort of self-authorship that would come into existence only through the labor of its citizens.

Brief Outline of the Book

This book is divided into two parts. Part I develops a theoretical and historical account of democratic citizenship in the United States. In Chapter 1, I argue that democracy requires solidarity in the form of identification among citizens on the scale of the whole state, and I distinguish this theory of democratic solidarity from both patriotism and nationalism. Chapter 2 outlines how the distinctive tradition of democratic membership that embodied this theory of solidarity arose in the context of the Civil War and declined about a century later. To use the terms developed in this book, the promotion of identification among Americans was an attempt to secure the democratic ideal of collective self-rule on terms of equality. This vision of democratic solidarity generated a distinctive understanding of American citizenship that has eroded since the end of the Second Reconstruction.

Part II traces the consequences of that decline in three chapters that illustrate, across a range of overlapping conversations, the absence of an ideal of political belonging that could helpfully respond to a range of crises facing American democracy. These crises include the resurgence of nativism (Chapter 3), the reversal of civil rights–era gains in racial integration (Chapter 4), and economic inequalities that threaten to replace democracy with oligarchy (Chapter 5). These chapters attempt to diagnose some pathologies of contemporary political debate, and they suggest that the road to democratic repair lies in recovering a vision of solidarity that has been misconstrued and rejected. In the Conclusion, I note connections between the erosion of democratic solidarity and the resurgence of white nationalism, placing this trend in the context of widespread contemporary worries about democratic decline.

Each of the problems discussed in this book has deep roots in American history, but today those problems face a novel circumstance: the relative lack of voices seeking to mobilize a robust vision of American peoplehood in the service of democracy. In trying to link popular political discourse to theoretical foundations, I am by no means suggesting that public debate observes the norms of philosophical argument. The views that predominate in public discourse often don't fit coherently together; they betray our professed commitments. They often maintain only a tenuous connection to conceptual foundations that, if acknowledged, might help clarify and resolve seemingly intractable disagreements. There remains a gap between the debate we now have and the one we might achieve.

This book aims to narrow that gap, assuming that it is possible to locate in both our present and past conversations the ingredients for a better one. By analyzing the actual discourse we are having, we can also suggest the kind of discourse we *could* have: a reframing of political questions that is within reach for members of this community, participants in this conversation, and inheritors of these traditions of thought and action.[25] From the perspective of democratic theory, I think there are good reasons to hold on to some version of state-bounded membership. From the perspective of American history, I think that the reconstitution of American democracy will require a revived conception of peoplehood, of the sort that democratic reformers attempted during the First and Second Reconstructions.

The figures who pioneered a new vision of citizenship after the Civil War embraced an expansive vision of peoplehood not just as a rhetorical strategy but more as an account of democracy with drastic implications. Seeking to reconstruct the republic out of the wreckage of a sectional rebellion fought for the cause of slavery, they posed a stark challenge to their fellow citizens: they could complete the work and choose government of the people, by the people, and for the people—with its sweeping implications for the meaning of membership—or they could choose white supremacy. The choice that remains for us today is not so very different.

PART I
THEORY AND HISTORY

Chapter 1
Identification and the Psychology of Democratic Citizenship

Imagine that a small group of people is trying to decide what to have for lunch, and they have chosen to make their decision democratically. Because each member of the group knows the roster of the luncheon, they know exactly on whose behalf the group is deciding. This information makes it possible to gather information not only about the food preferences that are the direct object of the group's deliberation (e.g., salad or sandwiches) but also any relevant factors influencing those preferences (this person is on a tight budget; that person has food allergies; a third is an ethical vegetarian). Suppose also that members don't merely consult their *own* preferences but that they revise them through deliberation, in conjunction with the other members. The diners may inform each other about new restaurants with unique offerings, or they may learn new facts through discussion that cause them to moderate or change their initial preferences. One person may, for instance, drop their initial suggestion of milkshakes upon learning that another person is attempting to diet, because they decide on reflection that they want to support that person's healthy choices more than they want to satisfy their own desire for dessert. In addition, because the group regularly dines together, each member recalls the group's history of decisions and looks forward to many more such lunches, which makes it easier to resolve disagreements via compromise, since members can expect that flexibility today will be met with reciprocity in the future. Because members of the group behave in this way throughout the whole process of deliberation and decision-making, they all perceive the resulting choice as *the group's* choice—even the dissenters, who do not consider themselves powerless or less than equal simply because they disagreed with one particular outcome (and who, in any event, look forward to the possibility of crafting a winning coalition next time).

This illustration is intended to highlight some of the distinctive elements of democracy as I will define it in this book: as collective self-rule on terms of equality. Defined this way, democracy's appeal lies not only in the fact that it promises a certain kind of power to the people (to rule themselves by shaping their common life), but that it also promises this power on terms of equality, without privileging

A Common Country. Nathan Pippenger, Oxford University Press. © Oxford University Press (2025).
DOI: 10.1093/9780197811771.003.0002

some members of the demos over others. This notoriously difficult (but irrepressibly captivating) wager suggests that when, and only when, the people share power in common can they be free. Wendy Brown characterizes the ideal this way: "For the people to rule themselves, they must be a people and they must have access to the powers they would democratize... Only democracy can make us free because only in democracy do we author the powers that govern us."[1]

This definition makes it easier to see something significant about the foregoing illustration: almost *none* of its distinctive elements follow from the standard features of a democratic decision-making process as it is commonly understood. Contemporary understandings of democracy tend to emphasize a handful of familiar formal elements, all of which turn out to be insufficient to account for those aspects of the process that make binding decisions compatible with the ideal of collective self-rule on terms of equality. Dominant understandings of democracy tend to include, at minimum, the following three components:

1. the chance to rule and be ruled in turn (*participation*)
2. in a system that protects basic rights and liberties (*rights*)
3. and that recognizes and promotes citizens' equality (*equality*)

This list is limited to elements that most would consider essential: today, a democracy that denied its citizens either opportunities to participate, basic rights protections, or (at minimum, legal) equality would be considered seriously deficient. But taken on their own, these familiar components of democratic citizenship cannot account for some of the most important features of the foregoing scenario. To illustrate this point, imagine once again that a group of individuals is choosing what to have for lunch—but this time, the behavior of the group's members adheres solely to these three components of democratic citizenship.

In order to satisfy the demands of participation, rights, and equality, the members of the lunch group could simply take a vote. Suppose that every member receives exactly one vote and that each has the right to speak freely and advocate their preferred option. In other words, participation, rights, and equality—these key elements of democratic citizenship—are achieved. But their achievement by no means guarantees that the voters actually discuss their decision together, that they listen to one another, or that they incorporate into their deliberation the perspectives or interests of their fellow members. Their voting process could still be marked by ignorance, mutual indifference, or selfishness. To that extent, the decision would fall short of democratic ideals, for as Charles Taylor writes, in a democracy "it is not enough for a vote to record the fully formed opinions of all the members"; rather, citizens' opinions must "take shape or be reformed in the light of discussion, that is to say by exchange with others."[2] But this exchange and mutual refinement of views cannot be mandated by law. Members must cultivate a willingness to allow their own deliberation to be modified by an awareness that they live in a community with significant and multifaceted relations. Some may refuse to seek out or consider the views of others; they may even regard some participants as subordinate members whose views can be disregarded. Among our hypothetical lunch deliberators, there may exist a number of members whose preference for a certain restaurant is unaffected by the objections of other diners that its staff behaves in a racist manner toward them. A vegan friend, tired of choosing from the same limited options on meat-and-dairy heavy menus, might find their complaints laughed at or might be met with churlish suggestions to lighten up and enjoy the occasional cheeseburger. When this occurs, and some "subgroup ... considers that it is not being listened to by the rest, or that they are unable to understand its point of view, it will immediately consider itself excluded from joint deliberation," observes Taylor. "Anyone who is excluded can have no part in the decisions that emerge, and these consequently lose their legitimacy for the excluded."[3] From the perspective of such disregarded minorities, it is as if some alien power had made the decision without consulting them at all. But the risk here is not limited only to the perceived legitimacy of democratic decisions. Even if these disregarded members of the demos did *not* question the legitimacy of decisions that excluded them, we would still have no warrant to say that the collective decision reflects the will of the group as a whole or that it is consistent with members relating to each other on terms of equality.

On their own, participation, rights, and equality are thus insufficient to realize the democratic aspiration of self-rule among equals. This insufficiency suggests that democracy not only requires the satisfaction of certain *formal* criteria, but that it also requires members to adopt certain mindsets appropriate to democracy and to relate to each other in a certain way. I refer to this relational ideal as *identification*: the tendency of citizens to identify each other as members of the same demos. Identification describes a common consciousness and mutual acknowledgment of belonging that enables a demos to collectively rule itself on terms of equality—not because members share a static identity (in the sense of some common trait), but rather because they habitually identify one another as fellow members. Identification is a dynamic, intersubjective phenomenon that emerges from the shared life of the demos itself. On this broadened definition, democratic citizenship encompasses the following:

1. the chance to rule and be ruled in turn (*participation*)
2. in a system that protects basic rights and liberties (*rights*)
3. and that recognizes and promotes citizens' equality (*equality*)
   +
4. within a group of people who identify each other as members (*identification*)

My claim about the kind of mindset required by democracy draws on Elizabeth Anderson's observation that democracy "can be understood on three levels: as a membership organization, a mode of government, and a culture."[4] At the first level (membership organization), democracy "requires equality as well as inclusion"—it cannot tolerate a permanent class within society to which either political voice or citizenship is denied. At the second level (mode of government), Anderson defines democracy as "government by discussion *among equals*,"[5] writing: "Democracy requires that citizens from different walks of life *talk* to one another about matters of common interest, to determine what issues warrant collective action, what kinds of action might make sense, and who is most trusted to hold political office."[6] At the third level (culture), Anderson argues that "democratic institutions amount to little unless citizens enact, in their day-to-day interactions, a spirit of tolerant discussion and cooperation"[7]—creating a culture, chiefly located in the institutions of civil society, "where citizens from different walks of life communicate with each other, in ways that shape their sense of what their proper goals are *as a public*."[8] Anderson interprets the act of listening as an expression of respect and equality among citizens;[9] in that sense, a democratic culture (in which people cultivate the virtues of tolerance and cooperation) is practically necessitated by a view of democracy as government by discussion. Identification refers to the mindsets characteristic of such an inclusive and communicative democratic culture, one in which citizens elicit each other's perspectives and assign them special weight in their political reasoning.

Identification is the starting point of democratic self-rule. For a people to rule themselves democratically, it must be the case that the course of their common life is not dictated by a monarch, or by tradition, or by divine command, but is rather determined by the citizens themselves. But citizens cannot collectively determine their goals unless they understand themselves to have a common life in the first place. This is because political problems are not straightforward facts about the world; they are the products of collective interpretation, the results of successful efforts to show that some set of circumstances is not a natural or immutable state of affairs but a problem to be solved by public action. And political problems are always problems *for* some particular set of people: they are obstacles to a certain group's goals, or a violation of a certain group's principles, or a distribution of power or goods that ought to have gone to some people rather than others. Even decisions that have a prominent technical dimension, such as whether to change zoning rules to allow for denser housing or where to develop public transit, require making judgments among competing visions of society. These determinations unfold against a background of beliefs about the nature of the association, who belongs to it, and what it is trying to achieve. They cannot be made in an inclusive and egalitarian manner unless citizens first identify each other as members. In other words, identification makes political problems legible *as problems* in the first place. This implies a loosely constructivist view of the common good, wherein the "What" of political problems is inseparable from the "Who."

The willingness of citizens to extend identification to *all* their compatriots, as well as the array of deliberative practices that go along with that extension, produces the difference between a genuinely collective decision and a mere aggregation of atomistic preferences. As Jürgen Habermas writes, "The political process of opinion- and will-formation in the public sphere" can be analogized either to "the acts of choice made by participants in a market" or to "the obstinate structures of a public communication oriented to mutual understanding." While the analogy of voting as consumer choice remains a common way of understanding democracy, only the latter model "preserves the original meaning of democracy in terms of the institutionalization of a public use of reason jointly exercised by autonomous citizens," because it alone "accounts for those communicative conditions that confer legitimating force on political opinion- and will-formation." When citizens of a democracy fail to communicate and act only on the basis of their individual preferences, "politics loses all reference to the normative core of a public use of reason."[10] An aggregation of individual preferences neither reflects a collective perspective nor advances a collective intention, so it cannot advance collective self-rule. Nor does it secure the equality of the members except in the merest formal sense, because preferences formed in isolation are by definition insensitive to the views, needs, and interests of others. Insofar as the perspectives of other members present facts relevant to a collective decision, any individual's failure to consider them means that they are treating the collective decision as a vehicle for advancing their own personal interests, at the expense of others who will be subject to that decision. Stripped of adequate concern for fellow-members, such a civic posture amounts to using the law to render some individuals mere instruments of other individuals' private wills, which fails to treat them as equals. (It may also reflect an undemocratic devotion to hierarchy if citizens underweight the views of those who they deem inferior and grant excessive deference to the views of those they revere as supposedly superior.) The risk posed by such failures of collective will-formation is not reducible to familiar worries about the "tyranny of the majority," for majority rule may be compatible with domination and mutual alienation even when it does not specifically violate minority rights. A society in which citizens exercise power without regard for each other falls short of a genuinely collective, democratic form of self-rule, even if it satisfies other observable criteria of democracy (such as universal suffrage and frequent, free elections).

For these and other reasons, theorists of democracy have long resisted the simple equation of democracy with the act of voting. As John Dewey maintained, voting is only one stage in the decision-making process and by no means the most important one: "What is more significant," Dewey wrote, "is that counting of heads compels prior recourse to methods of discussion, consultation and persuasion."[11] Only when these processes are robust and inclusive are we justified in interpreting the result of a vote as more than the mere summation of individual preferences formed in isolation. On a small scale, these forms of interaction and communication are comparatively simple. But on the scale of a state, where most of the other parties to public decisions are strangers, citizens must cultivate a tendency to extend their concern for distant others—to identify them as fellow-members and treat them accordingly, even if they never meet.

In these ways, identification generates the epistemic conditions for a democratic way of life—not just at discrete, episodic moments, but over time in a durably constituted demos. Citizens who identify with each other not only have a sense of the other people on whose behalf they are deciding, but they also commit themselves to seeking out the perspectives of their compatriots and according them special weight in their reasoning through processes of imagination, debate, discussion, and so on. This generates a collective democratic perspective: "a 'we,'" as Anderson writes, "from the perspective of which cooperative goals are framed, and appropriate policies selected and implemented."[12] No formal democratic institution can prevent self-centeredness or guard entirely against mutual alienation, thereby guaranteeing that citizens will identify with their compatriots in this way. Democratic self-rule may require identification, but democratic states cannot enforce it. There is no necessary means by which it must arise from a population's objectively shared features (whether ethnicity, history, shared citizenship status, or anything else). Nor can it be generated subjectively by an individual's own state of mind, considered apart from what others think. The identification that transforms a citizenry into a genuine demos is neither objective nor subjective but intersubjective: it requires a shared state of mind to come into existence. A democracy requires its citizens to think of each other as citizens, just as a friendship requires two people to think of each other as friends.

To claim that something as demanding as identification is crucial to democracy is to acknowledge that even in regimes with stable laws and institutions, democratic citizenship is a complex and fragile achievement, perpetually dependent on the dispositions and mindsets of the demos. Its conditions are not realized simply whenever citizens share an "identity," understood as some static, homogeneous set of attributes.[13] Identification suggests something more active, processual, intersubjective, and open-ended: it is something citizens do. For that reason, worries about the elusiveness of a shared "identity" need to be approached carefully, lest they suggest that any common feature could *by itself* perform the democratic functions under discussion here. To suggest (e.g.) that a shared culture unites citizens is to mistakenly reify culture—to attribute to it the ability to perform actions in the world. But cultures don't perform actions; people do. Whether citizens identify with each other is ultimately determined not by any set of features they share but by what they collectively do.

At the same time, it is impossible for human actions to be meaningful in a vacuum; they are always situated in discourses and traditions.[14] Practices of identification aim at reception within a group of individuals, which is to say that they occur within a context, against the backdrop of some history. While tradition and culture cannot perform the work of binding citizens together, they furnish the vocabularies and frameworks of meaning in which citizens can successfully develop practices of identification with each other. Here, my identity/identification distinction borrows from Hanna Pitkin's discussion of the two senses of "constitution." The term "constitution," notes Pitkin, sometimes refers to "a characteristic way of life, the national character of a people, their ethos or fundamental nature as a people, a product of their particular history and social conditions"—in short, "less something we *have* than something we *are*."[15] Yet at other times, "constitution" functions differently, as "a verbal noun pointing to the action or activity of constituting—that is, of founding, framing, shaping something anew . . . neither something we have nor something we are so much as something we *do*—or at any rate can do."[16] These two senses of constitution—as something we *are* and something we *do*—are interrelated, for as Pitkin writes, the act of constituting is not "just doing whatever one pleases, the expression in action of just any impulse or appetite" but rather an attempt to "establish something that lasts, which, in human affairs, inevitably means something that will enlist and be carried forward by others," something that is "lasting, inclusive, principled, and fundamental."[17]

On this view, successful political action in a democracy requires a high degree of collective self-consciousness. We can create something lasting only with other people (but which people?); we must be inclusive (of whom?); we must be principled (according to whose principles?); we must do something fundamental (fundamental to whose shared life?). "So, although constituting is always a free action," Pitkin concludes, "how we are able to constitute ourselves is profoundly tied to how we are already constituted by our own distinctive history. Thus there is a sense, after all, in which our constitution is sacred and demands our respectful acknowledgement. If we mistake who we are, our efforts at constitutive action will fail."[18] My invocation of identification similarly appeals to a productive tension between what we *are* and what we *do* (or could do), acknowledging that how we can identify with each other is neither completely open-ended nor wholly outside our power to revise. Any effort to transform mutual relations in a lasting way must, as Pitkin notes, be "carried forward by others," and so these transformations cannot be imposed from above or simply dictated by one individual; they must resonate with the others who are meant to carry the work forward. Because humans are the creators of contexts and the makers of meaning, reconstitution is possible—even if it cannot occur outside of history, or on a whim, or in a way that is indifferent to the uptake and reception of other people. New forms of identification are cultivated within a field of possibilities shaped, but not determined, by how we have identified ourselves up to now.

By now, it should be evident that identification is the most abstract component of citizenship. As will become clear in the following chapters, it is also the most controversial to defend and the most likely to be excised from theoretical models of democracy. Yet the abandonment of identification comes at the cost of a core democratic aspiration—for to the extent that members of a demos fail to engage in practices of identification on the scale of their whole polity, they will fall short of democratic self-rule.

Identification, Boundaries, and Democratic Epistemology

So far, I have argued that political problems are always problems for particular groups of people, and that, similarly, the common good for a citizenry cannot be defined (beyond a very general level) unless we know who belongs to that citizenry. To give an account of political problems and the common good, then, the boundaries of the demos must be reasonably clear and durable. But where should such boundaries be drawn? As I discussed in the Introduction, the principle of democratic self-rule implies that the boundaries of the demos—and therefore, the scope of identification—should be coextensive with the boundaries of the state. In other words, while there are countless ways individuals might circumscribe the political "We" with which they identify, democratic ideals give us reason to mark out a special circle of concern for compatriots—not on the basis of their race, religion, culture, ethnicity, or any other factor, but simply because they are fellow citizens.

Many democratic theorists are dubious of this form of identification, out of ambivalence or skepticism toward the bounded state as the site of democracy. The question of political boundaries became a prominent philosophical controversy in the wake of the 1971 publication of John Rawls's *A Theory of Justice*. One of Rawls's key assumptions in *Theory* was that his conception of justice applied to society "conceived for the time being as a closed system isolated from other societies."[19] As Michael Blake and Patrick Smith note, "Rawls is explicit, in his theory, that his principles should be taken as only describing the nature of justice within the political society represented by a territorial state," resulting in a "difference in treatment between the domestic and the international context" that "was immediately troubling to many philosophers."[20] That reaction, which spawned a vast literature on global justice, began from a recognizably Rawlsian intuition: Isn't an individual's place of birth another morally arbitrary characteristic that generates deep and persistent inequalities—the very problem to which liberal egalitarianism offers a response?

The resulting debate, which coincided with accelerating globalization, the spread of human rights discourse, and marked increases in migration, demonstrated the complex and uncertain relationship between global *justice* and global *democracy*. To theorists who viewed the scope of justice and democracy as necessarily overlapping (or who simply subordinated what they saw as democracy's particularistic claims to justice's universalist claims), liberal egalitarianism seemed to be edging closer to a coherent, universal framework in which citizenship beyond the bounded state would emerge as part of a broader vision of global justice. The expanding scope of justice seemed to stretch the domain of citizenship as well.

Early critics of this trend by no means disagreed with the basic moral claim that deep global inequalities demanded aggressive action, especially by the world's wealthier states. Rather, they expressed skepticism at the way Rawls and other liberal political philosophers portrayed the process of defining and implementing distributive justice. As Michael Walzer wrote in 1983:

> The deepest assumption of most of the philosophers who have written about justice, from Plato onward, is that there is one, and only one, distributive system that philosophy can rightly encompass. Today, this system is commonly described as the one that ideally rational men and women would choose if they were forced to choose impartially, knowing nothing of their own situation, barred from making particularist claims, confronting an abstract set of goods . . . I shall begin by doubting, and more than doubting, this standard philosophical assumption. The questions posed by the theory of distributive justice admit of a range of answers, and there is room within the range for cultural diversity and political choice.[21]

Walzer complicated Rawls's understanding of justice by insisting that distributive schemes are contextual and historical—since communities of people not only allocate social goods but also "conceive and create" those goods in the first place.[22] Walzer offered the example of bread, which may be variously "the staff of life, the body of Christ, the symbol of the Sabbath, the means of hospitality, and so on."[23] He maintained that even the obvious necessity of food for human survival does not mean that food's *meaning* is always obvious, in the sense that it could yield a universally valid distributive principle: "If the religious uses of bread were to conflict with its nutritional uses—if the gods demanded that bread be baked and burned rather than eaten—it is by no means clear which use would be primary."[24] This pluralist critique insisted that justice did not adhere to a one-size-fits-all model but rather varied according to culture and political choice. In this way, it provided grounds for a defense of boundedness that seemed to be missing from Rawls's theory.

Little wonder, then, that Walzer began his own account of distributive justice with a discussion of how membership itself is distributed, since it is only by virtue of being a member that individuals receive any other goods within a distributive scheme. My account of identification within democracy extends the logic of Walzer's claim: not only does membership confer a right to benefit from a particular distributive scheme, but it also embeds individuals within a range of social processes that produce interpretations of social meanings in the first place—meanings that influence not only the distribution of goods but also the whole range of political questions that face a society. Antecedent social processes of conception and creation are always already part of democratic self-rule because a demos carries out its shared life on the basis of how its members interpret their values, goals, circumstances, and history. This inevitably situated and contextual process tethers the entire enterprise of democratic self-rule to communities of meaning.

Identification and Temporal Continuity

My association of democratic self-rule with historically shaped communities of meaning brings to the foreground a key point that has so far been mentioned only in passing: democratic self-rule requires continuity over time. This is not only true in the straightforward definitional sense that "self-rule" presumes something more permanent and comprehensive than sporadically assembled sets of individuals making majoritarian decisions on discrete issues from time to time. Temporal continuity also underwrites, in complex ways, the psychology, dispositions, and virtues on which democracy relies.

The temporal durability of a democratic association helps mitigate the instabilities that might otherwise result from the often unsatisfying, even perplexing experience of democratic citizenship. As Danielle Allen has observed: "Democracy puts its citizens under a strange form of psychological pressure by building them up as sovereigns and then regularly undermining each citizen's experience of sovereignty."[25] Because democracies must reach decisions amid widespread disagreement, every citizen will at some point experience defeat, and democracies must ask them to assent to those defeats. Allen writes that defeated citizens, in giving their assent, "preserve the stability of political institutions," performing a "sacrifice" that "makes collective democratic action possible."[26]

Yet why would citizens be willing to sacrifice in this way or to engage in related behaviors such as reciprocity or peaceful power-sharing? Their willingness depends on their sense that they share a future with their compatriots. This provides a reassurance, even in moments of bitter defeat, that victorious majorities will treat their vanquished opponents not as subjects but as temporarily defeated fellow-citizens who may achieve future victories, and who may re-sort themselves into new and shifting coalitions in endless ways across future decisions (forming what social scientists sometimes call "cross-cutting cleavages"). This means that no set of winners and losers is permanent but rather can shift both *over* time and, potentially, at any given moment *in* time: each of us may experience democratic victories and losses simultaneously, finding ourselves in differently constituted majorities and minorities across a wide range of issues, living with some decisions that match our preferences and others that don't.

Democratic self-rule thus relies on a sense of shared futurity: the fellow citizen who was part of a victorious coalition today exhibits a spirit of accommodation based on the understanding that she may lose on some other issue tomorrow (or vice versa). This willingness to continue participating is premised on the rough stability of the roster of participants, who build up a history of reciprocity with one another, and who can credibly commit to collective action and fulfill obligations to each other over time. If democratic participation consisted of a set of discrete decisions in which the set of participants were constantly shifting, there would be no way for individuals to guarantee recognition of their sacrifices and no way to ensure reciprocity in the future. In contrast, when members of a demos identify with each other over time, they can achieve norms of reciprocity that promote peaceful institutional survival. As this account implies, the scale of identification that promotes reciprocal democratic decision-making should be coextensive with the boundaries of the democratic state, since it is through the state's institutions that citizens exercise rule over one other. By durably bounded, I don't mean a state that closes its borders to keep the composition of its citizenry as static as possible; rather, I mean a state where there is sufficient institutional continuity to enable citizens to see themselves as engaged in a common project that stretches into the future. (In fact, durability of this sort is compatible with high levels of immigration, depending on how the political association itself is understood—a point I return to in Chapter 3.)

So far, I have defended the claim that democratic self-rule requires bounded identification among all members of the demos. As will become evident in the chapters to follow, this is by no means a consensus view among egalitarians and democrats. But even among thinkers who are in some form sympathetic to bounded democratic solidarity, there remain substantial differences of interpretation about the nature of that solidarity. These differences have important consequences for a range of questions, including where the boundaries of the political community should lie, what its members need to share in common, the substance and nature of their obligations toward each other, and the extent to which they can alter what fundamentally constitutes them as a civic body in the first place. I turn to these disagreements next.

Identification: Neither Liberal Nationalism nor Constitutional Patriotism

The understandings of solidarity that predominate in contemporary political theory can generally be divided into two broad schools. The first, associated with liberal nationalists like David Miller, holds that solidarity is rooted in, bounded by, and given substance through a shared national culture. The second, associated with the constitutional patriotism of Jürgen Habermas and Jan-Werner Müller, instead looks to a liberal-democratic constitution to ground solidarity. Yet as I explain in this section, the emphasis on identification that distinguishes my theory of democratic solidarity does not neatly fit into either of these schools, and so I will generally avoid describing it as a variant of either nationalism or patriotism.

I share with liberal nationalists the belief that the maintenance of a liberal-democratic political society is reliant on a more robust sense of membership than is sometimes acknowledged by liberal theorists, as well as the conviction that it is possible (indeed, necessary) to maintain a strong distinction between this ideal of membership and the various exclusionary, belligerent, antidemocratic nationalisms that animate the contemporary far right. Yet in a variety of ways, liberal nationalism endorses a stronger ideal of cultural homogeneity, and assigns more of a substantive normative role to culture itself, than does the position I defend in this book.

Miller, for example, contends that co-nationals are better equipped "to solve collective action problems, to support redistributive principles of justice, and to practise deliberative forms of democracy"[27] because they share a distinctive "common public culture," defined as "a set of understandings about the nature of a political community, its principles and institutions, its social norms, and so forth"[28] and as "a set of ideas about the character of the community which also helps to fix responsibilities."[29] It seems quite plausible that shared understandings about a political community's institutions, values, and norms make it easier for members to cooperate and deliberate over matters of public concern. But Miller takes the argument further, claiming that it is the culture *itself*, not the fact of sharing a political community, that both generates normative obligations among co-nationals and promotes the discharge of those obligations. Not only does he argue that "obligations in their particular content are an artefact of the public culture of that nation,"[30] but he also asserts that "the [public] culture in question *is* a public phenomenon: any one individual may interpret it rightly or wrongly, and draw correct or incorrect conclusions about his obligations to compatriots as a result."[31]

In this way, Miller's account treats co-national obligations as a kind of moral fact derived from the particular public culture of the nationality and *not* from shared membership in a state. The gap between the thin obligations of citizenship and the thick obligations of nationality is potentially vast: Miller writes that citizenship is governed by an instrumental, self-referential logic, meaning that fellow-citizens who are *not* co-nationals would contribute to welfare schemes only to the extent that they expect to benefit from them.[32]

In contrast, I do not think it is necessary to appeal to shared culture to specify or justify citizens' duties to one another. Rather, I concur with Anna Stilz's argument that Miller "does not explain how a sense of identity and cultural relatedness could actually ground any political obligations."[33] Although culture provides a meaningful context in which citizens' mutual obligations can be debated and interpreted, culture does not itself determine whether those obligations among members exist or not. Second, as Stilz also notes, Miller's account of the sources of co-national obligations necessarily reifies public culture and imputes to it an implausible degree of coherence and transparency. Only a static, monolithic public culture could possess the straightforwardly factual character that would enable us to deem an individual's interpretation of its normative demands "correct or incorrect." As Stilz writes, it is unlikely that "we can individuate cultural wholes with one unitary set of understandings about their members' obligations."[34] Cultures themselves, to say nothing of their members' interpretations of them, are simply too complex and internally plural to enable the kind of certainty that Miller's account leans on.

If shared obligations are not a moral fact that can be derived from the transparent empirical reality of public cultures, and if they do not flow directly from cultural membership per se, then there is no reason to follow the liberal-nationalist contention that *shared culture* precedes and properly defines the boundaries and substance of *political membership*.

In rejecting this ordering of culture and politics, we can avoid some of the stark consequences that follow from adopting the liberal-nationalist position. For example, Miller claims that because shared citizenship cannot generate or motivate more-than-reciprocal shared obligations, a polity faces two basic choices whenever different national groups share citizenship within it. The first involves "slimming down the obligations of citizenship—turning the state into something closer to a minimal state"; the second involves "making state and nation coincide more closely" either by assimilating nonnationals or partitioning the state to craft "new political units [that] are more exactly isomorphic with national divisions."[35] Given the substantial diversity of the United States (as well as many other democracies), and the fact that the dispersion of different cultures within the U.S. does not follow clear, contiguous boundaries, liberal nationalism—which begins as an attempt to justify both the welfare state and solidarity—ends up suggesting, somewhat perversely in my view, that if the requisite cultural commonality proves unattainable, the alternatives are either libertarianism or an unpredictable, complicated process of carving the country into new, smaller political jurisdictions. These problems suggest that there are good reasons to reject the claim that shared national culture generates democratic obligations.

To better appreciate the difference between the liberal-nationalist view and the democratic tradition I describe in this book, it is helpful to consider how some of that tradition's early figures understood the genesis and scope of political membership. Significantly, the logic of their approach reversed the method of boundary-drawing typical of nationalists, including liberal nationalists: rather than proposing to redraw state borders to match the contours of an already-existing nation, these figures wanted Americans to imagine a nation composed of the already-existing population of their country. In practice, this definitional move linked Americans to a particular territory; it placed them in a morally relevant, institutionally defined association; and it made them common inheritors of a particular political legacy. But it did not rest on any premise that they shared a specific, antecedent quality that made them fellow-members. The figures who sought to build American democracy starting during Reconstruction simply took the existing population as more or less given and sought to redraw their political community so that it would extend throughout the boundaries of their country.[36]

This approach had an important precedent in Lincoln's assertion that the Declaration of 1776 had "brought forth ... a new nation" rather than simply delivering a state to an already-existing one.[37] It likewise finds expression in Sumner's claim that the meaning of nationhood had changed in the modern era: "Originally ethnological, it is now political."[38] When reflecting on the nature of membership in a diverse country, Sumner flatly denied that nationhood required ethnic or linguistic commonality: "The various accents of speech and the various types of manhood, with the great distinction of color, which we encounter daily, show that there is no such unity here. But this is not required. If the inhabitants are of one blood and one language, the unity is more complete; but the essential condition is one sovereignty, involving, of course, one citizenship."[39] A similar understanding is detectable in Frederick Douglass's 1889 remark about African Americans: "There can be but one American nation under the American government, and *we are Americans*. The constitution of the country *makes* us such."[40] In emphasizing that the constitution makes citizenship, Douglass was underscoring an important legacy of Reconstruction: the idea that membership in the American political community is not defined or predetermined by some quality that a group already shares (such as culture, race, ethnicity, language, or religion) but is guaranteed by a fundamental law that, in the wake of the 14th Amendment, extends citizenship to everyone born in the territory.

For all these reasons—to emphasize the novel method of boundary drawing that distinguishes this tradition of democratic thinking, to avoid confusion with right-wing positions that embrace similar terminology, and to maintain subtle yet important distinctions from contemporary liberal-nationalist theorists—I will avoid labeling the position I defend in this book as a "nationalist" one whenever possible. (At times, this term will be unavoidable because it was occasionally employed by the historical figures I discuss.) In this, I follow a number of popular and scholarly writers who (especially when discussing American politics) refer to national solidarity, distinguish the nation from the states, and more broadly use the language of nationhood, without intending thereby to endorse nationalism per se.

Nor, finally, will I invoke "civic" nationalism (which is often held up as the benign, liberal, and inclusive alternative to "ethnic" nationalism). If rendered as an empirical claim (i.e., an assertion that American identity is defined by devotion to liberal political values), civic nationalism seriously exaggerates the popularity of those values in American history—excluding many illiberal Americans from the scope of membership, even as it is simultaneously *over*inclusive with respect to liberals worldwide who do not live in the United States and who presumably do not identify as members of it. On the other hand, if it is rendered as a normative claim (i.e., Americans *ought to endorse* common political values), civic nationalism sheds no light on the question of who counts as a member, and in its attempt to cement the substance of membership in commonly endorsed values, it requires that the exact set of these fundamental values and their meanings reside, more or less, beyond contestation. By thus attempting to freeze the meaning of the values it holds up as the basis of belonging, normative civic nationalism perversely limits their expansion and transformation as they are reinterpreted and applied to new contexts (often controversially)—which is how concepts like freedom and equality have tended to expand in American history.[41] In other words, civic nationalism suggests conceptual fixity where it should, on the basis of its own liberal commitments, accommodate flexibility.

If nationalism is not an adequate characterization of this tradition, might patriotism be a more appropriate descriptor? As used in popular discourse, patriotism is generally understood as an ideal of political allegiance—of love for one's country. Yet thinkers in the tradition with which I am concerned were not primarily interested in promoting patriotic love; rather, they were primarily interested in reshaping how Americans understood the boundaries of the demos. Strictly understood, patriotism does not address this issue. It does not specify who belongs to the country, and although it offers an account of the feelings (affection, loyalty, sacrifice, etc.) that people arguably ought to have toward their country, the ideal conveys little about how members ought to relate to one another. In other words, patriotism—at least as popularly understood—does not offer an account of political membership.

However, some political philosophers have supplemented the concept in ways that partially address these issues. The most prominent such thinkers, who describe their position as "constitutional patriotism," see liberal democracy itself as generating a distinctive kind of culture. Jan-Werner Müller defines constitutional patriotism as "the idea that political attachment ought to center on the norms, the values and, more indirectly, the procedures of a liberal democratic constitution," in contrast to attachments centered on either a national culture or humanity in general.[42] Jürgen Habermas similarly maintains that a world which has discovered nationalism's dangers at painful cost needs "republican freedom ... [to] cut its umbilical links to the womb of the national consciousness of freedom that originally gave it birth."[43] The word "nation," writes Habermas, only came to mean both "community of descent" and "people of a state" around the time of the French Revolution, and the historical, "social-psychological" fusion of nationality and citizenship "does not mean that the two are linked at the conceptual level."[44] After that link is severed, Habermas argues, constitutional patriotism could supplant cultural nationalism as a basis for political allegiance—providing, in combination with a transnational public sphere and civil society, the basis for citizenship beyond the nation-state.[45] Habermas imagines a European citizenship whose political culture is isolated from the other cultural elements that shape the lives of its members: "In the future, however, a common *political* culture could differentiate itself from the various *national* cultures. A differentiation could appear between a Europe-wide *political* culture and the various *national* traditions in art and literature, historiography, philosophy, and so on, which have been branching out since early modernity."[46]

Constitutional patriotism's attempt to explain how common political allegiances could be fostered amid profound diversity is appealing. Nonetheless, it is far from clear that "liberal political culture" could stand apart from the other elements of culture—including art, literature, and philosophy—in which it is embedded and expressed.[47] Could Americans, for instance, draw on a purely political conception of freedom isolated from distinctive cultural elements such as Puritan religious ideals, slave narratives, Transcendentalist literature, the idea of the frontier, high levels of immigration, capitalist individualism, or jazz? This point holds even if the culture in question is a diverse one; one not defined by common descent. Hence Walt Whitman's contention that what American democracy needed was not only political reform but also the emergence of new cultural figures capable of "fusing contributions, races, far localities" across the "States, with all their variety of origins, their diverse climes, cities, standards, etc.": "a cluster of mighty poets, artists, teachers, fit for us, national expressers."[48] The misleading neatness of a culture/politics distinction invites an excessively decontextualized approach to the interpretation of political controversies.

Moreover, constitutional patriotism's understanding of constitutional values may, like liberal nationalism's invocation of a public culture, suppose the meaning of a deeply contested public object to be more coherent, transparent, and agreed upon than it actually is. For instance, what if a people's history, practices, and institutions are not (in their current form) a worthy object of patriotic love? What if they do not sustain a genuinely common liberty and could only be made worthy of patriotic loyalty if they were changed?

Like the normative implications of a public culture, the meanings of basic constitutional values are often the subject of deep disagreement. For example, in the United States (which Habermas has suggested may provide evidence about the feasibility of constitutional patriotism),[49] an explicit invocation of liberal and democratic principles during the nation's founding in no way secured a stable consensus over the meaning of basic concepts such as freedom and equality.[50] These disagreements found expression in the ambiguous character of the nation's fundamental law, so much so that prior to the Civil War, even abolitionists disagreed intensely about whether the American Constitution was a proslavery or an antislavery document. Because they disagreed about whether that document supported or subverted republican liberty, abolitionists also disagreed about whether they owed political allegiance to the American constitutional order. In this way, interpretive disagreements led to disagreements about obligation, allegiance, and the duty to support one's Constitution—precisely those elements of citizenship about which constitutional patriots hope to secure a rough consensus.[51] The experience of Reconstruction further suggests that although subsequent reforms might clarify and deepen the liberal and democratic commitments of a constitutional structure, disagreement about fundamental values can still persist—even as political debate is saturated, as it is in the United States, with constitutional veneration and appeals to constitutional meaning. The figures in the tradition described here raised questions that complicate any straightforward application of the various provisos offered by contemporary theorists of patriotism. Their aim was not to cultivate a love of country per se but something conceptually prior to it: a willing belief among Americans that they formed a common country in the first place, one that extended to include everyone living within the boundaries of the state.

These issues with constitutional patriotism and liberal nationalism show that we can neither bracket democracy from culture nor collapse the boundaries between them. The former approach leads to the implausible position that a society could be characterized by a democratic ethos without that ethos finding expression in its folkways. At the same time, it is no less problematic to argue that culture both demarcates the scope of a democracy and defines its way of life. That position not only requires us to reify culture, but it also constrains the malleability of social meanings and entails unjust forms of exclusion. Instead, I try here to strike a middle position, acknowledging that culture could help encourage democratic solidarity without taking the reified and implicitly assimilationist position represented by liberal nationalism. Analytically, I admit culture into the background of my account, as a wellspring of meaning without which we could not explain the sources or deployment of political ideas or motivate their adoption or transformation. In all these senses, politics is always shaped by culture, but because culture itself is the product of creative human agents, we can never determine in advance what form of relevance it will take in any given instance.

For example, think of how civil rights activists justified their goals by drawing on, and in some cases effectively reinterpreting, potent American cultural resources such as the Declaration of Independence. The success of this effort by no means demonstrates, as civic nationalists might have it, that Americans are united by the core liberal and democratic values that they all trace to their founding documents, such that citizens need merely to be reminded of these shared commitments in order to embrace further democratic reform. As I discussed in the previous chapter, the Declaration was indeed an important touchstone for many significant figures in the United States' long process of democratization, including Charles Sumner and Abraham Lincoln. But their readings of the document were far from uncontested; in fact, the scope and meaning of the Declaration was a matter of deep disagreement. Chief Justice Roger Taney, in his notorious *Dred Scott* ruling, maintained that while the famous words "all men are created equal" might "*seem* to embrace the whole human family," it was nonetheless "too clear for dispute, that the enslaved African race were not intended to be included"—if they had been, "the conduct of the distinguished men who framed the Declaration of Independence would have been utterly and flagrantly inconsistent with the principles they asserted." Since Taney found it inconceivable that the framers could have been such brazen hypocrites, it followed that their intended meaning was obvious. "They perfectly understood the meaning of the language they used, and how it would be understood by others; and they knew that it would not in any part of the civilized world be supposed to embrace the negro race," he declared. "They spoke and acted according to the then established doctrines and principles, and in the ordinary language of the day, and no one misunderstood them."[52]

Yet Taney's conclusion—that the Declaration, despite its somewhat imprecise wording, plainly did not mean to encompass black people—was disputed even by other white supremacists. Detecting in the document the universalism whose existence Taney denied, they decided not to endorse his cramped reading of it but rather to repudiate it altogether. As Confederate Vice President Alexander Stephens explained, Jefferson and the other "leading statesmen at the time of the formation of the old constitution" may not have believed that slavery could be eradicated in the short term, but they nonetheless thought it was "wrong in principle, socially, morally, and politically" and hoped that it would someday "pass away." But such beliefs, declared Stephens, were "fundamentally wrong"—they "rested upon the assumption of the equality of races. This was an error. It was a sandy foundation, and the government built upon it fell when the 'storm came and the wind blew.'" Stephens allowed that many Northerners "still cling" to "the errors of the past generation," but he contended that such people were simply "fanatics"; their belief in human equality was "a species of insanity."[53] In characterizing the basic error of these egalitarian fanatics, Stephens made a pointed allusion to the Declaration's most famous phrase: "They were attempting to make things equal which the Creator had made unequal."[54]

As these examples indicate, it was not inevitable that the Declaration would come to be understood as a statement of universal egalitarianism. Nor was it inevitable that, if the document *did* come to be understood in this way, it would enjoy broad approval from Americans. The contemporary meaning and status of the Declaration in American politics is just one example of how new cultural forms are constantly emerging from human ingenuity, as well as how the process of bringing those new forms into political life is not controllable by any person. We can't know in advance what people in a culture will do, or how they'll do it, or whether any given cultural innovation will be a successful instance of "constituting," in Pitkin's sense of achieving recognition or affirmation from other people. Not only that, by attempting to isolate certain elements of our culture as fundamental and/or sacrosanct, we risk becoming chauvinists for our own cultural status quo, generating hostility toward the kind of creativity that can improve political life in ways we can't anticipate. Because culture is the terrain of meaningful human action, we can't insulate politics from it; but because its content is not fixed and its boundaries are fuzzy, we can't rely on it to define the scope and content of political membership.

These challenges surrounding constitutional meaning, political allegiance, and the scope of membership began to seriously concern many American egalitarians during the Civil War and Reconstruction era, and their response is instructive. The solution on which their thought eventually coalesced is that democracy requires more than the abstract affirmation of values such as freedom and equality, and indeed more than the affirmation of a particular constitutional structure. What it further requires is an imagined projection of the demos that stretches to include everyone in the state—a projection that is not simply guaranteed either by shared culture, or by formal equality, or by the presence of a liberal-democratic constitution. Citizens must be willing to identify all their compatriots as equal participants in a shared project of democratic self-rule.

If the kind of identification characteristic of a democratic way of life is neither derived from a shared culture in precisely the way liberal nationalists argue nor is oriented toward purely political values and norms in precisely the way constitutional patriots argue, then how else might we describe it? I contend that the tendency of citizens to identify one another as co-members, and to act on the basis of their concern for co-members, should be considered a form of bounded solidarity—an extension of mutual concern that is rooted in associational ties.

Identification and Bounded Solidarity

Solidarity, as theorists have argued, denotes a kind of mutual concern that is rooted neither in instrumental logic nor any particular interaction among individuals; rather, it stems from their relationship *itself* and takes varied forms depending on the nature of that relationship.[55] Identification fits this description. It is a form of mutual concern among democratic citizens that entails distinctive obligations rooted in their civic bond. Notice the contrast to liberal nationalism, which roots obligations in a shared *culture* that may or may not map onto shared civic relationships since citizens of the same democracy may belong to different national cultures, and members of the same national culture may be dispersed across several democratic states. Identification describes a kind of solidarity that is not vulnerable to some of the most familiar critiques of nationalism; it does not require either treating the demos as a prepolitical group or bounding it by reference to (partly or wholly) immutable group characteristics, such as language, culture, or descent. As Anderson argues, "People do not need some *prior* sense of fellow feeling or mutual identification to have reasons to include one another as equals in cooperative projects. But the kind of inclusion entailed by seeing one another as fellow citizens joined in a common project of living together democratically *constitutes* a form of mutual identification."[56] The goal of such identification is to sustain processes of democratic self-rule.[57]

Yet is this kind of fellow-feeling truly necessary for democracy? In this final section, I answer the skeptical claim, articulated by Jacob Levy, that solidarity is at best superfluous to democracy and at worst is an actively malevolent force. In an essay titled "Against Fraternity: Democracy Without Solidarity," Levy writes that

> fellow citizens are in a fundamental sense moral strangers to each other, united *only* by the shared circumstances of inhabiting a common political jurisdiction, and not by any prior relationship that legitimizes, grounds, underlies, or stands outside of those circumstances. Our moral relationship to one another differs in degree, not in kind, from the relationship among the strangers locked in a room, or passengers on a bus, or any other collection of persons thrown together by happenstance. Statehood is a big happenstance, much bigger than a bus; but it is still a happenstance.[58]

Since many regimes manage to achieve basic justice despite this civic estrangement, Levy reasons that solidarity's defenders have greatly exaggerated its importance. Solidarity, on this reading, is simply not necessary to motivate citizens to discharge their obligations of justice toward one another. Nor, Levy argues, should we *wish* for citizens to feel motivated by solidarity, even in supposedly benign guises such as civic nationalism. Such putatively "civic" forms of fellow-feeling are suspect: they tend to mask an underlying cultural nationalism, they threaten intolerance toward political dissenters, and they share with organic visions of membership a tendency—indeed, an imperative—to exaggerate both insiders' similarities and outsiders' differences.[59] This exaggeration suffocates internal diversity and often obstructs the achievement of humane relations with outsiders by rationalizing indifference or even violence against them.[60] As Levy summarizes:

> I don't at all deny that our social life together requires some degree of moral commitment, some sense of justice, in order to have some chance of *being* just. My claim is not that just institutions are likely to arise or be stable out of nothing but calculative self-interest . . . But at *best*, it seems to me that bounded solidarity is a way of describing an unnecessary loop in the path between the beginning

sense of justice and the eventual willingness to pursue just policies: I believe in justice, therefore I feel an affective connection to my co-nationals and co-citizens, because it is through such affective connection that I will be motivated to pursue just policies. And at worst, it can be much worse than that: a moral-psychological perversion of the sense of justice into action that promotes injustice. The strategy of indirection, of trying to cultivate an enhanced sense of justice by cultivating a stronger commitment to national solidarity seems to me both unnecessary and dangerous.[61]

Levy maintains that we require no appeal to solidarity to justify political obligation and secure the "core" elements of justice: "life and limb, property and contract," as well as "distributive justice of various kinds."[62] Following an argument advanced by David Hume, he contends that the justificatory and motivational work often associated with solidarity can instead be performed by the obvious fact that the state is a useful institution. Of "bounded solidarity as a foundation for decent liberal democratic politics," Levy concludes "that we *can't have it* and *shouldn't want it*," and that "this is not a counsel of despair, because we don't need it."[63] If citizens' obligation or motivation to pursue justice required fellow-feeling or a shared prepolitical identity, justice would sit on wobbly foundations—since that kind of fellow-feeling simply doesn't exist among people whose ties to each other are solely accidental. The obvious fact of the state's usefulness, requiring no appeal to such chimerical sources of unity, provides a far more secure justification. "We are capable," he writes, "of cooperating under institutions that we don't feel deep allegiance to, that we view as only provisionally and instrumentally useful: the political procedures of Babylon, as it were."[64]

My account of identification provides reasons to be skeptical of this conclusion. In particular, it calls attention to the gap between democratic self-rule and what Levy calls the "core" elements of justice: "life and limb, property and contract," as well as "distributive justice of various kinds."[65] None of these elements of justice is specific to democratic regimes; a government of technocrats or philosopher-kings could ensure these forms of justice without instituting a democracy. This is a key element of what is at stake, conceptually, in current debates about solidarity: to regard a state without solidarity as capable of achieving democracy would require treating political problems as self-evident facts about the world and/or the aggregation of individual preferences as epistemically sufficient for collective self-rule. Yet social processes of interpretation and argument among individuals who recognize each other as fellow-members are necessary for a demos to define common problems *in the first place*. As Anderson notes, "Democratic discussion is a critical way for the public to come to an understanding of what its aims are as a public—to decide *which* concerns are properly matters of public interest, entitled to lay a claim on collective resources and cooperation to secure their fulfillment."[66] If we endorse that view, we have reason to follow Margaret Moore in valuing "a special concern with, and attachment to . . . people who share a specific political and institutional structure," since it is through those structures that democratic citizens address the problems they have collectively defined for themselves, thereby realizing "the value attributed to being collectively self-determining—to shaping the conditions of our existence, including our collective life together."[67] To value democratic self-rule is, by extension, to value those mindsets that make it possible. Here, solidarity is not an unnecessary loop or a mere motivational force that carries citizens from a baseline belief in justice to a will-to-justice. Rather, solidarity is integral to the process of determining what justice is for a particular community, especially if justice extends beyond the relatively minimal elements laid out in Levy's account.

Such an allocation of psychological resources, in which the concerns, needs, and aspirations of one's compatriots register as essential elements of political reasoning, struck Reconstruction-era democratic thinkers as an essential condition of the nascent regime they were trying to build. As Walt Whitman observed in 1871, "The great word Solidarity has arisen."[68] He went on:

> Of all dangers to a nation, as things exist in our day, there can be no greater one than having certain portions of the people set off from the rest by a line drawn—they not privileged as others, but degraded, humiliated, made of no account. Much quackery teems, of course, even on democracy's side, yet does not really affect the orbic quality of the matter.[69]

For Whitman, to be denied solidarity is to be "made of no account"; it is to be ignored or disregarded. In other words, it is to be denied identification as a compatriot. If democratic decisions are impossible when "certain portions of the people" are placed outside the scope of concern that ought to govern citizens' reasoning ("set off from the rest by a line drawn"), then by the same logic, democratic decisions are impossible when *all* citizens disregard one another. So understood, solidarity can be significant even if shared citizenship is, as Levy writes, a "happenstance." The happenstance quality of citizenship provides no reason for thinking that citizens can safely disregard a particularistic concern for their compatriots and still preserve a democratic way of life.

This is because effective democratic citizenship is not defined solely by participation, rights, or formal equality. To realize the core aspiration of collective self-rule on terms of equality, democracies also require identification among all members of the demos. Yet since identification cannot be readily observed, and since it raises controversial issues about the boundaries of democratic belonging, it is the component of democratic citizenship most likely to be overlooked or dismissed. Dismissals of identification rest on a misunderstanding of the nature of democratic self-rule and generate flawed answers to many of the problems facing contemporary democracies. In the following chapters, I apply this argument about identification to ongoing debates over immigration, racial segregation, and economic inequality. Cultivating a defensible form of identification is one of the most difficult tasks facing the United States and many other democracies, but if the foregoing analysis is correct, it is a project of paramount importance.

Chapter 2
American Democracy Between the First and Second Reconstructions

For about one century, between the 1860s and the 1960s, the United States intermittently pursued democratization by broadening the scope of the demos to the boundaries of the state. The process—which proceeded in fits and starts, with conspicuous exceptions and devastating reversals—began with what Eric Foner identifies as "the emergence during the Civil War and Reconstruction of a national state possessing vastly expanded authority and a new set of purposes, including an unprecedented commitment to the ideal of national citizenship whose equal rights belonged to all Americans regardless of race."[1] This attempt to realize democratic ideals through an expanded conception of the political community persisted until the so-called Second Reconstruction, a similarly ambitious attempt to remake the American polity during the civil rights era. As Nelson Lichtenstein has observed, "All of America's great reform movements, from the crusade against slavery to the labor upsurge in the 1930s, defined themselves as champions of a moral and patriotic nationalism, which they counterpoised to the parochial and selfish elites who stood athwart their vision of a virtuous society."[2]

Although this tradition is best represented by the two Reconstructions which bookend it, partial antecedents can be traced to the Revolutionary era, which saw the emergence of what James Kloppenberg calls a "lively American cultural tradition" of "egalitarian, aspirational nationalism." In the process of coming to reject British authority, Americans of the period developed what Kloppenberg calls "the most important innovations of American constitutional thought, the idea of popular sovereignty and the institution of the constitutional convention."[3] During the spring and early summer of 1776, Americans produced at least ninety "declarations of independence"— a range of related documents, adopted by both colonies and localities, that either announced the end of British rule or otherwise took steps toward independence.[4] By the time the most famous of those declarations was adopted in Philadelphia, the colonists had already begun to develop not only a new procedure for announcing their political authority but also a new conception of themselves as a collective actor—a *people* legitimately entitled to found a basic set of rules by which it will govern itself.

During the debate over ratification, proponents of the new Constitution marshaled this idea of an expansive peoplehood against those who endorsed a more confederal vision of the new republic. In *Federalist* no. 2, John Jay posed the question—"one of the most important," he wrote, "that ever engaged [Americans'] attention"—of "whether it would conduce more to the interest of the people of America, that they should, to all general purposes, be one nation, under one federal Government, than that they should divide themselves into separate confederacies, and give to the head of each, the same kind of powers which they are advised to place in one national Government."[5] Jay's vigorous defense of a unified system was supplemented by James Madison's argument for an extended republic in *Federalist* no. 14, which concluded on a rhetorically ambitious note: "Hearken not to the unnatural voice which tells you that the people of America, knit together as they are by so many chords of affection, can no longer live together as members of the same family; can no longer continue the mutual guardians of their mutual happiness; can no longer be fellow citizens of one great respectable and flourishing empire . . . Shut your hearts against the poison which it conveys; the kindred blood which flows in the veins of American citizens, the mingled blood which they have shed in defense of their sacred rights."[6]

Still, the social and economic changes that would transform the relatively rural, agricultural, and decentralized early republic into a modern nation-state would not emerge until the 1820s and 1830s. The United States in the first half of the nineteenth century witnessed, as James McPherson writes, "an unparalleled rate of growth" in "three dimensions: population, territory, and economy."[7] Between 1789 and 1850, the size of the country quadrupled, GNP increased sevenfold, and per capita income doubled. Between 1810 and 1860, the urban share of the population rose from 6 percent to 20 percent and the nonagricultural share of the labor force more than doubled. In the 1820s, the annual number of immigrants had remained below 13,000. In the next decade, that number quadrupled; in the early 1840s, during an economic downturn, it grew another 40 percent. In the decade after 1845, about 3 million immigrants came to the U.S.[8] The U.S. had undergone dramatic change between the Revolution and the War of 1812, but as one historian summarizes, the changes after 1815 "were so substantial as to render its contours practically unrecognizable compared with what they had been at the founding . . . It had assumed a place as one of the most important economic producers in the world, its citizens had acquired confidence in themselves as individuals and collectively as a nation, and it seemed to demonstrate the brilliant if raucous possibilities for republican government."[9]

How would Americans make sense of this emergent society? One response, represented by prominent politicians such as Daniel Webster, was to embrace a nationalist conception of American union—not only in "doctrine" but also in "imagery and myth," to use Samuel Beer's formulation.[10] Webster believed that a sense of nationhood was necessary in order to orient democratic politics during a period of rapid and drastic transformation.[11] As Beer notes, one of Webster's most famous pieces of rhetoric—his oration on the fiftieth anniversary of the Battle of Bunker Hill—did not directly "make an argument for the union" but rather opted to "tell a story about it—a story about its past with a lesson for its future."[12] Webster's story, with its call to "let our conceptions be enlarged to the circle of our duties,"[13] promoted a unified idea of American nationhood by celebrating the revolutionary colonists' solidarity against British pressure. This mythology of national origins was mobilized in the service of a consensus politics: "Let us cultivate a true spirit of union and harmony. In pursuing the great objects, which our condition points out to us, let us act under a settled conviction, and an habitual feeling, that these twenty-four States are one country."[14] But the events of subsequent decades exposed the fragility of this hoped-for national unity. As the political crisis over slavery deepened, it became clear that an ideal of national unity could not satisfy the imperatives of comity while maintaining substantive political content. This dilemma raised questions about what form of American unity, if any, it was still possible to champion.

Few perceived the problem as clearly as Abraham Lincoln, who was deeply influenced by Webster's rhetoric,[15] and who deployed its themes in a direct challenge to the compact-based understanding of American politics endorsed by many representatives of the South. The conception of American peoplehood that runs through Lincoln acquired its distinctively democratic character through this encounter with an ideological foil, a political narrative that cast in starkly different terms not only the basis of American union but also, increasingly, the substantive commitments of American democracy.[16] In Foner's summation: "The crisis of the Union, among other things, was a crisis of the meaning of American nationhood."[17]

In the antebellum era, the democratic commitments implicit within the Unionist idea came into view through the struggles against nullification and later against secession, both of which claimed legitimacy through a narration of American political community which held, as John Calhoun contended in 1831, that "the very idea of an *American People*, as constituting a single community, is a mere chimera. Such a community never for a single moment existed—neither before nor since the Declaration of Independence."[18] Calhoun's position does not directly challenge the ideal of popular sovereignty; it simply denies that the American people, taken as a national whole, are the relevant sovereign. Opponents of this states' rights view wanted to advance an interpretation of American popular sovereignty that could vindicate federal authority, but for obvious reasons they could not invoke the narrative of a primordial, organic community that tended to accompany such arguments. Circumstances thus prodded them into ideological innovation: a theory of the American people as called into existence by a collective political action consciously undertaken at a precise moment in historical time.[19] In this way, a crucial feature of democratic thinking in the United States was born of necessity. As David Armitage has argued, "the United States might be seen as a, perhaps the only, spectacular example" of "a beast we might call the state-nation, which arises when the state is formed before the development of any sense of national consciousness."[20] From this unusual sequence of events, the figures who hoped to create that collective consciousness developed a narrative that offered powerful rhetorical, intellectual, and moral resources.

That narrative found its most influential expression in Lincoln's interpretation of the Civil War, which has served as a touchstone for a range of subsequent thinkers in the United States' democratic tradition. The Gettysburg Address concisely expresses this interpretation from its first sentence: "Fourscore and seven years ago our fathers brought forth on this continent a new nation, conceived in liberty and dedicated to the proposition that all men are created equal."[21] These words introduce most of the key themes in Lincoln's argument, which explains the meaning of the nation's deepest crisis by reaching back to a pregnant interpretation of its origins. The next sentence immediately links these origins to contemporary events (a theme to which the speech returns at its close): "Now we are engaged in a great civil war, testing whether that nation or any nation so conceived and so dedicated can long endure." The war for Union is a test of whether a polity created in historical time ("fourscore and seven years ago"), one tracing its legitimacy to a collective and purposive political action, can survive.

The purposive element—specifically, the "proposition" of equality—is the most difficult part of Lincoln's interpretation: both the gendered language of "all men" and the obvious fact of slavery call attention to the limits of the founders' egalitarianism and the difficulties of claiming their legacy in the present.[22] (Indeed, Lincoln himself had never taken the radical step of endorsing political equality for black Americans, although he was beginning to endorse a limited form of black male suffrage at the time of his death.) But the gap between ideals and practice was a problem that Lincoln had confronted before, and one that proved generative for his thinking and his oratory. Gettysburg was by no means his first attempt to make sense of, and to creatively exploit, the contradiction between the words of the Declaration and the reality of the country it had called into being. As Garry Wills notes, Lincoln had long insisted that Americans' proslavery views and their reverence for the Declaration were incompatible. In their debates, Stephen Douglas had responded that this was a false dilemma: Jefferson himself had evidently seen no inconsistency in declaring the equality of men while owning slaves, and in any case, it was the Constitution of 1789—which, as Wills writes, "countenanced slavery"—that was the country's fundamental law, not the Declaration of 1776. "It was at this point in the argument," observes Wills, "that Lincoln distinguished between the Declaration as the statement of a permanent ideal and the Constitution as an early and provisional embodiment of that ideal, to be tested against it, kept in motion toward it."[23] Lincoln's "dialectic of the ideal with the real," already developed in his 1858 debates, was at "the very heart of his Gettysburg Address" in 1863.[24]

The arrival of war enabled Lincoln to powerfully augment this argument with rhetorical invocations of birth and death that would likely not have resonated with audiences before the experience of national breakdown. At the speech's outset, Lincoln refers to the American nation being "conceived" by "our fathers" in the year 1776, subtly underscoring his view that the Declaration, not the Constitution, properly represents the nation's founding. The war is a test of whether the eighty-seven-year-old nation can "endure," whether it "might live." At the end of the speech, when Lincoln refers to "the unfinished work" that the soldiers at Gettysburg advanced, and the "great task remaining" before Americans, he returns to this imagery, defining the task as a "new birth of freedom" and implying that this second birth will more fully realize the principles latent in the first.

This was, in a significant if limited respect, what Union victory achieved: the centralized state that emerged from the Civil War, especially in the wake of the 13th, 14th, and 15th Amendments, was expressly tasked with what Foner calls a "new set of purposes."[25] At Reconstruction's outset, Lincoln's party was home to a faction of radicals who, as Richard White puts it, "were nationalists committed to a homogeneous citizenry of rights-bearing individuals, all identical in the eyes of a newly powerful federal government."[26] Their ideal of "homogeneous citizenship" did not refer to ethnic or racial sameness: as discussed previously, radicals like Charles Sumner concluded that the United States didn't have this kind of homogeneity and didn't need it. Rather, the kind of homogeneity favored by radicals referred to "full civil, political, and social equality for freedpeople and confiscation and redistribution of land in the South"[27]—a vision of uniformity informed by their bitter struggle against the antebellum system of "localized rights" that were defined within complex webs of group memberships. These radicals were sensitive to the fact that "as long as citizenship remained local, as it always had been in the United States, citizens were manifestly unequal."[28] As Sumner explained in 1867: "The partisans of State Rights, plausibly professing to *decentralize* the government, have done everything possible to *denationalize* it. In the name of self-government they have organized local lordships hostile to Human Rights. In the name of the States, they have sacrificed the Nation."[29] Against this decentralizing/denationalizing tendency, Sumner promoted a vision of civic unity characterized by a uniform set of basic rights:

> The constant Duel between the Nation and the States must cease. The National Unity must be assured,—in the only way which is practical and honest,—through the principles declared by our Fathers and inwoven into the national life. In one word, the Declaration of Independence must be recognized as a fundamental law, and State Rights, in all their denationalizing pretensions, must be trampled out forever, to the end that we may be in reality as in name, a Nation.[30]

This effort was only partly successful. Although they helped secure the passage of constitutional amendments that advanced the codification and nationalization of democratic citizenship,[31] the radical Republicans never represented a broad ideological consensus, and even when they were able to pass legislation (which they often were not), they struggled with poorly resourced implementation.[32]

The situation worsened with Reconstruction's end in 1877, when two superficially divergent trends operated in concert to undermine this nascent democratic polity. First, Calhounian sectionalism resurfaced after the federal government's retreat from Reconstruction, in the form of Jim Crow—which renewed nullification in practice by hollowing out the Reconstruction amendments, the war's most significant democratizing and nationalizing legacies. Second, the desire for reconciliation after the war produced a racialized discourse of national unity that deliberately downplayed bitter controversies over slavery and emancipation in favor of a unifying narrative emphasizing the heroism demonstrated by (white) soldiers on both sides of the conflict. As David Blight has shown, this "reconciliationist vision" purchased sectional healing for white people at the cost of racial justice for black people. It overwhelmed the "emancipationist vision" of the war, which had stressed the agency of African Americans, the radicalism of Reconstruction efforts, and above all an understanding of the war as "the reinvention of the republic and the liberation of blacks to citizenship and Constitutional equality."[33] Such an interpretation was deemed too polarizing, too likely to reopen old wounds and obstruct the necessary work of national reconciliation, conceived of as a process among white people. Thus, in a dark irony, the resurgence of a Calhounian politics of nullification and sectionalism was actually enabled by a discourse of national unity—the opposite of what democratic reformers had envisioned when they invoked the ideal of a unified American people during radical Reconstruction.

This perverse outcome highlights the divergent ends to which the ideal of *unity* can be marshaled. The ideal implies that divisions in the body politic are always to be resisted, but as Danielle Allen argues, this subtly misconstrues the proper aspiration of a demos—which is not to be unified as one, but rather to achieve wholeness, understood as "integrity and solidarity."[34] "We long ago abandoned modes of citizenship that laid claim to unity by means of domination, acquiescence, hypocrisy, and the production of invisibility," writes Allen of the United States, but "we have met the challenge to develop new forms of citizenship with only limited success."[35] Neither "citizens" nor "theorists of democracy," argues Allen, have "adequately articulated positive alternative visions of the citizenly practices that might foster wholeness through acknowledging difference."[36]

This distinction—between national unity and democratic solidarity—is subtle and difficult to maintain, and it was not always recognized even by egalitarians seeking to articulate a broader ideal of American peoplehood during and after Reconstruction. The way some of these leading figures addressed the question of Indigenous peoples is illustrative. Even Frederick Douglass and Charles Sumner were guilty at times of appealing to contemporary prejudices against Indigenous peoples—perversely, as a means of advocating equality in *other* contexts. In one respect, this was by no means unprecedented. As Joseph Fishkin and William Forbath note, the Jacksonian movement that came to power in the decades before the war "wedded white farmers' and workers' democratic egalitarian aspirations to the racist causes of Southern slavery and Indian removal"; the Jacksonians' egalitarian goals for white male workers produced a "Herrenvolk democracy" that promoted a racist and sexist vision of citizenship and that relied on a "murderous new policy of mass expulsion of Native peoples."[37] But Douglass and Sumner were no Herrenvolk democrats, and neither endorsed the most notorious policies that the United States adopted toward Indigenous peoples, including forced removal and attempts to achieve assimilation through coercion and violence. Even so, their significantly broader conception of democratic peoplehood struggled with the issue of Indigenous populations.

In 1866, for example, Douglass told a white audience that black Americans were eager to become full members of American society; that they were "incomparably more like you in all the elements that go to make up civilized man than the Indian," who "disdains your civilization."[38] The very next year, Sumner similarly argued for a uniform regime of legal equality by drawing a contrast with Indigenous peoples, whose political decentralization he offered as evidence of their tragic backwardness. In illustrating "the incalculable mischief of State Rights," he invoked "our Indians, the Aborigines of the soil, split into tribes, possessing a barbarous independence, but through this perverse influence kept in constant strife, with small chance of improvement. Each chief is a representative of State Rights. Turning their backs upon Union, they turn their backs upon civilization itself."[39]

These remarks share a troubling invocation of American "civilization"—one which is defined in contrast to Indigenous peoples, who "turn their backs" on it (per Sumner) in "disdain" (per Douglass). In attempting to capitalize on an unprecedented opportunity to realize the equality of *other* groups, Douglass and Sumner invited their audiences to imagine an idealized American society into which these groups might be incorporated. The contours of this imagined society are made all the sharper, and the seeming strength of those arguments for incorporation are augmented, by way of contrast with people whose supposedly alien cultural and political traditions mark them as unincorporable. While it is worth keeping in mind the differences between persuasive oratory and careful philosophical argument—especially since these remarks are somewhat out of character for each figure—these lapses illustrate the dangers of failing to observe Allen's distinction between *unity* and *solidarity*.[40] As I argued in the previous chapter, democratic solidarity need not rely on any specific, antecedent commonality among members of the demos, and as Allen argues, it does not require strictly uniform modes of citizenship.

Indeed, for a statist logic of membership like the one defended here, demanding uniformity is not only unnecessary but also perverse—and this perversity is most acute in the case of Indigenous peoples. Because Indigenous peoples were forcibly incorporated into the American state, a theory that takes the state as providing the boundaries of the demos, but which fails to consider *how* those boundaries were formed, bases its approach on historical injustices that it consigns to oblivion and thus risks perpetuating the oppression that a theory of democratic solidarity is intended to counteract.[41] Calling attention to this risk, scholars of Indigenous politics maintain that "taking the claims of Indigenous peoples seriously" requires that we "challenge the standard assumption that the state and its boundaries are justified."[42] Below, I will argue that the tradition of democratic thinking reconstructed here eventually developed resources that make it capable of taking up this challenge—albeit in response to a slightly different array of questions. But before discussing how these conceptual tools were developed in the early twentieth century, it is worth making a few observations about the issues raised by the status of Indigenous peoples.

First, it is not the case that normative questions surrounding democratic inclusion and Indigenous peoples could be dissolved simply by endorsing strong forms of separatism, up to and including secession. For as scholars of Indigenous politics frequently note, "secession is something rarely appealed to by Indigenous polities."[43] Since Indigenous peoples rarely demand secession, their political status is likely to involve continued subjection to state authority in some form—which raises inescapable normative questions about how that subjection could be made democratically legitimate. Second, if Indigenous peoples are likely to remain subject to the authority of a democratic state (rather than seceding from it), we need to ask which models of democracy are likely to respond satisfactorily to their claims. Here, it is relevant to note, following Philip Pettit, that a "thin," "electoral" version of democracy "is not particularly hospitable to special minority claims"—including those of Indigenous populations.[44] Pettit's observation parallels the previous chapter's rejection of a thin, electoral account of democracy, on the basis of its inability to account for significant relational dimensions of democratic self-rule. If we reject that model, we need to offer a *replacement* account of how democratic citizens must relate, if not through the largely individualistic and aggregative method of counting votes in an electoral contest. The kind of relation that best promotes democratic equality between Indigenous peoples and other citizens will depend on the details of different cases, as well as the nature of the claims that Indigenous peoples make against the state (which usually include claims to a degree of self-government, land rights, acknowledgment of historical injustices, treaty observations, and so on). Generally speaking, the imperative of identification lends support to some common demands of Indigenous peoples: that democratic states recognize how their settler-colonial history generates specific obligations to Indigenous communities, including the obligation to engage in ongoing processes of dialogue with them and to acknowledge what may be their uniquely compelling claim to the maintenance of partly separate cultural and political institutions.

From the claim that settler states can only adequately respond to Indigenous claims, and hence progress toward democracy, through such processes, it follows that the *existing* political order may turn out to be in need of reform if it is to attain democratic legitimacy in the eyes of all its citizens.

This signals an important difference between my argument and some of the most common ways in which other theorists invoke civic nationalism and constitutional patriotism. In different ways, both constitutional patriots and civic nationalists assume that there is a set of broadly shared values whose meaning is more or less static, that these values accurately capture the nature of the state's constitution and/or its citizens' normative commitments, and that this set of basic values (or constitutional structure) is *already* just, such that it is a worthy object of loyalty. Rather than beginning from this set of assumptions, my account asserts that citizens can only *render* their shared order democratic, and can only *generate* a shared perspective or common values, by committing themselves to solidaristic processes of deliberation and contestation that include everyone within the state. Only such processes can achieve a genuinely common realization of civic values, one that covers previously excluded groups and unanticipated circumstances. It is likely, moreover, that such processes will produce a translation of or variation in the meanings of such values so that they can reflect the perspective of newly included members.[45]

In this way, my approach heeds the warning, often issued by theorists of Indigenous politics, that we should not begin our inquiry by assuming the legitimacy of the liberal state as presently constituted. The claims of Indigenous groups present an opportunity, as Duncan Ivison puts it, to promote "modes of public reasoning" that are "open to counter-assertions and contestations of existing normative orders and authorities," and that present a chance to "(re)form the bases of new sources of legitimacy, and thus of new forms of political community."[46] That this will require institutional innovation is not necessarily a problem for liberal-democratic states, since—as Ivison writes, in a passage that echoes the core of my own argument about identification—"we should look for the glue of liberal democratic belonging not in pre-existing cultural or national traits, but rather in the way in which our democratic practices grapple with difference and disagreement." From this perspective, the changes called for by many Indigenous movements present "an extraordinary resource for free societies, as opposed to a threat to them."[47]

By the early twentieth century, democratic thinkers in the United States were beginning to systematically theorize such resources. Thinkers of this era exhibit a notable sensitivity to the possibilities presented by difference—while demonstrating a growing consciousness that certain homogenizing assumptions about American civilization risked undermining the kind of democracy they were trying to build. Even then, however, progress was fitful. Consider, for example, the Progressive thinker Herbert Croly, who appreciated more keenly than nearly any other thinker of his era how Americans' political imaginations exhibited partialities and parochialisms that lagged behind the implicitly broader scope of the democratic ideals they professed. Croly offered an especially clear diagnosis in his 1909 book *The Promise of American Life*:

> For better or worse the American people have proclaimed themselves to be a democracy, and they have proclaimed that democracy means popular economic, social, and moral emancipation . . . The economic and social changes of the past generation have brought out a serious and a glaring contradiction between the demands of a constructive democratic ideal and the machinery of methods and institutions, which have been considered sufficient for its realization. This is the fundamental discrepancy which must be at least partially eradicated before American national integrity can be triumphantly re-affirmed.[48]

Croly perceived that the traditional Jeffersonian association of democracy with localism was ill-equipped to address the problems of a country reshaped by war, Reconstruction, and industrialization. He envisioned replacing this obsolete tradition with new self-interpretations, revised historical narratives, and major changes to political institutions and the state-federal balance of power. The United States, he wrote, must become "a democracy devoted to the welfare of the whole people by means of a conscious labor of individual and social improvement; and that is precisely the sort of democracy which demands for its realization the aid of the Hamiltonian nationalistic organization and principle."[49] Yet thinkers in the Progressive era were sharply divided over the question of how to understand "the whole people," as Croly put it— and many, Croly included, endorsed views on race, gender, immigration, and empire that were at odds with a genuinely inclusive and egalitarian vision of the demos.[50]

It is in the Progressive-era debate over these issues that we can locate, in germinal form, a theorization of American peoplehood that also contains resources to respond to the claims of Indigenous peoples. Other figures of the era—those who shared Croly's diagnosis of the United States' obsolete, dysfunctional, and undemocratic political traditions, but who lacked his imperialist sympathies and questioned his elitist vision of efficient social control—began to develop a more inclusive conception of the American demos. Jonathan Hansen calls these turn-of-the-century American thinkers "cosmopolitan patriots." At the outset of the twentieth century, Hansen writes,

> All sorts of internal distinctions constituted the American people: not Indian, not African American, not female, not Catholic, not Jewish, not Asian, not southern or

eastern European—the list goes on and on. Alleged to be inherently, permanently *different* from the white male Protestant majority, these people were thought to be, ipso facto, fundamentally unequal to it, hence unworthy of democratic citizenship. The foremost aim of the cosmopolitan patriots was to end the invidious conflation of citizenship with cultural homogeneity at the heart of American nationalism... As mature adults, Eugene V. Debs, Jane Addams, and W. E. B. Du Bois would work to make the so-called imaginings of the American national community more generous, more encompassing, a task made possible by the protean quality of national identity.[51]

Alongside figures like Debs, Addams, and Du Bois, another major proponent of this "cosmopolitan ideal," as he put it, was the radical writer Randolph Bourne, who in 1916 called for "a genuine integrity, a wholeness and soundness of enthusiasm and purpose which can only come when no national colony within our America feels that it is being discriminated against or that its cultural case is being prejudged."[52] That same year, John Dewey wrote that Americans faced "the difficulty of developing the good aspect of nationalism without its evil side; of developing a nationalism which is the friend and not the foe of internationalism." This, Dewey cautioned, was not a question of perfecting any "outward machinery"; rather, it was "a matter of ideas, of emotions, of intellectual and moral disposition and outlook."[53] "We must ask what a real nationalism, a real Americanism, is like," Dewey continued. "For unless we know our own character and purpose we are not likely to be intelligent in our selection of the means to further them."[54] On that deeply contested issue of the nation's "character," Dewey is worth quoting at length:

> The American nation is itself complex and compound. Strictly speaking it is interracial and inter-national in its make-up. It is composed of a multitude of peoples speaking different tongues, inheriting diverse traditions, cherishing varying ideals of life. This fact is basic to *our* nationalism as distinct from that of other peoples. Our national motto 'One from Many' cuts deep and extends far. It denotes a fact which doubtless adds to the difficulty of getting a genuine unity. But it also immensely enriches the possibilities of the result to be attained... Such terms as Irish-American or Hebrew-American or German-American are false terms because they seem to assume something which is already in existence called America to which the other factor may be externally hitched on. The fact is the genuine American, the typical American, is himself a hyphenated character. This does not mean that he is part American, and that some foreign ingredient is then added. It means that, as I have said, he is international and interracial in his make-up.[55]

Significantly, Dewey characterized this search for "a real Americanism" not as an effort to restore a bygone ideal, or even to identify a present-day commonality, but as a goal "to be attained." This suggestion—that an American demos did not yet exist but could only be brought into being by an effort that the country had not yet undertaken—echoed earlier figures in the United States' democratic tradition, who frequently reminded their compatriots that the American demos was an unachieved and daunting ideal. Frederick Douglass, writing in 1862, declared to readers of his *Douglass' Monthly* that "great duties and responsibilities are devolved upon us."[56] Reminding them that "the structure of the American Constitution and Government imply the existence among the whole people of a fraternal good will, an earnest spirit of co-operation for the common good, a mutual dependence of all upon each and of each upon all,"[57] Douglass warned that merely "putting down the rebels in arms" would not achieve the war's ultimate goal. "The work before us," he wrote, "is nothing less than a radical revolution in all the modes of thought which have flourished under the blighting slave system."[58] In the title of his essay, Douglass described this succinctly as "the work of the future." The next year, as Lincoln memorialized the dead at Gettysburg, he similarly spoke of "the great task remaining before us" and "the unfinished work" that fell upon living Americans who sought a "new birth of freedom."

These intertwined themes of responsibility, work, and futurity are likewise present in Walt Whitman's 1871 contention that democracy had "few or no full realizers and believers" and was "not yet . . . the fully-receiv'd, the fervid, the absolute faith."[59] Whitman compared the struggle for democracy's achievement to the demanding regimen of a gymnast. "Political democracy" was "life's gymnasium," and Americans were "freedom's athletes": "Whatever we do not attain, we at any rate attain the experiences of the fight, the hardening of the strong campaign, and throb with currents of attempt at least."[60] Concluding that "the fruition of democracy, on aught like a grand scale, resides altogether in the future,"[61] Whitman further maintained, in contrast to nationalists who judge their political community by the standards of a traditional culture, that the criteria appropriate for evaluating the American people would have to be entirely original. What he maintained of American poetry he also believed of the country itself: "Like America, it must extricate itself from even the greatest models of the past, and, while courteous to them, must have entire faith in itself, and the products of its own democratic spirit only."[62] A similar sentiment was expressed by Randolph Bourne in 1916:

> As long as we thought of Americanism in terms of the "melting-pot," our American cultural tradition lay in the past. It was something to which the new Americans

were to be moulded. In the light of our changing ideal of Americanism, we must perpetrate the paradox that our American cultural tradition lies in the future. It will be what we all together make out of this incomparable opportunity of attacking the future with a new key. Whatever American nationalism turns out to be, it is certain to become something utterly different from the nationalisms of twentieth-century Europe.[63]

A similar consciousness of opportunity and responsibility can be detected in James Baldwin's 1962 statement that "everything now ... is in our hands," which immediately precedes his call to "achieve our country."[64] This latter phrase from Baldwin inspired the title of Richard Rorty's 1997 lectures on the American left, which noted the risk involved in this "thoroughgoing experiment in national self-creation."[65] To regard America as an unachieved experiment, a country whose "existence is in the future,"[66] is to reject two common myths: the reactionary myth of a once-idyllic America corrupted by social change (and awaiting restoration), and the complacent myth of an America perfected in the here and now. The American intellectual tradition is replete with democratic thinkers who, in rejecting these myths, accepted responsibility for undertaking an experiment, with a clear understanding of the risk of failure that accompanies all experimentation. As Whitman predicted: "The United States are destined either to surmount the gorgeous history of feudalism, or else prove the most tremendous failure of time."[67] Quoting this line of Whitman's, Rorty observed: "The price of temporalization is contingency."[68]

Such contingency was repeatedly demonstrated in the century following Reconstruction—including during Redemption and Jim Crow, the period of anti-Chinese sentiment culminating in the Chinese Exclusion Act of 1882, and the reactionary years between the onset of World War I and the Great Depression. Even during the height of the New Deal, which was, as Gary Gerstle writes, "an experiment in state building without precedent in [American] history,"[69] the Roosevelt administration acceded to the demands of segregationist Democrats who would consent to a welfare state only on Jim Crow terms.[70] Nonetheless, after the grim decades following Reconstruction's end, the twentieth century witnessed a succession of democratizing movements that took inspiration from a broad, solidaristic ideal of American peoplehood, beginning with Progressivism and continuing through to the New Deal, the Great Society, and the civil rights movement. "The appeal to a common destiny—to a sense that we, as Americans, are all in it together—has been a vital element in the mobilization of state power on behalf of a number of worthy causes," the historian David Hollinger writes, even if the deployment of such appeals "has always been episodic."[71]

This episodic tradition of democratization, however, would begin to crumble in the 1960s. Since that time, the United States has experienced a steady erosion of many of the gains that were achieved between the First and Second Reconstructions. What is striking about this long period of decline is not the strength of the reactionary countermobilization; American egalitarians have always faced strong opposition. Rather, the striking feature of this era is that for the first time in a century, egalitarians seemed increasingly disinclined to tether their ambitions to a solidaristic vision of shared peoplehood.

Regarding the precise timing of this change, Rorty approvingly cited Todd Gitlin's estimate of August 1964, the month in which "the Mississippi Freedom Democratic Party was denied seats at the Democratic Convention in Atlantic City, and . . . Congress passed the Tonkin Gulf Resolution."[72] After Atlantic City, according to Gitlin, a "liberal-radical rift widened . . . too fast for anyone to straddle"; it was in that "fateful month" that "a sharp line" was drawn "through the New Left's Sixties."[73] Similarly, Gary Gerstle argues that as a result of the compromises forced on them by Democratic elites at the 1964 Convention, a number of activists for racial justice "repudiated their faith in the civic nationalist tradition," a seismic development that "triggered the unraveling of the Rooseveltian nation."[74] As Rorty noted, "It is certainly the case that the mid-Sixties saw the beginning of the end of a tradition of leftist reformism which dated back to the Progressive Era."[75]

The faltering of this reformist tradition was fueled by a swift and consequential collapse of the distinction between a solidaristic vision of American peoplehood and simple nationalism. As Michael Kazin and Joseph McCartin write, "By the late 1960s, Americanism had become virtually the exclusive property of the cultural and political right," a transformation largely attributable to the "politics of the Vietnam War":

> Young radicals did not seek to draw attention to the distance between America's promise and its reality as much as to debunk the national creed itself as inherently reactionary and destructive. Many black, Native American, and Chicano militants viewed themselves as victims of Americanism, while white New Leftists dismissed appeals to patriotism as a smokescreen for imperialist war and the squelching of dissent.[76]

The American right had never accepted the democratizing implications of the narrative favored by radical Republicans, New Dealers, and civil rights activists; now, in the wake of this Vietnam-era change, it scarcely needed even to acknowledge them. For unlike earlier egalitarians who promoted an understanding of the United States that rejected both reactionary and complacent national mythologies, many thinkers after the 1960s came to view the ideal of a common country as hopelessly intertwined with those very myths. The result was a perverse conflation of democratic solidarity with its familiar ethnonationalist and inegalitarian nemeses. As James Kloppenberg observed in 2002: "During the last four decades, many Americans on the left have tried to demonstrate their radicalism by dismissing this tradition of aspirational nationalism as a form of apology or celebration of America's profoundly flawed, inegalitarian past."[77] In a similar vein, Jefferson Cowie argues that "in recent decades, progressive forces in the United States" have "surrender[ed] a robust and hopeful sense of national citizenship," whereas "before the 1960s, dissenting and progressive movements regularly invoked nationalist and patriotic themes."[78] Recalling his experience in the social movements of the 1960s, including his time as an early president of Students for a Democratic Society, Gitlin observed that the New Left "had to find the right relation to the American nation; having taken America's dream of itself seriously, it was quick to feel betrayed when the dream turned into nightmare, quick to relocate the promised land on some revolutionary soil elsewhere."[79] For all their other disagreements, reactionaries and egalitarians increasingly concurred on the essentially conservative and exclusionary nature of American peoplehood.

With few egalitarians willing to invoke the language of shared peoplehood in support of their agenda, public understandings of what it meant to belong to the United States gradually became dominated by those favoring what Rogers Smith calls the "inegalitarian ascriptive" tradition of American identity—characterized by various iterations of the belief "that 'true' Americans are 'chosen' by God, history, or nature to possess superior moral and intellectual traits associated with their race, ethnicity, religion, gender, and sexual orientation," with the consequence that "nonwhites, women, and various others should be governed as subjects or second-class citizens, not as equals, denied full individual rights, including many property rights, and sometimes excluded from the nation altogether."[80] By the time that concerns about democratic decline became widespread in the twenty-first century, the politics of American peoplehood had chiefly become a matter of specifying which Americans do *not* belong. As Gerstle observes, this collapse can be traced back to the decisive years marking the end of the New Deal order:

> The 1970s crisis in American nationalism did not trigger, of course, a literal fragmentation or unraveling of the American nation ... The nationalist crisis occurred

primarily in the realm of *ideology, culture, and institutions*. Many people who resided in America no longer imagined that they belonged to the same national community or that they shared a common set of ideals. The bonds of nationhood had weakened, and the Rooseveltian program of nation building that had created those bonds in the first place had been repudiated. A nationalist era that had begun in the early decades of the twentieth century had come to a stunning end.[81]

Gerstle's careful wording makes an important distinction between a breakdown in civic imagination and a form of fragmentation caused by difference per se. The changes of the postwar era did transform the United States, and political activism from the 1960s onward was increasingly marked by the assertion of difference—a trend that was not lost on cultural critics and academic observers, from whose ranks emerged numerous studies attempting to make sense of a pervasive feeling of dislocation.[82] But the United States had long been characterized by diversity, and although it presented (then as now) complicated questions for national solidarity, this diversity was by no means an insurmountable obstacle for earlier generations of democratic thinkers. Moreover, the suggestion that "difference" necessarily undermines solidarity risks reifying racial, ethnic, sexual, and other traits whose political salience is socially constructed and malleable. The forces that reshaped American politics and displaced this major tradition of democratic thinking cannot therefore be traced simply to demographic changes or the celebration of difference; they came from changes in styles of thought and argument. As Daniel Rodgers writes, if we are to understand this era, we must look to "struggles over the intellectual *construction* of reality," to "the ways in which understandings of identity, society, economy, nation, and time were argued out," and how, in the postwar era, "imagined collectivities shrank." What we find in such an investigation is a wide-ranging and complex tendency in public thought, elegantly captured in Rodgers's simple phrase: the "age of fracture."[83]

The consequences of this broad shift in political thinking would hardly have surprised intellectuals of the early twentieth century. In 1914, *The American Journal of Sociology* circulated a letter on the theme "What Is Americanism?" to 250 "carefully selected" Americans,[84] asking their views on the "ideals, policies, programs, or specific purposes" Americans should emphasize in the "immediate future."[85] Among the recipients was W. E. B. Du Bois, who responded that "Americans in the immediate future should place most stress upon the *abolition of the color line*."[86] His brief elaboration succinctly captured the connections between an inclusive vision of American peoplehood and the pursuit of democracy:

> Just so long as the majority of men are treated as inhuman, and legitimate objects of commercial exploitation, religious damnation, and social ostracism, just so long will democracy be impossible in the world. *Without democracy we must have continual attempts at despotism and oligarchy, with the resultant failure through the ignorance of those who attempt to rule their fellow-men without knowing their fellow-men.* America, instead of being the land of the free, has made herself a hotbed of racial prejudice and of despicable propaganda against the majority of men.[87]

Du Bois's response amounts to a succinct defense of identification on the scale of the whole polity. Democracy fails—it degenerates into despotism and oligarchy—insofar as citizens attempt to rule over each other without knowing each other.

Part II: Applications

Building on the theory and history outlined in these opening chapters, the second half of this book critically examines how thinkers in the age of fracture have addressed three problems confronting American democracy: the return of nativism, the stalled progress of racial integration, and the twinned ascendance of economic inequality and political oligarchy. Each of these problems has worsened since the end of the Second Reconstruction, and responses to each have been hampered by egalitarians' reluctance to invoke compelling visions of a common American people. Indeed, as I will show, in each case there is a tendency not to think of these problems as primarily problems of *membership* at all. To insist otherwise—to frame these problems as fundamentally about the meaning and scope of membership in American democracy—is to confront directly the question of identification and its scale. In Chapter 1, I argued that identification is essential to democratic self-rule, and that its proper scope is coextensive with the entire population of a state. In this chapter, I traced the emergence and development of this view among democratic thinkers whose reformulation of American peoplehood adopts that same logic of inclusive solidarity.

In the chapters to follow, I will critically survey a range of views that either downplay the importance of identification or otherwise locate it somewhere besides the whole population of a state. In many cases, these approaches are informed by understandable worries about the homogenizing, violent, exclusionary, or otherwise oppressive tendencies that have often marked the pursuit of shared peoplehood. But there is another tradition of peoplehood in American politics. If my account of identification is persuasive, that tradition and its account of democracy should not be ignored or discarded. Accordingly, each chapter combines historical reconstruction with theoretical argument, in an attempt to recover the normative logic of democratic membership embodied by this discarded intellectual tradition. Through this approach, I hope to show that while these problems are newly urgent, they are by no means new—and that there is much to be learned from an examination of how earlier generations of egalitarian thinkers addressed them.

PART II
APPLICATIONS

Chapter 3
Migration, Membership, and Democracy

"I have been in California my whole life," explained Luisa Argueta. This statement contained a minor inaccuracy of major importance. To be precise, Luisa had lived in California since she was four months old, when her mother had brought her there from Guatemala. Now, Luisa was nineteen years old and facing deportation. She and her mother had received a removal order from U.S. Immigration and Customs Enforcement (ICE), signed "Very truly yours," with instructions to report for removal at 9:00 a.m. on September 12. The forty-pound weight limit on their baggage was stricter than most U.S. airlines impose on vacationers checking a suitcase. After a failed asylum appeal and multiple stays of removal, Luisa and her mother were facing the prospect of a life without her stepfather (a legal permanent resident) and her two half-sisters (both U.S. citizens), one of whom suffered from a rare medical condition that could not be treated in Guatemala.[1] Removal would mean family separation.

It was the summer of 2011, and Luisa and her mother were caught directly in the administrative manifestation of a national ambivalence: the government was hardly extending them a warm welcome, but at the same time, it had a torturous tendency to vacillate on their removal. Just months before their scheduled removal to Guatemala, ICE's director had released a memo advising the agency to exercise "prosecutorial discretion" in accordance with "civil immigration enforcement priorities." The memo declared that scarce enforcement resources should be focused on "the promotion of national security, border security, public safety, and the integrity of the immigration system,"[2] not on migrants like Luisa, who posed no threat to public safety, who had been present for a long time, who had family ties with U.S. citizens, who were pursuing an education (an honor roll student in high school, Luisa was enrolled at Diablo Valley College), and so on.

Yet many of ICE's agents were openly contemptuous of these instructions. A year earlier, its union had issued a no-confidence vote in the agency's leadership, warning of "amnesty,"[3] and implementation of the agency's discretionary criteria was inconsistent at best.[4] As a result, many migrants found themselves selected for removal just when they believed they had been selected for relief. In such a context, "I have been in California my whole life" should not be read merely as a statement of (near) fact but as a claim of membership: despite the fact that its government was trying to remove her, Luisa was asserting that she belonged in the United States.

If she had been able to put this membership claim to the American public, Luisa would not have found a universally warm reception. In the previous decade, major immigration reform bills had failed repeatedly; this latest ICE memo was an attempt to partially accomplish, through administrative maneuvering, what could not pass a deadlocked Congress. That winter, as Luisa (granted a temporary reprieve until the end of the school year) wondered would happen next, Republican presidential hopeful Mitt Romney announced his support for a policy of "self-deportation," hoping to attract primary voters from his party's right wing. As *The New York Times* explained: "The idea is to make it so difficult for illegal immigrants to live in this country—by denying them work, driver's licenses and any public benefits and by stepping up enforcement—that they will give up and go home."[5] Romney carried the primary yet lost the general election, receiving just 27% of the Hispanic vote against President Obama's 71%.[6] In the wake of this performance, the Republican National Committee (RNC) commissioned a report (widely termed an "autopsy") that predicted that "unless changes are made, it will be increasingly difficult for Republicans to win another presidential election in the near future."[7] Deeming it "imperative that the RNC changes how it engages with Hispanic communities,"[8] the autopsy issued a warning: "If Hispanic Americans perceive that a GOP nominee or candidate does not want them in the United States (i.e. self-deportation), they will not pay attention to our next sentence."[9] Going so far as to declare that "we must embrace and champion comprehensive immigration reform,"[10] the report was interpreted by many as a sign that the party was ready to change its approach.

Less than three years later, Donald Trump launched his bid for the GOP's presidential nomination. As he announced his campaign, Trump made it clear that immigration would be his primary issue, declaring: "When Mexico sends its people, they're not sending their best . . . They're bringing drugs. They're bringing crime. They're rapists. And some, I assume, are good people."[11] Trump's call for expanded deportations along with an "impenetrable, physical, tall, powerful, beautiful" border wall were the signature policies of his successful campaign.[12]

Trump's ascent was an obvious repudiation of the conclusion reached by Republican elites after 2012. Yet it also signaled a deeper, broader challenge to what the legal scholar Robert Tsai calls "the political settlement of the 1960s"[13]— which reshaped America's political order through not only the Civil Rights Act and the Voting Rights Act but also the 1965 Immigration and Nationality Act. Although the Immigration Act occupies a lesser place in popular historical memory, Tsai argues that it deserves to be ranked alongside its better-known contemporaries as a similarly "monumental" and "transformative" achievement that enshrined "a basic set of deeply-rooted principles concerning an egalitarian polity . . . that politicians of both parties embraced."[14] Those principles are reflected in the 1965 law's repeal of the national origins quotas that Congress had imposed in the so-called Johnson-Reed Immigration Act of 1924. The culmination of a series of restrictive measures dating back to 1882's Chinese Exclusion Act, the 1924 law favored migrants from Northwest Europe and limited—or in many cases banned outright—immigration from those parts of the world populated by groups deemed racially incompatible with American society. Its quotas were explicitly justified on the basis of pseudoscientific ideas of racial hierarchy. When President Lyndon Johnson signed the 1965 Immigration Act four decades later, he rebuked the 1924 law in remarks that invited comparison to concurrent civil rights legislation. Arguing that the United States had "flourished because it was fed from so many sources—because it was nourished by so many cultures and traditions and peoples," Johnson called the national origins quota system a "harsh injustice" that "violated the basic principle of American democracy" and was "un-American in the highest sense."[15]

The architects of the first Trump's administration's immigration policies—including his attorney general, Jeff Sessions; his chief strategist, Steve Bannon; and his senior adviser, Stephen Miller—took a different view. To these figures, it was the 1965 law that deserved scorn and condemnation. Sessions, who as a U.S. senator had been known for opposing immigration reformers within his own party,[16] tended to frame his concerns about "uncontrolled immigration" in economic terms.[17] But in a 2015 interview with Bannon—at that time, executive chairman of the far-right Breitbart News—Sessions raised another point:

> In seven years we'll have the highest percentage of Americans, non-native born, since the founding of the Republic. Some people think we've always had these numbers, and it's not so, it's very unusual, it's a radical change. When the numbers reached about this high in 1924, the President and Congress changed the policy, and it slowed down immigration significantly, we then assimilated through the 1965 [sic] and created really the solid middle class of America, with assimilated immigrants, and it was good for America. We passed a law that went far beyond what anybody realized in 1965, and we're on a path now to surge far past what the situation was in 1924.[18]

Disdain for the 1965 law was also a running theme of the frequent correspondence between Breitbart's editors and Stephen Miller, a Sessions aide who would later design immigration policy in both Trump administrations. In 2015, Miller began emailing Breitbart editors in order to shape the site's immigration coverage.[19] In messages that included several links to white nationalist websites, Miller praised the immigration system of the 1920s–1960s. He also made seemingly approving reference to a novel, popular among white nationalists and neo-Nazis, which graphically depicts an apocalyptic invasion of France by nonwhite immigrants.[20] In summer 2016, by which time Miller had sent more than 900 such emails, *The Wall Street Journal* reported that "more than anyone else on the campaign, [Miller] has achieved a mind-meld with the candidate."[21] For his part, President Trump was frank about his desire to admit more immigrants from Norway, and fewer from Haiti, El Salvador, and African nations—wondering aloud, in a 2018 meeting with lawmakers, "Why are we having all these people from shithole countries come here?"[22]

The ascent of these perspectives well into the twenty-first century indicates the enduring potency of reaction against the Second Reconstruction's attempt to reshape the meaning of democratic membership in the United States. It is therefore unsurprising that contemporary opposition to Reconstructionist reforms should crystallize in part around the issue of immigration: the nexus of questions regarding who should be admitted, and on what terms, ultimately concerns the nature of belonging in the political community.

Both public and philosophical debate, however, frequently obscure this fact. In policy briefs and op-ed pages, immigration is often framed as a largely utilitarian matter of increasing GDP or maximizing the efficiency of labor markets. Among political theorists, discussion tends to emphasize the urgent humanitarian and/or economic needs of many migrants. In short, membership is not always the top concern of either host states, which often prioritize economic goals, or migrants, who often need work or refuge more urgently than they need to join the political life of the host country. But regardless of a migrant's reason for crossing a border—whether they are seeking better economic options, refuge from oppression, escape from violence, reunion with family members, or simply a change of scenery—they become subject to the authority of a host state when they enter its territory. This is a fact of special significance for democratic states since their claim to be democracies at all rests on whether they include everyone residing in the polity as a member—not merely in formal terms but informally as well, as part of a demos characterized by solidaristic identification.

Among philosophers who write about immigration from liberal, cosmopolitan, and democratic perspectives, this strong ideal of membership is often viewed with suspicion. These thinkers broadly agree that many states, especially wealthy ones, ought to admit more migrants than they currently do, and they fear that political support for immigration in destination states will erode if new migrants are extended generous terms of incorporation. Moreover, they take seriously the "numbers-rights trade-off" identified by economists: as migrants are granted more generous rights to equal wages, welfare benefits, and so on, they will become more expensive to employ, and the number of migrants will correspondingly decline.[23] Insisting on strong norms of solidarity, as well as formal political and economic inclusion, thus threatens to reduce the overall level of migration, which restricts individual freedom of movement, cements deep global inequalities of wealth and income, traps desperate people in dire circumstances, and obstructs economic growth that would benefit humanity in general. For these reasons, many philosophers support withholding the full extension of citizenship, and other ways of thinning down membership, if doing so would help maximize the overall level of migration.

In this chapter, I aim to show that this trade-off is not only undesirable but also unnecessary—that in principle, democratic states do not need to choose between strong ideals of membership and openness to higher levels of migration. My argument shares the basic moral premises from which these other approaches begin, and it does not presume that democratic inclusion is of greater moral weight than global distributive justice or freedom of movement. Rather, I take the view that because there are other ways of promoting global distributive justice and freedom of movement, we are not required to dilute democratic membership to advance these goals. A more open, more just, and more democratic system of international migration does not require weakening particularistic bonds among citizens. To the contrary, it requires both migrants and host citizenries to cultivate a robust and expansive form of solidarity capable of incorporating new members into an ongoing project of collective self-rule.

Nativism's resurgence threatens this ideal, insofar as it rests on the assertion that immigration is generally at odds with a genuine sense of shared peoplehood. In this way, the new nativists risk confirming many political theorists' suspicion that fellow-feeling among citizens is likely to prove incompatible with openness to outsiders. This seems to present a dispiriting choice: either solidarity can be achieved on xenophobic terms or openness can be achieved by sacrificing equal political status, economic rights, and/or solidarity. The former promises a *Herrenvolk* democracy; the latter augurs a society where democracy has been transformed into a project of domination, with legally defined underclasses, complex webs of hierarchy and dependence, and pervasive social alienation.

The rejection of these bleak alternatives begins with an account of democracy that emphasizes the central importance of full and inclusive membership, while also showing how that membership (properly understood) can be broadly shared even among people of diverse origins and characteristics. Drawing on historical precedents in the American political tradition, I show how democratic thinkers from the mid-nineteenth century onward mobilized an aspirational vision of American peoplehood that expresses this ideal. The thinkers in this tradition show that a robust ideal of membership can be marshaled in the service of openness, not opposition, to immigration. They offer a way of thinking about migration that opposes nativism without sacrificing the potent moral, conceptual, and rhetorical resources contained by an aspirational ideal of shared democratic peoplehood. A clearer account of that ideal is essential to addressing the complex set of disagreements that mark the contemporary landscape of immigration politics. In the final section of the chapter, I use this account of democratic membership to draw a contrast with other liberal, democratic, and cosmopolitan theorists to show how it offers greater power to defuse contemporary forms of ethnonationalism, nativism, and xenophobia, without sacrificing core democratic principles and goals.

The aim of this engagement is to correct the misconception, potently exploited by the far right, that liberal and cosmopolitan normative commitments necessarily entail a rejection of civic belonging. This misconception rests on both theoretical oversimplification and the historical erasure of a significant strand of American democratic thinking—one that offers lessons for responding to the contemporary descendants of earlier generations of nativists who similarly attempted to claim sole right to define the American people.

Immigration and Democratic Membership in American Political Thought

As I noted in Chapter 2, the United States' "state-nation" sequence of political development led its democratic reformers to abandon the nationalist approach of drawing a state around the boundaries of a prepolitically defined people. Instead, the distinctive aim of these egalitarians, beginning during the Civil War and Reconstruction, was to democratize the U.S. by encouraging Americans to imagine themselves as a demos on the scale of their newly nationalized state.

Amid the turbulent politics of the mid-nineteenth century, this attempt to seize the meaning of American peoplehood and reinvent it for democratic ends had both internal and external dimensions: many of the same figures who first marshaled this ideal against the states' rights defense of slavery also opposed the era's powerful nativist currents. The connection was evident by the 1850s, as growing sectional divides over slavery divided and dissolved the Whig Party, while growing nativism led to the emergence of the American Party, or the "Know-Nothings." Formed in response to the high levels of immigration during the previous two decades, the Know-Nothings' "main goal," as James McPherson writes, "was to reduce the power of foreign-born voters in politics": they proposed extending the waiting period for naturalization to twenty-one years, along with other measures that "might discourage immigrants from coming to the United States."[24] An 1854 questionnaire for admission to the party dictates the sworn responses required to questions such as, "Are you by religious faith a Roman Catholic? (I am not)," "Were you born in this country? (I was)," and "Are you willing to use your influence to elect ... none but native born citizens of *America*, of this *Country*, to the exclusion of *all* foreigners, and *all* Roman Catholics ... regardless of all party predilections *whatever*? (Answer I am)."[25]

The Know-Nothings' exclusionary logic is explained at length in what historian Bruce Levine has called the party's "Bible"[26]: the extravagantly titled *A Defence of the American Policy, as Opposed to the Encroachments of Foreign Influence, and Especially to the Interference of the Papacy in the Political Interests and Affairs of the United States*, published in 1856 by the prominent nativist Thomas R. Whitney. As Levine writes, Whitney—elected to Congress in 1854 under the party's banner—"sneered at" and "spurned" the assimilationist view, held by many Whigs, that immigrants would embrace American culture if offered relatively generous terms of political incorporation.[27] Assurances of assimilation did little to placate Know-Nothings like Whitney; instead, they favored restricting full citizenship to the native born and allowing immigrants only "passive citizenship rights," not "the right actively to shape the polity."[28]

Whitney's *Defence* rejects the possibility of entrusting immigrants with citizenship. "The word naturalization may be appropriately called a *misnomer*, because the process of naturalization is one of the most unnatural of all proceedings," Whitney wrote. "You may, indeed, invest an alien with the rights and privileges of a native citizen, or subject, but you cannot invest him with the *home sentiment* and feeling of the native."[29] Reasoning that people who emigrate from the land of their birth have, by that act, proven themselves devoid of natural home sentiments, Whitney warned that "the man who could coldly renounce that natural allegiance to his home, is not the man who ought to be trusted in his professions of fealty in any other country."[30] Professions of allegiance to the new country would "doubtless be prompted solely by selfish motives" and would be "unreliable."[31] Yet "on the other hand," Whitney mused, if an immigrant *did* retain "his natural instincts, while yet he forswears those instincts, and renounces all attachment, association, or allegiance to his native land, his trustworthiness is still in doubt, because, in making the oath of allegiance, there is a mental reservation, not palpable, perhaps, at the time, even to his own perception, but liable to development through the pressure of after circumstances."[32] In short, immigrants could not be trusted because they had renounced their native loyalties, but they also could not be trusted because they might retain those loyalties. Lamenting the naturalization process that perpetuated this "moral fraud,"

Whitney asked: "Could not a system be devised that would protect alike the individual interest of the alien, and the interests of the State, without demanding this unnatural sacrifice?"[33] He proposed "a system of *affiliation*, instead of that which is called naturalization. A system that would identify the respectable resident immigrant with the *social family*, but not with the *political* family of the country and afford to him all the advantages of citizenship, except the right to take part in the government."[34] Here was a theory of membership fit for a nativist movement.

Many critics of the Know-Nothings objected to their conception of American peoplehood. In an 1855 letter, Abraham Lincoln expressed his disagreement with nativists by appealing to the Declaration of Independence—the same rhetorical move that marked his critique of slavery. He explained:

> I am not a Know-Nothing. That is certain. How could I be? How can any one who abhors the oppression of Negroes be in favor of degrading classes of white people? Our progress in degeneracy appears to me to be pretty rapid. As a nation, we began by declaring that *"all men are created equal."* We now practically read it "all men are created equal, *except Negroes*." When the Know-Nothings get control, it will read "all men are created equal, except Negroes, *and foreigners, and Catholics*." When it comes to this I should prefer emigrating to some country where they make no pretence of loving liberty—to Russia, for instance, where despotism can be taken pure, and without the base alloy of hypocrisy.[35]

Of course, Lincoln knew well that the universal scope of the Declaration's egalitarianism was not so obvious to other Americans.[36] But as he demonstrated throughout his career, the gap between the Declaration's words and the country's practices made it possible to invoke this potent text in the service of advancing democratic equality. At other times, Lincoln expressed his opposition to nativism more plainly, and more publicly, than he had in the 1850s. As he told an audience of Germans in 1861: "In regard to the Germans and foreigners, I esteem them no better than other people, nor any worse ... if there are any abroad who desire to make this the land of their adoption, it is not in my heart to throw aught in their way, to prevent them from coming to the United States."[37]

Charles Sumner likewise objected to the Know-Nothings, declaring in an 1855 speech that a party that "arraigns Catholics and foreigners ... is not the party of Freedom which we seek."[38] Like Lincoln, Sumner expressed his opposition by directly challenging the nativists' vision of American peoplehood. Sumner hoped that the incorporation of immigrants into American political life would help bring about a new kind of diverse republic, a "fusion of all races here." Noting that the "condition of isolation" in which different provinces and nations once lived had "gradually passed," Sumner declared: "In our country a new example is already displayed. From all nations people comingle here."[39] Addressing the Know-Nothing view that "Catholics are mostly foreigners, and on this account are condemned,"[40] Sumner asked whether there could be any reason in such hostility:

> More than one quarter of a million are annually landed on our shores. *The manner in which they shall be received is a problem of national policy.* All will admit that any influence which they bring, hostile to our institutions, calculated to substitute priestcraft for religion and bigotry for Christianity, must be deprecated and opposed. All will admit, too, that there must be some assurance of their purpose to become *not merely consumers of the fruits of our soil, but useful, loyal, and permanent members of our community, upholders of the general welfare*. With this simple explanation, I cannot place any check upon the welcome to foreigners.... The history of our country, in its humblest as well as most exalted spheres, testifies to the merit of foreigners.[41]

Sumner's complex response to nativism begins by briefly allowing that some immigrants *could* potentially harbor bigotry or hostility toward American institutions and that such attitudes should be "deprecated and opposed." However, Sumner quickly turns this familiar nativist argument back on its proponents: since there is no basis for assuming that immigrants generally *do* harbor these attitudes, they cannot plausibly be invoked as a justification for restrictive policies. Subtly reversing the logic of nativist fears, Sumner suggests that insofar as the country needs "assurances" from immigrants, those assurances point toward inclusion, not exclusion. Like Lincoln, Sumner appeals to a resonant national text—in this case, by referencing the Constitution's preamble ("upholders of the general welfare"). This reference not only defends but also celebrates the changing face of the nation. It also grounds a distinction crucial to a democratic theory of immigration: between "[mere] consumers" of the society's wealth, on the one hand, and "permanent members" and "upholders of the general welfare," on the other. The resulting vision of immigration and membership reverses the "affiliationist" model promoted by Whitney, with its denial that immigrants could fully join the political community. For Sumner, the reception of migrants "is a problem of national policy" because the demos has an interest that they join as *political* members who contribute to an ongoing project of collective self-rule. In other words, democrats like Sumner reached for an argument against nativism by appealing to a demanding vision of democratic citizenship—doing so in the service of inclusion, not exclusion.

This strategy was consistently adopted by democratic thinkers attempting to rescue the concept of American peoplehood from nativists, xenophobes, and racists. Perhaps no formulation of this ideal is more prescient than Frederick Douglass's vision of a "composite nationality," articulated in an 1869 speech endorsing Chinese immigration:

> I have said that the Chinese will come, and have given some reasons why we may expect them in very large numbers in no distant future. Do you ask if I would favor such immigration? I answer, *I would*. Would you admit them as witnesses in our courts of law? *I would*. Would you have them naturalized, and have them invested with all the rights of American citizenship? *I would*. Would you allow them to vote? *I would*. Would you allow them to hold office? *I would*.[42]

Douglass's support for a broadly open immigration policy was fused to a vision of political inclusion and an expansively defined demos: "If we would reach a degree of civilization higher and grander than any yet attained, we should welcome to our ample continent all nations, kindreds, tongues and peoples, and as fast as they learn our language and comprehend the duties of citizenship, we should incorporate them into the American body politic. The outspread wings of the American eagle are broad enough to shelter all who are likely to come."[43] He further envisioned a fusion of peoples who were united without abandoning their particularities:

> We shall spread the network of our science and civilization over all who seek their shelter, whether from Asia, Africa, or the Isles of the Sea. We shall mold them all, each after his kind, into Americans; Indian and Celt; negro and Saxon; Latin and Teuton; Mongolian and Caucasian; Jew and gentile, all shall here bow to the same law, speak the same language, support the same government, enjoy the same liberty, vibrate with the same national enthusiasm, and seek the same national ends.[44]

The imagery here—of "molding" Americans—may seem initially to gesture toward an assimilationist policy, but notice the crucial qualifier: "each after his kind," which suggests that the creation of a "composite" identity does not involve the sacrifice of distinctive characteristics. Of course, Douglass's view did not prevail in his day; in 1882, Congress banned the entry of Chinese laborers entirely. Yet if this vision of the American demos was never dominant, neither was it wholly absent from public discourse, even during periods of extreme nativism and racism.

In fact, periods of nativism seem to have inspired egalitarians to sharpen their arguments in order to show that another kind of Americanism was possible.

This became a democratic imperative in the years during and after World War I, when American immigration policy grew increasingly conservative and coercive, codifying racial and ethnic hierarchies and instituting disciplinary programs of assimilation in immigrant communities. Public and private organizations both pursued campaigns of "Americanization," while the state censored publications, arrested labor activists, deported aliens suspected of political radicalism, and criminalized antiwar statements.[45] "Americanization was not necessarily incompatible with respect for immigrant subcultures," notes Eric Foner.[46] Yet the onset of World War I "transformed Americanization into a government-sponsored campaign to instill undivided loyalty in immigrant communities and gave the concept 'American' a deeply conservative new meaning."[47]

Following the approach developed by nineteenth-century opponents of the Know-Nothings and anti-Chinese sentiment, opponents of this coercive Americanization attempted to reclaim, rather than disclaim, the ideal of shared American peoplehood. A "strength of cooperation, this feeling that all who are here may have a hand in the destiny of America, will make for a finer spirit of integration than any narrow 'Americanism' or forced chauvinism," wrote Randolph Bourne in 1916.[48] Similarly, John Dewey declared: "No matter how loudly any one proclaims his Americanism, if he assumes that any one racial strain, any one component culture, no matter how early settled it was in our territory, or how effective it has proved in its own land, is to furnish a pattern to which all other strains and cultures are to conform, he is a traitor to an American nationalism."[49] Dewey continued: "I wish our teaching of American history in the schools took more account of the great waves of migration by which our land for over three centuries has been continuously built up, and made every pupil conscious of the rich breadth of our national make-up."[50]

Dewey envisioned the patient, persistent deployment of such a program in America's public schools, but other social institutions took up the task as well. Here, the example of the Foreign Language Information Service (FLIS) is illustrative. First organized in 1918 as part of the Committee on Public Information, the wartime coordinator of federal government propaganda, the FLIS was responsible for communicating a wide range of information (regarding draft registration, Liberty Loans, and much else) to non-English speakers.[51] Continuing as an independent organization after the war, it was for a brief period run by the Red Cross,[52] and by the mid-1930s, it began receiving federal support from the Roosevelt administration.[53] Over the course of its sometimes independent, sometimes quasi-official existence, the FLIS came to promote a vision of America that rejected the assimilative, conservative pressures of its era. In a circa 1921 document summarizing its work, the Service drily summarized the attitude that it existed to counteract:

> In recent years have come the "Americanizers." They have discovered that the immigrant is a Problem and have maintained that something must be done to him to lessen this problematical quality with which they have gratuitously endowed him. He must be "Americanized." The very term repudiates any recognition of the immigrant's own efforts to become an American. It insists that the immigrant conform, take on a sameness of customs and manners, rather than that he participate with the native born in a common purpose of effecting national unity and progress.[54]

Against this view, the Service insisted that "assimilation cannot be forced on the immigrant," and that it was rather the "prejudices of the native born toward the immigrant" that "must be overcome" since such attitudes posed the true "barrier to assimilation."[55] Noting that many immigrants were "not only uninformed, but misinformed, concerning laws, regulations, and customs, their own rights and their own obligations," and that an immigrant "cannot wait for this knowledge until he has mastered the language of the country," it furnished immigrants with information about the United States in more than a dozen languages, while simultaneously providing native-born Americans with information about new immigrants, often from foreign sources translated into English.[56] Perhaps surprisingly, given its origins in the Committee on Public Information, the FLIS announced its intention to remain "free from all taint of propaganda" and described its work as "dedicated" to a core belief:[57] "Understanding means sympathy, and sympathy begets unity."[58]

The organization's work during the height of the xenophobic 1920s underscores the sincerity of this belief. Its publication, initially titled *The Bulletin*, was by 1923 rechristened as *The Interpreter*—better reflecting its slogan, "to interpret America to the immigrant and the immigrant to America." In addition to its regular coverage of life in, and issues facing, different immigrant communities, *The Interpreter* published numerous meditations on the cultivation of an inclusive Americanism. These essays demonstrate a keen awareness of the complexities of aspiring to national unity, especially in light of that aspiration's vulnerability to assimilative cooptation. One 1923 article, titled "Americanization vs. 'Americanization,'" affirmed that "the bringing together of all [a community's] parts, foreign born and native born, is an excellent thing in itself and is conducive to the promotion of the best ideals of citizenship."[59] But it cautioned that such togetherness "can come only as the result of the right attitude *within* the community, an attitude made up of mutual friendliness, understanding and the spirit of cooperation between the foreign born and the native born, an attitude developed naturally and steadily over a long period of time."[60] A "*sine qua non* of this attitude," it went on, is the foreigner's sense of "standing shoulder to shoulder with their native born neighbors," something that proponents of Americanization had wrongly "tried to *hand down* from the *top*," when it "should have *grown up* from the *bottom*."[61]

How should such sentiments of solidarity grow up, cooperatively, among new immigrants and citizens? Sociologist Julius Drachsler, writing in the September 1924 issue, offered some reflections on the question. He acknowledged that incorporating new migrants was "a problem ... of no small proportions." But in an echo of Sumner's 1855 statement that "the manner in which they shall be received is a problem of national policy," Drachsler maintained that "of infinitely greater importance for American life is the *method and the meaning* of this process of incorporation. For what we do and *how we do it and why we do it*, will affect the future structure and complexion of American civilization."[62]

Generalizing, Drachsler suggested that earlier periods in American history had been marked by two broad strategies of incorporation. Until World War I, "the characteristic policy of the white settlers was either extermination, as in the case of the Indian, or subjugation, as in the case of the Negro," but toward other white immigrants, a "laissez-faire policy with reference to assimilation" prevailed.[63] During and immediately after the war, however, the government shifted to a policy of "compulsion, of forced conformity to a supposedly general social type," including the "compulsory study of English by the foreign born, the compulsory registration of aliens, [and] the prohibition of the foreign language press," all in the name of "national unity."[64]

Few, Drachsler supposed, would "question the need for national unity," but even so, neither policy provided a suitable model for achieving it.[65] The laissez-faire approach had subordinated everything to the goal of "rapid and profitable industrial expansion and exploitation of natural resources," resulting in a "magnificent wastefulness of human capacities and a sweeping disregard of human sensibilities and human loyalties."[66] What Drachsler called "the great steam roller of modern industrialism" had "flattened out and is continuing to flatten out stimulating variety into deadening uniformity."[67]

If the laissez-faire approach subordinated human needs to the pitiless demands of the market, the compulsory approach substituted "animal intelligence (using force)" for "human intelligence (using reason and reasonableness)," Drachsler continued. "The surest way to create disharmony, disunity and ultimately social chaos in America is to practice the policy of compulsion."[68] Concluding that "neither drifting nor coercion" could secure incorporation, Drachsler recommended instead "a conscious and deliberate policy of harmonization." This harmony would be based on three principles: "the inviolability of the immigrant's essential humanity"; a "sincere effort to work *with*" (and not simply *for*) immigrants as they "learn how to feel at home in America"; and—most intriguingly—the "encouragement of a generous, constructive criticism of American life on [the immigrant's] part, instead of the demand for absolute unthinking conformity to it."[69]

These principles of humanity, collaboration, and constructive criticism amount to a model of political—and, more specifically, democratic—inclusion that, on Drachsler's interpretation, had never before been attempted in American history. The laissez-faire policy reflected an economistic perspective that treated the immigrant population as merely a labor pool; the compulsory policy attempted to model the demos on an ethnos. The approach endorsed by democratic thinkers going back to the nineteenth century attempted something distinct from each of these. Unlike the compulsory policy (whose logic led easily to sharp restrictions), it took a broadly open attitude to entry: consider Lincoln ("if there are any abroad who desire to make this the land of their adoption, it is not in my heart to throw aught in their way"), Sumner ("I cannot place any check upon the welcome to foreigners"), and Douglass ("we should welcome to our ample continent all nations, kindreds, tongues and peoples"). Unlike the laissez-faire policy, it did not merely welcome foreigners as laborers. Rather, its endorsement of that open immigration policy was predicated on a vision of active citizenship. Sumner specifically welcomed immigrants as "upholders of the general welfare," and Douglass imagined them participating in an array of civic tasks, such as voting, holding office, and testifying in court, arguing that they should be incorporated "as fast as they learn our language and comprehend the duties of citizenship."

Not only that; for these thinkers, political activity *alone* was not sufficient to realize this ideal of democratic membership. "When we let the process of naturalization become a meaningless, unseemly scramble for an empty political privilege, rather than make it a dignified procedure leading to a genuinely coveted citizenship, we are doing violence to [the immigrant's] humanity," Drachsler warned.[70] The activities of citizenship had to be invested with certain mindsets and dispositions appropriate to the task of collective self-rule. As Douglass had elsewhere remarked, "The structure of the American Constitution and Government imply the existence among the whole people of a fraternal good will, an earnest spirit of co-operation for the common good, a mutual dependence of all upon each and of each upon all."[71] While a despotic government demands "mere cold obedience," a government that is "of, by and through the people" requires "a cordial co-operation," for its "whole machinery is deranged when one of its parts fail to perform its functions."[72] Douglass's vision is a natural match with Drachsler's view that Americans should work with new immigrants and encourage them to constructively criticize national life.

Efforts to articulate this ideal against nativists who claimed ownership over the meaning of American identity faced a perennial difficulty: How could these thinkers define what it meant to *join* the people without endorsing homogeneity or appealing to some essentialized source of unity? The distinctive way in which democratic thinkers responded to this challenge was by subtly changing the sought-after ideal, from shared identity to shared identification. This intellectual project took on special urgency in the early 1920s as the nation's immigration laws were being tightened by a Congress gripped by fears of so-called mongrelization and determined to combat so-called racial impurity.[73] As the prominent eugenicist Harry H. Laughlin, an expert witness to the House Committee on Immigration and Naturalization, explained during a 1922 hearing: "We in this country have been so imbued with the idea of democracy, or the equality of all men, that we have left out of consideration the matter of blood or natural inborn hereditary mental and moral differences."[74]

Rejecting the view that political unity stemmed from hereditary or natural similarities, the thinkers who articulated a democratic immigration policy in the early twentieth century preferred to speak of dynamic, intersubjective processes—a shift evidenced by the conspicuous rise of musical metaphors in their arguments. For Drachsler, the sought-after ideal was "harmonization," a metaphor stressing the mutual adjustment of different parts. This expressed an insight that his nineteenth-century predecessors would have endorsed: a democracy cannot function unless citizens make a sincere effort to identify with each other, and to adjust the work of citizenship accordingly. Here, Drachsler may have been drawing on Horace Kallen's well-known 1915 essay "Democracy Versus the Melting-Pot." In that essay, Kallen had famously likened a diverse democracy to a "symphony of civilization" wherein each ethnic group contributes "its spirit and culture" as "its theme and melody," leading to "the harmony and dissonances and discords of them all." Yet as Kallen went on to observe, a *civilizational* symphony was marked by "this difference: a musical symphony is written before it is played; in the symphony of civilization the playing is the writing, so that there is nothing so fixed and inevitable about its progressions as in music, so that within the limits set by nature they may vary at will, and the range and variety of the harmonies may become wider, and richer and more beautiful."[75]

This insistence on the openness of a democratic future follows directly from the refusal to name any *particular* characteristic as the definitive criterion of membership in the American demos. If Americans were defined by some specific quality that they all shared, it would be possible to predict the outcome of "Americanization" with at least some precision: to know what notes would be played in the "fixed and inevitable" score of national identity. But because they resisted this pressure to define Americanism in terms of any such static quality, democratic thinkers denied their project any antecedently given purpose that existed beyond the creativity of its participants. As Rabbi Stephen S. Wise wrote in 1922, in an essay reprinted in the FLIS's *Bulletin*:

> Americanism, being ever in the making, is of present content and not of ancient context; is not a birthright privilege but a lifelong responsibility.... America is an atmosphere, an ideal, a vision as yet unfulfilled.... All this is only another way of saying that an American is a conscious, vigilant, fraternal, unwearied *creator of America* who scorns the notion that America bears a charmed life, and that democracy, even though it be of the American brand, guarantees the automatic solution of its own problems.[76]

Drachsler was similarly explicit on this point: "But, you will ask me what is the ultimate aim of this conscious policy of harmonization? What will be its outcome? What is your conception of the future American civilization? I frankly say, I do not know. I do not believe any one knows. Nor can any one, in the nature of the case, know."[77] Drachsler's insistence that it was impossible to predict the future of a "harmonized" United States draws a striking contrast with the confident forecast of Sen. David Reed, co-sponsor of the 1924 Immigration Act. As the law's details were being finalized in conference committee, Reed took to *The New York Times* to promote its benefits in an essay titled "America of the Melting Pot Comes to an End." Reed promised that with the new law, the "racial composition of America at the present time thus is made permanent," adding that with its passage, the "America of our grandchildren will be a vastly better place to live in."[78] Neither Drachsler nor Reed lived to see the 1965 Act, although Reed survived into the 1950s, while Drachsler died in 1927 at the age of thirty-seven.[79]

Drachsler's insistence on the unpredictability of a genuinely democratic United States would have been well understood by his Reconstruction-era predecessors. "Thus we presume to write, as it were, upon things that exist not, and travel by maps yet unmade,"[80] Walt Whitman had announced in 1871. Democracy, Whitman averred, was "a word the real gist of which still sleeps, quite unawaken'd.... It is a great word, whose history, I suppose, remains unwritten, because that history has yet to be enacted."[81] Again and again, these thinkers invoked shared democratic peoplehood as the ideal that would expand and transform as it incorporated new members while rejecting familiar nationalist premises: that the people are prepolitically unified, that they constitute an ancient community awaiting recovery by a predetermined set of descendants, or that this community can be achieved through the state's peremptory coronation of one particular vision of culture.

Minimizing Membership, Transforming Membership

Distinguishing an ideal of democratic membership from both ethnic homogeneity and mere economic inclusion, American thinkers between the First and Second Reconstructions mobilized a demanding vision of political incorporation in the service of greater openness to immigration. As I mentioned at the outset of this chapter, such strong ideals of political belonging are viewed skeptically by many thinkers today since migrants often need higher wages or refuge more immediately, and more profoundly, than they need citizenship. If meeting these urgent economic and humanitarian needs is in tension with a robust form of political inclusion, then on this view, membership must either be minimized or transformed to better accommodate a more open migration regime.

Arguments for minimizing membership are common in the political theory of immigration, especially among advocates of open borders. While every state in the world claims the right to control entry into its territory, political theorists have generally viewed this claim skeptically. This skepticism was initially spurred by Joseph Carens's seminal article on the topic, which influentially contended that on nearly every leading theory of justice, borders should "generally be open."[82] Noting that most migrants "are ordinary, peaceful people, seeking only the opportunity to build decent, secure lives for themselves and their families,"[83] Carens argued that if that opportunity does not exist in a migrant's home state, then the question of whether they will be granted entry into another one poses weighty issues of freedom and justice.

Carens's agenda-setting argument in favor of open borders introduced, but did not resolve, complex questions about membership and belonging. While he stressed that "*our* society ought to admit guest workers to full citizenship," since "anything else is incompatible with our liberal democratic principles," there is no necessary logic by which a given entrance policy dictates a corresponding policy of membership.[84] Many proponents of open borders accommodate greater openness of entry by retreating from the ideal of citizenship and instead promoting a policy of denizenship, in recognition of the fact that thicker forms of inclusion might come at the cost of other priorities. In this vein, Chandran Kukathas defends the dilution or restriction of political membership as a meaningful step toward the ultimate goal of open borders. Kukathas observes that border openness is actually multidimensional, encompassing a progressively thicker set of rights: first entry, then participation (understood mainly in economic terms), and finally membership (understood mainly in political terms).[85] "Membership is not a trivial matter," writes Kukathas, "but morally speaking it does not matter nearly as much as the freedom or the opportunity to enter and participate in a society. It is restrictions on entry and participation that are of most concern from the perspective of an advocate of open borders."[86]

Similarly, some thinkers contend that states might permit higher levels of migration if they were not asked to grant citizenship and its attendant costly benefits (such as education and healthcare) to those who enter. Howard F. Chang detects a perverse consequence haunting the commitment to extend the various benefits of membership to migrants: "Our commitment to treat them as equals once admitted would cut against their admission and make them worse off than they would be if we rejected such a commitment.... These aliens would be better off if we agreed never to care about their welfare and never to treat them as equals."[87] Given this reality, argues Chang, "guest worker programs may represent the only alternative to exclusion for many aliens,"[88] and so "cosmopolitan liberals should support liberalizing reforms that include guest worker programs, even while seeking the broadest rights possible for aliens within the constraints of political feasibility."[89] On this consequentialist view, restrictions on membership are a reasonable price to pay for more open border policies. (I use the language of prices intentionally, since in effect this system envisions migrants trading—at least for a period of time—civic equality in exchange for the rights to enter and work.[90])

The adoption of such policies establishes a denizen class—a group of people subject to the state's authority, but lacking equality and political voice. This sacrifices the commitment to universal citizenship that is essential in a democratic state, replacing egalitarian relationships with hierarchical ones and leaving migrants vulnerable to exploitation. Additionally, by restricting access to certain rights enjoyed by citizens (such as public education, welfare, etc.), such policies effectively announce that certain goods otherwise deemed necessary for participation on equal terms in society will be denied to *this* group of migrants, thereby designating them as outside the scope of social equality. These and other consequences of denizenship policies might be tolerable if there were no other way to satisfy the underlying justice and freedom-related goals that they aim to advance. But of course, there are a variety of means by which global distributive justice and freedom of movement could be promoted; policies aimed at maximizing migration are not the only, or even the best, means of pursuing those goals.[91] Addressing the most important concerns of global justice and freedom does not require relegating migrants to a second-class status of resident nonmembership, and in that way sacrificing a core requirement of democratic self-rule.

Indeed, the same egalitarian commitments that proscribe the sacrifice of equal membership within the polity also demand that wealthier, migrant-receiving states address these global concerns. It follows, from a commitment to the equality of persons, that states' powers to regulate migration and membership are, as

Jorge Valadez writes, "*morally conditional* on the observance by states of certain global moral obligations," including obligations to ensure greater distributive justice and freedom.[92] If states fail to address these drivers of migration, their insistence on maintaining strong norms of inclusion (norms that plausibly rule out many forms of temporary migration) becomes perverse, invoking a supposedly principled egalitarianism in support of chauvinism and indifference toward outsiders. To reiterate a point I made in the introduction and will revisit in Chapter 5, a belief in the universal equality of persons is compatible with an endorsement of more particularistic civic obligations, since equality's demands are sensitive to facts about the nature of human relationships and hence vary by context.[93] For that reason, it is possible to insist on maintaining strong norms of democratic inclusion internally, while *also* insisting—on the same egalitarian grounds—that any consequent restrictions on entry or membership are legitimate only if they are accompanied by measures that address the relevant justice- or freedom-related drivers of migration in other ways. In other words, if the legitimacy of immigration controls is morally conditional, and if the moral costs of immigration control increase along with the inequalities among different states, then a democratic approach to migration policy must pair its general opposition to (for example) guest worker programs with expanded efforts to promote global justice, since such efforts render that position morally legitimate. Democratic states can neither pursue a nativist egalitarianism that ignores the global injustices driving migration into their territory nor restrict membership to maximize overall levels of entry. Either policy is inconsistent with the core principles to which they trace their legitimacy.[94]

While the foregoing arguments give reasons to reject proposals that would minimize or restrict membership in violation of democratic ideals, bounded forms of political membership face a different criticism: one that appeals directly to democratic principles rather than circumventing them in the name of other goals. This alternative approach, prominently developed by Arash Abizadeh, argues for "unbounding" the demos on the grounds that democratic principles are inconsistent with states' unilateral control of their borders. Abizadeh writes that

> *by its very nature*, the question of boundaries poses an *externality problem*: while democracy claims to legitimate the exercise of political power by reference to those over whom power is exercised, civic boundaries, which by definition distinguish between members and nonmembers, are always instances of power exercised over both members *and nonmembers*—and nonmembers are precisely those whose will, views, or interests the bounded democratic polity claims to be able legitimately to ignore.[95]

Existing practices of unilateral border control are usually justified on grounds of state sovereignty, but Abizadeh contends that this justification is at odds with an equally prevalent belief in popular sovereignty. A sincere endorsement of popular sovereignty, he contends, cannot be compatible with a system in which states unilaterally control their borders, since such a system coerces outsiders without granting them any say in the decisions that coerce them. Against this practice, Abizadeh argues that "according to democratic theory, *the democratic justification for a regime of border control is ultimately owed to both members and nonmembers*."[96] Acknowledging this conclusion requires that we "abandon this implausible picture of the demos as a prepolitically constituted, really existing corporate entity"[97]—an entity that could democratically decide to erect against outsiders the very same boundaries it presupposes when denying them a say in the decision. A truly democratic border policy, Abizadeh writes, would require explicit, participatory consent, such as a vote,[98] since democratic theory's principle of legitimation is rooted in mutual justification, not in the prior existence of some collective entity. The reach of that democratic principle of legitimacy, concludes Abizadeh, "extends as far as practices of mutual justification can go, which is to say that the demos is in principle unbounded."[99]

From a democratic perspective, Abizadeh's approach has several advantages. It identifies practices that are, at the very least, in tension with the professed ideals of democratic states, and unlike the other approaches surveyed above, it addresses the problem of borders without trading away or diluting democratic membership, at least formally. Nonetheless, this proposal to unbound the demos would transform the nature of democratic membership in ways likely to undermine the pursuit of collective self-rule on terms of equality.

The transformation implied by Abizadeh's account stems from his adoption of the *all-coerced principle*—the claim that "a democratic theory of popular sovereignty requires that the coercive exercise of political power be democratically justified to all those over whom it is exercised, that is, justification is owed to all those subject to state coercion."[100] Such justification cannot be hypothetical; in order for it to be genuinely democratic, the coerced must actually have the opportunity to participate in decision-making procedures.[101] Some critics have responded to Abizadeh by critiquing his characterization of coercion, but here I take a slightly different approach, focusing on what an "unbounded" theory entails for how we should characterize the demos itself.[102]

To appreciate the magnitude of the implied transformation, it is important to begin with a point raised by other critics: the all-coerced principle generates an episodically constructed demos. In other words, if the demos were composed of the parties coerced by a given decision, then its composition would depend on the issue in question rather than remaining stable over time. (A related principle draws lines of democratic inclusion by reference to all those *affected* rather than *coerced*. Abizadeh adopts the more restrictive standard of coercion, which produces less expansive implications,[103] but the point applies in either case.) As Sarah Song has observed, "What the affected interests and coercion principles actually require is *different demoi for different decisions.* Who will be affected or coerced by any single decision will vary from decision to decision, and as a result, democratic boundaries are not fixed but constantly changing."[104] Indeed, since multiple political decisions across a range of issues are always occurring at any given moment, the application of either principle would make it impossible to speak of "belonging to a demos" at all. Instead, individuals would (at different moments) belong to different fleeting, overlapping, crisscrossing, ad hoc demoi. This would fundamentally change the practice of democratic politics in ways that go well beyond the rejection of unilateral border controls.[105] The episodic tendency of the all-coerced/all-affected principles would obstruct identification in two ways, which I will call the *stability* problem and the *legibility* problem.

Stability problems arise whenever the demos lacks continuity over time. The importance of such temporal continuity is indicated by Charles Taylor's distinction between sporadic acts of majority decision-making, which "can be adopted by all sorts of bodies, even those which are the loosest aggregations" and the kind of decision-making that is characteristic of a democratic society.[106] A group of people who rule themselves collectively must bargain, compromise, credibly commit to promises, and engage in a range of other practices that presume a roughly stable set of participants who interact under what they understand to be the shadow of a shared future. This stably shared future is, as Bernard Yack has noted, at odds with "continual adjustments of [a community's] boundaries. For these communities need to know exactly whom the state is serving and where the limits of its authority lie. Without sharp and relatively settled boundaries the liberal project of rendering coercive authority accountable to the people who created it is impossible."[107] The all-affected and all-coerced principles present a basic departure from these conjoined assumptions—that the demos's membership roster is both transparent and continuous over time. As Song writes, they would introduce "a serious problem of indeterminacy," leading to a world in which "the lion's share of democratic contestation would likely be devoted to determining who ought to have a say rather than to the policy issues at hand."[108] These questions of composition are further complicated by the fact that the parties affected/coerced by a decision cannot be known until a decision has been reached, as well as by the unstable distinction between all those coerced/affected by a decision and all those *potentially* coerced/affected. If any given decision comes to unexpectedly encompass a new group, does it still stand? And when and how are we to make such determinations? Since there is no way of determining with certainty how a decision made today will affect the world in the future, even expansive applications of these principles threaten to be underinclusive and illegitimate on their own terms.[109] Such stability problems would be endemic, making it all but impossible for a project of collective self-rule to be sustained over time.

Even more fundamentally, an unbounded demos would obstruct the processes by which political problems become legible *as problems* in the first place. As I argued in Chapter 1, most political problems are irreducibly interpretive.[110] They are not objective facts about the world; rather they are problems *for* specific groups of people, as interpreted in light of their beliefs, aspirations, and values. For that reason, they cannot be defined with any specificity until we know what group of people we are dealing with and how they understand themselves and their circumstances. This general observation about the nature of political problems applies with special force to democracies because collective self-rule requires the demos to define its problems and goals for itself, rather than simply accepting a definition of problems and goals provided by tradition, social elites, divine revelation, or any other source. For this process of definition to advance the self-rule of the whole demos, it must unfold inclusively and on terms of equality. Through processes of identification, citizens must intersubjectively generate a collective perspective, eliciting one another's views with sensitivity to the social positions and historical experiences of different groups within the demos. If the composition of the demos constantly varied from decision to decision, then citizens would share no common fate, identification of this kind would be impossible, and the ideal of self-rule would be obstructed.

A robust and expansive form of identification enables democratic citizenries to reconcile the imperatives of openness and solidarity—to respond to urgent concerns of global justice without sacrificing core ideals of democracy. The nativists, xenophobes, and ethnonationalists who have powerfully shaped the past and present of American immigration politics deny the possibility of this reconciliation: they assert that fellow-feeling is possible only among people who antecedently share a common identity and that immigration therefore threatens solidarity. These are claims about the nature and preconditions of political membership. When these claims have surfaced, democratic thinkers have historically answered them not by diminishing or discarding a robust vision of membership in the name of global justice but rather by *reinterpreting* the ideal of membership in ways that sustain democracy while enabling a much greater openness to migration.

While this account of democratic membership is demanding, its unique ability to synthesize goals that are often thought to be in tension makes it worthy of sympathetic reevaluation. Its proponents remind us not only that the life plans of most migrants are perfectly compatible with the self-determination of citizens in the destination polity but also that citizens who enjoy a common formal membership status, but who do not otherwise understand themselves to be engaged in a common political enterprise, share a democracy only in an incomplete sense. As Anna Stilz argues, a democratic citizen

> must be capable of regarding herself as a *member* of the body politic if that body is to be able to produce a general will capable of legitimately defining each citizen's rights. Once this transformation occurs, the interests of each individual—while still privately held—are the interests of a different kind of self, of an individual citizen who is considering herself as a citizen.[111]

On this understanding of democracy, proposals to minimize democratic membership invoke significant moral concerns, but ultimately they do not provide an available immigration policy to democratic states. My critical engagement with these proposals has intended to show that one can (and should) acknowledge the force of these underlying concerns without ceding the terrain of political membership. Because migration raises inescapable questions about membership, it remains urgent for contemporary democracies to cultivate forms of belonging that resist the illiberal, exclusionary, and homogenizing logic of nativism. This is the lesson that the tradition of figures like Sumner, Douglass, and Drachsler has to offer: not only do we not have to choose between robust democratic identification and a more just system of migration, but it would also be a profound mistake to pit them against one another.

Chapter 4
Racial Integration and the Project of National Definition

In the final days of May 1969, fourteen black intellectuals convened at Haverford College in Pennsylvania. It was a distinguished group, counting among its members the writer Ralph Ellison; the historian John Hope Franklin; the sociologist St. Clair Drake; the economist Phyllis A. Wallace, the first woman to gain tenure at MIT's Sloan School of Management; the literary scholar J. Saunders Redding, thought to be the first black faculty member at an Ivy League university;[1] William Hastie, the first African American federal judge; Robert C. Weaver, the first African American cabinet secretary; and Kenneth and Mamie Phipps Clark, the educational psychologists whose "doll experiments" had famously influenced the Supreme Court's decision in *Brown v. Board of Education*.

The previous years had witnessed the most momentous advances for racial equality in a century. Six decades of activism following *Plessy v. Ferguson*'s endorsement in 1896 of "separate but equal" public facilities had finally produced, in *Brown*, an iconic endorsement of integration from a unanimous Supreme Court. Landmark civil rights and voting rights legislation had followed. But the Haverford Group had not gathered to celebrate the recent past. Rather, they were united by a shared worry about the future, especially the next generation's "repudiation of what we consider some important values and goals": specifically, they feared that younger African Americans were coming to consider "integration a dirty word."[2]

In response to this development, the members of the Haverford Group hoped to spearhead a collaborative restatement of the premises, social philosophy, and political goals of integration, and in so doing reclaim some lost momentum for their cause. They considered publicizing their conversations, producing a journal, scheduling speaking events, seeking mass-media attention, and reaching out to young activists. But such plans for a coordinated intervention in public debate never materialized; the group's organization faltered, and its funding dried up. The May 1969 conversations were not published until 2013, and three subsequent meetings (later in 1969, and again in

1972 and 1975) remain unpublished today. Viewed in retrospect, the elegiac tone of the Haverford Group's conversations assumes a somewhat prophetic quality, and the fate of their efforts embodies in miniature their central worry: that *Brown* was not the herald of a new, integrated American democracy but rather a brief and thrilling apex preceding a long decline.

In many ways, subsequent decades have vindicated this worry. In 2019, *Brown*'s sixty-fifth anniversary was marked by a report warning that "intense levels of segregation—which had decreased markedly after 1954 for black students—are on the rise once again" and had been since the 1990s, "placing the promise of *Brown* at grave risk."[3] In 2016, a Brooklyn-based writer for *The New York Times Magazine* documented the complexities of choosing a school for her daughter in a diverse, liberal city that had largely given up on integrating its public schools. At one town hall meeting, the city's school chancellor, declaring that "you don't need to have diversity within one building," proposed an alternative: "Poor students in segregated schools could be pen pals and share resources with students in wealthier, integrated public schools." After all, the chancellor reasoned, "We adopt schools from China, Korea or wherever." A frustrated city councilman from the Bronx summed up the city's resignation: "The moral vision behind *Brown v. Board of Education* is dead."[4]

But *Brown* was not only a "moral vision." The chancellor's unwittingly revealing comparison—likening other American schoolchildren a few blocks away to students on the other side of the globe—serves as a reminder that *Brown*'s vision was also political. Chief Justice Warren's opinion had encouraged Americans to understand the ruling in expansive terms: "We must consider public education in the light of its full development and its present place in American life throughout the Nation ... It is the very foundation of good citizenship."[5]

This vision of an integrated national democracy met with immediate and massive resistance from segregationist whites, but as the Haverford Group came to realize by the late 1960s, it also faced deep skepticism—obviously on quite different grounds—from a number of black critics who feared that integration would subject black Americans to unfair and overwhelming assimilative pressures. These critics concluded that the pursuit of equality faced more favorable prospects in separate settings insulated from such pressures. The growing prominence of this argument, as well as the corresponding decline of integration, marks a key point when American egalitarians' democratic aspirations began to detach from a vision of shared peoplehood.

But even as these separatist arguments came to displace integration, many of their key premises were gradually abandoned. In particular, midcentury critics of integration often appealed to strong notions of racial identity that came to be criticized in subsequent decades as romantic and essentialist and which are now largely out of favor among scholars. During that same time, a large and disturbing body of empirical research demonstrated the undeniable contribution of pervasive separation (especially residential segregation) to numerous, lingering inequalities between black and white Americans.[6] In the face of these developments, many skeptics of integration became convinced of the necessity to reformulate their critiques without appealing to racial identity as such. As Tommie Shelby has written, this endeavor recognized "race, as commonly understood"[7] to be "a problematic foundation for African American identity and black political solidarity," and it set out to be "forthrightly anti-essentialist."[8] Accordingly, contemporary critics tend to eschew any suggestion that integration threatens a unitary or essential racial identity, while nonetheless maintaining that there are many other downsides to its pursuit, at least in the present. For reasons I will discuss below, their proposed alternatives generally do not include mass emigration or a fully independent nation. Rather, they encompass a family of related approaches variously termed "community nationalism,"[9] "egalitarian pluralism,"[10] "voluntary separation,"[11] and "limited separation."[12]

There are differences among these various accounts, but they share a crucial feature: like the critiques of integration that rose to prominence in the late 1960s, they too relocate the site of democratic citizenship from the multiracial nation to its relatively monochromatic localities. This strategy of argument generally avoids what Shelby calls "questions of social identity as such."[13] Instead, it invokes familiar *political* values—like civic virtue, solidarity, and democracy—and interprets them in ways that aim to vindicate the kind of locally centered citizenship that, as a practical matter, is entailed by separatist and quasi-separatist arguments. If the un-integrated neighborhoods and regions where many Americans live can flourish politically, then integration is not, as Elizabeth Anderson has prominently argued, "an imperative of justice and democracy."[14]

In recent years, localist critics of integration have revived this argument in response to Anderson's 2010 book *The Imperative of Integration*. The most comprehensive philosophical defense of integration to date, Anderson's work is notable for situating its defense of integration within a broader account of democracy. As she explains, the argument is intended to "demonstrate the importance for democracy of integration, of cooperation and communication *across group lines*, for the purposes of forging *shared* norms and goals of the democratic polity as a whole, and to that extent forging a shared identity of citizens."[15] For Anderson, pervasive racialized separation among

Americans obstructs the achievement of this collective sense of selfhood, which in turn inhibits democracy. Accordingly, she argues that integration "requires the construction of a superordinate group identity, a 'we,' from the perspective of which cooperative goals are framed, and appropriate policies selected and implemented."[16] She is explicit about the polity-wide scale of this ideal: "In a democratic society, this 'we' is most importantly a shared identity as citizens."[17]

Contemporary argument over black-white integration thus turns on disagreements over identification: its nature, its role, and its appropriate scope in a democratic society. (While Anderson does use the term "identity," her meaning is much closer to my preferred term because it does not refer to a shared, prepolitical quality; rather, it refers to a range of practices, such as the construction of a perspective, the framing of goals, and the selection of policies.) Anderson's account of democracy endorses integration because it accords a central role to identification on the scale of the whole polity, viewing such identification as systematically obstructed by racial separation. In response, her critics argue that identification of this kind is either impossible or unnecessary.

This chapter reconstructs the history of these anti-integration views and argues that they misconstrue the nature and role of identification among democratic citizens. I first trace this misconstrual to midcentury debates over integration, which in retrospect were plagued by a consequential ambiguity between *identity* (something *individuals have*) and *identification* (something *citizens do*). This ambiguity gave credence to arguments that integration would amount to assimilation, rather than mutual transformation (to use Sharon Stanley's term).[18] As I have argued throughout this book, what matters from the perspective of democracy is not that citizens share a static, homogeneous identity but rather that they identify one another as fellow-members in a way that enables them to collectively self-rule on terms of equality. We should understand integration in terms of this latter ideal, as many of its proponents did.

With the identity/identification distinction more clearly drawn, the chapter next turns to contemporary arguments against integration, showing that while they avoid some problematic aspects of earlier accounts, they too fail as alternative visions of American democracy. Because they eschew the ideal of identification on the scale of the whole polity, contemporary arguments against integration cannot fully promote the various political values (such as freedom, civic virtue, solidarity, and justice) on the basis of which they are justified. Their prioritization of the local over the national is ultimately in tension with the imperatives of American democracy.

The ideal of a genuine American demos, marked by robust identification among all its members, is recoverable from the often-overlooked political thought of some of integration's proponents. Inattention to their arguments has at times fostered an overly narrow understanding of integration as simply a policy of racial mixing (or even worse, as one of assimilation). But in the thought of its most perceptive proponents, integration was neither. Nor was it intended solely to redress concrete inequalities. In its broadest and most important sense, integration represented a transformative view of what the American demos could be. It envisioned the development of a new way for Americans to live together that would both express and promote a deep democratization in the psychology of citizenship—a needed step, and one that systematic separation would inevitably obstruct. The power of this vision gives us reason to sympathetically reevaluate integration as a political theory, even amid the obstacles currently facing it as a policy agenda.

Because integrationist intellectuals were sensitive to the importance of identification among *all* citizens, their democratic aspirations ultimately rested on how they viewed the prospects of American peoplehood. In reconstructing that vision of an integrated democracy, this chapter urges a reconsideration of the conclusion reached by Anderson and, before her, by members of the Haverford Group: in a racially divided American polity, there is no route to democratic equality except through integration—and integration presumes a broad vision of the American demos.

Integration, Assimilation, and Homogenization

Pessimism about integrated equality seems to have crested sometime around the mid- to late 1990s, in the wake of a set of Supreme Court decisions that made it easier for school districts to be released from desegregation orders.[19] "Integration, the ideal that once inspired an interracial mass movement to dream of a better America, has lately fallen into disuse or disfavor," wrote Eric Foner and Randall Kennedy in 1998.[20] By the early 2000s, short obituaries for integration were a staple of scholarly work on contemporary racial politics. As Andrew Valls wrote in 2002, "Optimism about progress toward racial justice has fallen on hard times," meaning that "the traditional civil rights strategy of integration, with its assimilationist tendencies, must be scrutinized and perhaps discarded in favor of alternative strategies that favor black-dominated institutions, institutions that both reproduce black culture and offer a refuge from racism."[21] In 2006, Michelle Adams summarized the intellectual landscape: "Integration no longer captivates the progressive imagination; it no longer moves those concerned with eliminating racial inequality."[22]

Integration, of course, had never been popular among white supremacists. But over time, its standing had fallen among egalitarians as well. In the ecstatic wake of *Brown*, many activists believed themselves to be in possession of the tools necessary to effect rapid desegregation; even a figure as experienced as Thurgood Marshall predicted that school segregation could be ended nationwide within five years.[23] This expectation of rapid progress was due not only to the legal mechanisms the decision provided but also to a widespread optimism that *Brown* signaled the general decline of America's racial hierarchy, a trend with repercussions far beyond public schools.[24] The historian C. Vann Woodward, seeking a term that would capture the changes underway, began to write of a "Second Reconstruction."[25] The comparison's connotations could be read with both optimism and some measure of apprehension—for these two Reconstructions resembled each other not only in their ambition but also in the uncertainty of their ultimate trajectory. Opponents of segregation shared a common desire to dismantle Jim Crow, but like the factions who struggled for control over Reconstruction, they had deeply different visions of precisely what else their project entailed.

In particular, they disagreed about the role, and indeed the very meaning, of integration. "The implications of the philosophy of 'racial integration' vis-a-vis the idea of a legitimate Afro-American racial culture in the United States is a subject which is not being publically debated and clarified," observed Harold Cruse in 1957. "Yet it lingers beneath the surface of a choppy sea of racial and interracial events like a powerful unseen social tide, inexorably flowing despite the agitation and clamor above."[26]

Cruse's remark proved prescient. The progress of the civil rights movement in the years following *Brown* revealed divergent understandings of its basic goals. In 1964, at a roundtable discussion featuring James Baldwin, Nathan Glazer, Sidney Hook, and Gunnar Myrdal, *Commentary* editor Norman Podhoretz surmised that a split had emerged in the last "two or three years," pitting a nascent radical faction against the "traditional liberal mentality": "those liberals whose ultimate perspective on race relations ... envisages the gradual absorption of deserving Negroes one by one into white society."[27] Two years later, the Pulitzer Prize–winning historian Oscar Handlin declared that since *Brown*, "Americans concerned with resolving the dilemma posed by the Negro's plight in a society committed to equal rights have lived in a state of crisis." *Brown*'s implications, wrote Handlin, "were not immediately clear," had not become clearer "in the intervening eleven years," and were indeed so uncertain that the civil rights movement could maintain "the pretense of unity only by a resolute determination not to think of long-term objectives."[28]

Handlin understood the post-*Brown* agenda in predominantly negative terms, as a project of desegregation. But the movement, he worried, had shifted "from desegregation to integration, but without adequate awareness of the consequences and often with a profound ambiguity about the nature of the desirable goal."[29] Did proponents of integration merely favor a greater "openness of society," a "leveling of all barriers to association other than those based on ability, taste, and personal preference," or did they favor "a condition in which individuals of each racial or ethnic group are randomly distributed through the society so that every realm of activity contains a representative cross section of the population"? The two paths were "antithetical": the first sought merely to break down barriers to opportunity, "even though the group may remain as separate as before," but the second aimed for "racial balance" in different sectors of society.[30]

Drawing on a pluralist framework informed by his scholarship on early twentieth-century immigrant groups,[31] Handlin asserted that many of the problems facing black people in Northern cities were not unlike those faced by Irish, Jewish, and Polish immigrants in earlier decades.[32] Desegregation, he maintained, would soon "eliminate the vestiges of discrimination inherited from the Jim Crow era," and although "it may open the way to full participation by Negroes in the political and economic life of the nation," such a process would occur "within the terms of some approximation of the group life already developed."[33] Yet Handlin believed that the civil rights movement, rather than allowing desegregation to work such a course, was tending toward the "racial balance" version of integration, which would upend this healthy pluralist process: "Integration, defined as the elimination of differences ... demands of both Negroes and whites an impossible surrender of identity."[34]

The worry that integration would destroy identity was invoked by a range of critics. Some, such as Handlin, feared a universal dissolution: "Is the ultimate objective to eliminate the differences that actually divide the population of the United States and thus dissolve its people into a single homogeneous and undifferentiated mass?"[35] Others, such as Cruse, saw a loss of identity disproportionately borne by black Americans. At least as far back as the mid-1950s, Cruse had criticized integration as the policy of an out-of-touch black middle class, who "meant to further their own class aims, and the aspirations of the masses only incidentally."[36] Despondently comparing the American civil rights movement to the anticolonial struggles then underway in Africa, Cruse lamented that it is "we Afro-Americans who are out of step with the rest of the colonial world. They are seeking their identity while we are endeavoring to lose ours in exchange for a brand of freedom in a never-never-land of assimilated racial differences—the great dream of the integrationists but hardly visible on the horizons of reality."[37] A related worry informed Kwame Ture and Charles Hamilton's 1967 denunciation of integration as "unrealistic" and "despicable," as "a subterfuge for the maintenance of white supremacy."[38] "The fact is that integration, as traditionally articulated, would abolish the black community," contended Ture and Hamilton. "No person can be healthy, complete and mature if he must deny a part of himself; this is what 'integration' has required thus far."[39]

By the second half of the 1960s, the intellectual and political winds were clearly shifting. In 1967, the economist and separatist thinker Robert Browne declared that integration was "being written off"; increasingly, it was understood to be "not only unattainable but actually harmful."[40] Browne proclaimed a "momentous realization by many 'integrated' Negroes that, in the U.S., full integration can only mean full assimilation—a loss of racial identity."[41] "There is the general skepticism that the Negro, even after having transformed himself into a white blackman, will enjoy full acceptance into American society," wrote Browne, "and there is the longer-range doubt that even should complete integration somehow be achieved, it would prove to be really desirable, for its price may be the total absorption and disappearance of the race—a sort of painless genocide."[42]

In proposing that integration would harm self-respect, such arguments effectively reversed the reasoning that had prevailed among many prominent racial egalitarians in the previous decade. At the time *Brown* was decided, the "doll test" research performed by Kenneth and Mamie Phipps Clark—showing that black children preferred white dolls and viewed black dolls negatively—was cited as evidence of segregation's harmful effects on the self-respect of African American children, buttressing support for integrationist policies.[43] But Browne's critique suggested that the end of separation had the potential to inaugurate a new, more insidious form of subordination. Any form of integration that amounted to "absorbing" racialized fellow citizens into the "mainstream" of a democratic society would necessarily cast the assimilated as an inferior group—uniquely in need of change in order to deserve inclusion into the dominant group (still coded as white) who deigns to incorporate them. (In this respect, as john a. powell has written, assimilation shares segregation's premise that there is something wrong with the racial other.)[44]

Although he was keenly sensitive to these attitudes, Kenneth Clark nonetheless could not sanction separatist responses. As he explained in a 1968 letter:

> As a psychologist I try to understand the depths of frustration and bitterness out of which these racial separatist demands arise... In understanding this, however, I do not accept or agree with the variety of demands which some Negroes are making

> for racially segregated facilities and institutions. I particularly do not agree with the demands for racially segregated educational institutions or facilities. My studies of this problem have convinced me that all forms of racial segregation institutionalize racism and thereby intensify the basic American disease. Furthermore the consequences of voluntary or self-imposed racial segregation are as detrimental—at times more insidiously so—as that of involuntary segregation.[45]

Yet as his decision to gather at Haverford the next year showed, Clark understood that this integrationist response to racial inequality was rapidly losing ground to separatist alternatives that, as Browne put it, "unmistakably revealed ... the depth of the despair about white America which is now prevalent in the black community."[46]

The democratic implications of despair are profound. As I argued in Chapter 1, democratic self-rule requires that members of the demos see themselves as having a shared future. Many of democracy's key virtues and activities, such as sacrifice,[47] reciprocity,[48] and what Amy Gutmann calls "conscious social reproduction,"[49] are comprehensible only within the context of a shared fate with a particular collective. For a century, starting with what Lincoln had called a "new birth of freedom," democratic reformers had consistently and hopefully appealed to this shared fate in order to lend substance to what Lincoln called "the unfinished work" and "the great task remaining before us," and what Frederick Douglass called "the work of the future."[50] In contrast, despair expresses the conviction that the future *cannot* be improved from within current conditions, that an ongoing project of democracy is not possible with this set of compatriots—leaving, as the only alternative for a hopeful future, exit and the establishment of some different political order, of the sort longingly invoked by separatist rhetoric and buoyed by the example of anticolonial revolution abroad.

Yet what form would this new politics take? In the late 1960s, its contours had not yet become clear. What primarily united integration's diverse critics was not a positive alternative vision but a negative conviction that the integrationist project of multiracial democratic peoplehood was proving futile.

Identity and Citizenship: Pessimistic Diagnoses and Alternative Prescriptions

Few critics of integration perceived the dilemma as acutely, and imagined the possibilities as expansively, as did Robert Browne. In 1967, Browne described the task facing African Americans as a "search for a place where they can experience the security which comes from being a part of the majority culture, free at last from the inhibiting effects of cultural repression and induced cultural timidity and shame." Those who had pursued this search through emigration to Africa had felt racial solidarity but experienced "cultural estrangement"; their experience proved that African Americans "are left with only one place to make our home, and that is this land to which we were brought in chains."[51]

In short, Browne concluded that African Americans should neither emigrate nor integrate—not into a society of alien norms, values, and standards:

> To convince a black child that she is beautiful when every channel of value formation in the society is telling her the opposite is a heart-rending and well-nigh impossible task. It is a challenge which confronts all Negroes, irrespective of their social and economic class, but the *difficulty of dealing with it is likely to vary directly with the degree to which the Negro family leads an integrated existence*. A black child in a predominantly black school may realize that she doesn't look like the pictures in the books, magazines and TV advertisements, but at least she looks like her schoolmates and neighbors. The black child in a predominantly white school and neighborhood lacks even this basis for identification.[52]

To confront this situation "as an integrationist," contended Browne, is to accept that the child *is* ugly, at least "by prevailing standards," and to simply urge them "to excel in other ways." Only the separatist has the resources to reassure the child that she is "not a freak but rather part of a larger international community of black-skinned, kinky-haired people who have a beauty of their own, a glorious history and a great future." Separatism, not integration, is capable of replacing "shame with pride, inferiority with dignity."[53]

For some critics, arguments like these underscored the value of separatist enclaves, but Browne pursued the logic of his claims further. If a broad cultural transformation that would enable black self-respect was impossible, the solution was the creation of a new and independent polity. Browne proposed "a formal partitioning of the United States into two totally separate and independent nations, one white and one black,"[54] with a black state possibly located in some region of the South already heavily populated by African Americans.[55] He advanced this argument in the pages of radical journals like *Ramparts* and mainstream ones like *The New York Times Magazine*, as well as in public dialogues with civil rights leaders like Bayard Rustin.[56] His writing directly addressed the divergent possibilities that stemmed from separatist arguments:

> If one inquires about the spokesmen for the new black nationalism, or for separatism, one discovers that the movement is locally based rather than nationally organized ... To a black who sees salvation for the black man only in a complete divorce of the two races, these efforts at ghetto improvement appear futile, perhaps even harmful. To others, convinced that coexistence with white America is possible within the national framework if only the whites permit the Negro to develop as he wishes (and by his own hand rather than in accordance with a white-conceived and white-administered pattern), such physically and economically upgraded black enclaves will be viewed as desirable steps forward.[57]

Browne's writings offer a clear expression of the dilemma facing separatist thinkers at midcentury: they lacked the confidence of some earlier black nationalists in the prospects of emigration to Africa, but they could not envision "joining" an American nation that, in their view, was unlikely to renounce its devotion to white supremacy. Facing the futility of exit and the impossibility of loyalty, they were left with either secession or the decidedly partial solution of organizing locally while ultimately remaining citizens of the larger polity. Favoring secession but sympathetic to the prudential judgments underlying enclave separatism, Browne perceived that citizenship was, at least in part, being relocated to a place where self-respect and autonomous development were possible. While an observer committed to "complete divorce" might see these efforts as "futile, perhaps even harmful," they might also be seen as a next-best solution.

Amid the growing popularity of such views, members of the Haverford Group continued to dispute separatist accounts of identity, insisting not only that a non-assimilative form of integration was possible but also that it was the only plausible democratic future for black Americans. In his post-meeting statement, for example, Ralph Ellison pointedly affirmed "integration without the surrender of our unique identity as a people to be a viable and indeed inescapable goal for black Americans."[58] He added that as a writer, "the object of my fictional imagination is the American society and the American experience as experienced fundamentally by Negroes and I find it impossible to deal with either in isolation, for they are intricately united in their diversity."[59]

J. Saunders Redding expressed a similar view in his post-meeting statement, which was mainly a critique of proposals for separatist education. But Redding's views on that issue were informed by a sociological understanding of race that had implications beyond education and that had long pitted him against anti-integration thinkers, including Cruse. As the literary scholar Michael Lackey has written, Redding understood identity in "sociological and anthropological" terms, and he objected to the tendency of separatists like Cruse to "use the word Afro in a metaphysical sense and the word American in a sociocultural sense."[60] In later essays, Redding would express concerns about what he called Cruse's "metaphysical" belief in inherent racial differences,[61] against which he contrasted his own view "that culture is the product of a people in a given environment; that culture-building and culture-possession are continuing processes, and that these processes are vitalized and set in motion by social circumstances and historical experiences commonly shared."[62]

Redding's Haverford statement reflected this view of culture. A complex problem faced "black Americans," he explained, since they "could not drop out of a society of which they had never been a part, and of course they could not drop in."[63] In other words, while much of American society remained closed to them, black people did not—could not—live wholly apart from it. What was distinctive about black Americans had been shaped by the United States; by the same token, much of what was distinctive about the United States had been shaped by black Americans. On this point, he was adamant: "Except when we put it in the context of Africa," he argued, "there is no such thing as 'black studies'—no black history, language, philosophy, physics, chemistry, ethics, etc. in the context of the United States. There *is* such a thing as *American studies*, and in courses such as American history, literature, sociology, economics, the ideal is to structure into these courses the substantive facts about black Americans." Warning that "knowledge that is not shared is useless,"[64] he contended that separatism in education would undermine black Americans' political goals: "One of the difficulties of our present American situation is due to the ignorance of white people about Negroes."[65]

Redding had defended this position for years, but in the period following the Haverford meeting it came to seriously affect his standing among intellectuals. In a later essay titled "The Black Revolution in American Studies,"[66] Redding extended the critiques he had made during the Haverford meeting, arguing that the proponents of "black studies" presumed a "genetic constant" that harkened back to discredited biological theories of race.[67] "All this is to say that Afro-American studies is basically American studies," concluded Redding, adding that until scholars seriously investigated how the "line of historical continuity and development peculiar to what is now the United States has generated a new breed of black man with a new 'Americanized' orientation to life," the field of American studies would "remain diminished and of questionable validity," and Americans would "remain poorly equipped to deal with the problems that confront them."[68] In an acerbic response, Amiri Baraka dismissed Redding's "house-servant fantasy"[69] and charged him with conservatism, complicity in black oppression, and white chauvinism—accusations that fail as characterizations of Redding's position but which succeeded in significantly damaging his reputation.[70]

As Lackey has noted, the irony of Redding's "defeat" in these debates is that this reputational damage has persisted, even though his views, however unpalatable in the late 1960s, eventually came to gain scholarly favor over Cruse's and Baraka's.[71] Contemporary thinkers prefer to speak of plural, shifting, hybridized, and contextual aspects of identity; they note that aspects of identity may differ greatly in their mutability, flexibility, and political salience. Not only that: if, as Redding and Ellison argued, African American identity could only be understood in terms of the broader context of the United States, it was an unpromising source of justification for this particular project of political separatism.[72]

Yet as the work of contemporary thinkers demonstrates, it is possible to drop such appeals to identity and defend quasi-separate forms of localist citizenship on other, more directly political grounds.[73] These thinkers contend that even if racial identity is not existentially threatened by integration, it nonetheless remains the case that black-white integration in the U.S. would disproportionately burden black Americans, all in order to advance political goals whose realization does not actually depend on integration and may even be threatened by it. The main political values to which these thinkers appeal include freedom of choice, civic virtue, justice, and solidarity. Such values, they contend, would be more effectively promoted if citizens prioritized local ties and affiliations over integrated life and fellow-feeling on the scale of the whole polity.

Contemporary Critiques of Integration

Contemporary skeptics of integration endorse a localist understanding of democratic citizenship that reformulates familiar political concepts as liberty, civic virtue, and justice to fit within the context of a political community whose boundaries do not align with those of the broader democratic state. Here, I examine some representative examples of this approach, proceeding in two steps. First, I consider whether a theory of racial justice should, as Andrew Valls has argued, focus on achieving free conditions of choice with respect to where individuals live, work, go to school, and so on, and remain agnostic toward the patterns of racial clustering that result from these free choices. On the account of identification defended here, I contend that Valls's agnosticism is untenable.

If a theory of racial justice cannot be agnostic toward integration, then the second step is to answer whether racial egalitarians should pursue or reject integration. Accordingly, I next turn to contemporary critics of integration who offer two main arguments: one, that the proper scope of identification is, in principle, local; and the other, that while a broader form of civic identification *may* be desirable *under some conditions*, it cannot justly be demanded now in the context of black-white racial integration in the United States. The first of these positions I associate with Michael Merry's redefinition of civic virtue as good neighborliness, and the second I associate with Sharon Stanley's and Tommie Shelby's arguments that just forms of integration on a national scale must await achievement in the future. It bears emphasizing that Stanley is not an unqualified critic of integration; in fact, her work attempts to develop a justifiable account of it. However, she concludes that a just form of integration could reasonably delay a call for multiracial national solidarity, and in this respect her argument overlaps with Shelby's more critical position. I discuss these arguments in turn.

1) *Conditions of Choice.* Seeking to develop a theory of racial justice that proceeds "on liberal grounds,"[74] Andrew Valls has proposed reframing familiar debates over integration and separation in terms of conditions of choice. This professedly liberal, choice-based approach generates a "provisional" defense of the "community black nationalist" perspective[75]—Valls's term for the view that makes "modest demands for community and institutional autonomy"[76] but stops short of advocating full secession. Valls notes that African Americans often face unfair pressures when deciding where to live, attend school, and so on, since the profound material deprivations facing black institutions strongly encourage "integration into white institutions," generating an objectionable "assimilation pressure."[77] Valls argues that our priority should be achieving fair conditions of choice and respecting those choices rather than stipulating any particular pattern of spatial clustering or mixing. This approach, he explains, "cuts across the integration/separation debate by focusing on the terms on which the debate should be decided."[78] From this perspective, he contends that

> in principle, it is a mistake to equate racial clustering with failure. This is one of the main upshots of the black nationalist position: racial clustering is not in itself a bad thing, and may in some respects be a good, valued thing, as long as it results from uncoerced individual choices under just conditions. It is a mistake to say that "If racial segregation is the problem, then racial integration is a remedy" (Anderson 2004, 20). De jure segregation was certainly a "problem" but it does not follow that integration is the remedy.[79]

This "conception of racial justice ... is agnostic about what should be the ultimate spatial distribution of residences along racial lines"[80] and "takes no position on what the right mix is, or the degree of racial clustering that is desirable."[81] "As long as these individual choices are made under fair conditions, conditions that support the liberty and equality of those making them," contends Valls, "the resulting pattern is compatible with justice."[82]

Although this liberal focus on choice calls attention to an important dimension of the integration/separation debate, I think there are two complicating considerations that argue for qualifying its agnosticism. First, the account adopts a predominantly materialistic understanding of coercive pressure,[83] which generates an overly permissive interpretation of what counts as an uncoerced choice. If it aims to ground a plausible agnosticism toward the outcomes of individual choices, a standard of "fair choice" should set not only legal and material criteria but also criteria related to social respect. The underlying reason here is captured by Valls himself, who notes that even today, "black schools, as well as other predominantly black institutions, still provide a refuge in an often hostile and racist society."[84] The continued need for such refuges indicates that if material deprivation creates an unfair pressure to integrate, racial hostility creates a similarly unfair pressure to separate. If, under conditions of material equality, black Americans declined to participate in majority-white institutions where they would be disrespected and alienated, we would have limited warrant to infer that their living a mostly separated existence implied consent to a pattern of racial clustering. This possibility suggests that the absence of materially coercive pressures does not signal the absence of coercive pressures generally; in such a situation, we would have grounds to doubt whether the choice was truly fair and thus to qualify our deference to it.

Second, the agnosticism of Valls's account rests on an unstated assumption that whatever patterns of clustering result from voluntary choice will not undermine the liberal and democratic ideals to which his theory is committed.[85] In contrast, the account of democracy I have defended throughout this book calls attention to the risk that pervasive separation would undermine citizens' tendency to imagine and regard one another as equal fellow-members. To the extent that citizens are pervasively separated, they will not be able to collectively articulate and pursue a vision of the common good that emerges from inclusive, egalitarian processes of public interpretation and discussion. This conception of identification tracks Anderson's understanding of "a democratic *culture* pervading civil society," marked by "habits and sentiments of association on terms of equality."[86] In the settings of civil society, writes Anderson, democratic citizens engage in "cooperation and communication *across group lines*, for the purposes of forging *shared* norms and goals of the democratic polity as a whole, and to that extent forging a shared identity of citizens."[87] Notice that "shared identity" here is not a static quality that automatically inheres in citizens. It emerges only from their cooperative interactions with each other. This suggests that a segregated society, where citizens consistently interact only within group boundaries, will generate a corrupted, distorted sense of membership: it will lead even well-intentioned citizens to believe, earnestly but mistakenly, that they are listening to their compatriots and pursuing a shared vision of the common good.

It is impossible to specify in the abstract when any given individual is living a pervasively separated existence since the array of spaces in which any individual life plays out—neighborhoods, schools, workplaces, friend groups, religious organizations, professional societies, clubs, and so on—may be more or less integrated. Nonetheless, it *is* reasonable to assert that, in principle, the totality of individual citizens' associational ties should not substantially obstruct democratic identification. Such obstruction undermines the epistemic conditions of democracy and so inhibits the ability of citizens to live together in a free and equal manner. To endorse this requirement is to rule out a strong form of agnosticism about clustering: Even free conditions of choice cannot launder forms of pervasive separatism that undermine democracy.[88]

One possible alternative, not comprehensively explored by Valls but compatible with his approach, would be to explain how a polity-wide democratic epistemology is to be maintained when spatial and associative barriers are voluntarily constructed among citizens who must understand each other's perspectives when making decisions that affect the whole. But as I will argue below, contemporary defenders of separatism tend to *assume* a civic whole, rather than showing how it can be sustained through the more circumscribed (and racially clustered) practices and imaginaries of citizenship that they endorse.

2a) *Civic Virtue, Defined Locally.* Michael Merry's defense of "voluntary separation" represents one attempt to resolve this problem by defining the civic whole in predominantly localist terms. Merry's argument begins with the observation that segregation—by which he simply means "the de facto situation of spatial concentration"[89] among some group that shares a characteristic—is a common feature of life. Groups that are segregated (i.e., spatially concentrated) are often, but not always, stigmatized in some way; but while stigmas and harm are not a *universal* feature of this spatial concentration, lack of choice generally is: segregation is "the state of affairs into which many of us are born and grow up."[90]

Merry's account concerns how individuals might respond to such unchosen conditions of spatial concentration, including in cases where it entails harmful stigmatization. "Contrary to the integrationist creed," writes Merry, "I espouse the view that both equality and citizenship can be fostered and realized in segregated communities, even under nonideal conditions."[91] He proposes the alternative approach of "voluntary separation": an attempt to "resist, reclaim, and rearrange the terms of one's segregation when those terms are counterproductive to equality and citizenship," to "change the conditions under which one's segregated experience occurs" in a manner that enhances liberal democratic equality and citizenship—which may, in some cases, be normatively preferable to integration[92] since minority groups often have good reasons for clustering.[93]

Merry's contention that "neither equality nor citizenship is dependent on integration"[94] rests on a "pluralist" account of citizenship that is "less robust" than more demanding alternatives that emphasize, beyond the fulfillment of basic civic responsibilities, such capacities as imaginative engagement with others, a willingness to disagree reasonably, and so on. As an alternative to these demanding visions, he proposes "a less explicitly political version of civic virtue."[95] Merry understands virtues as "dispositions, habits, and actions whose excellence promotes individual and collective well-being," and he deems them *civic* "to the extent that they contribute to, and strengthen, the communal good."[96] Civic virtue therefore entails "dispositions and actions that promote the good of the community," but it "does not collapse into *political* virtue."[97]

In this account, civic virtue is less the sine qua non of effective membership in a polity and more a set of qualities that could be described as good neighborliness. Its geographical scope is correspondingly narrower: Merry acknowledges that "civic virtue typically begins with the local"[98] since its "possibility . . . begins with attachments nourished by those with whom we have daily interaction."[99] He does not claim that these good local habits are incapable of a broader application, but neither does he insist that they will, or should, have one. His characterization of civic virtues' extension beyond the local is consistently provisional: civic virtues "need not eclipse more remote concerns";[100] they "do not exclude" an outward-facing application;[101] their benefits "*may* very well move outward";[102] and the local "*may* significantly overlap with the national or global."[103] The reach of effective civic virtue "will arguably depend on the good being promoted,"[104] but in any case, it is not to be "conflated with republican notions of citizenship that accentuate national over communal attachments and their attendant expressions of common good."[105] Merry characterizes these expressions of communal attachment, and their political salience, in this way:

> Civic virtue may include political acts such as lobbying, town meetings, and voting, but it need not. Instead, it might include coaching little league baseball, good parenting, volunteering one's time at a homeless shelter, or planting trees. What gives these activities civic import is their impact on the lives of others. Here, *civic* draws attention to people's roles as citizens and their relation to the state and to others within the same country, most of whom they do not know. If and when conditions change, persons may choose to participate in overtly political acts . . . But civic virtues need not be overtly political; indeed, nonpolitical actions often contribute more to the common good within a particular community.[106]

Although Merry contends that "*civic* [virtue] draws attention to people's roles as citizens,"[107] this array of actions offers little guidance on democratic citizenship's role-specific obligations—since it is not the case that democratic citizenship flourishes wherever people exhibit care for their communities. One need only consider the many communal virtues that could flourish among, say, the subjects of a medieval monarch to appreciate the gulf between such virtues and those distinctive to modern democratic citizenship. The essential difference between subjects in a monarchy and citizens in a democracy is not the character of actions that each group might engage in to enhance neighborhood life but the fact that the latter share the power to shape their common life as equals. To the extent that there are virtues specific to this form of political life, they cannot be limited to a local scope and have an ambiguous or provisional relationship to politics, because the relevant ties of responsibility are constituted by shared subjection to the democratic state—meaning that they necessarily stretch *beyond* the locality.

For this reason, I contend that it is shared state subjection, not shared neighborhood residence, that demarcates the scope of civic virtue and determines (to at least some extent) its substance. Merry's account effectively naturalizes the local community as the "real," or at least the more fundamental, site of belonging, but because local communities *as such* have no special political character, this account of political community offers little guidance to democratic citizens other than that they should comply with "basic civic responsibilities and obligations" (Merry's example is the duty "to operate within the parameters of the law").[108]

Merry's account of civic virtues must necessarily have this apolitical and localist character if it is to be plausibly marshaled in defense of separation. The reason can be found in the significant qualification that accompanies his endorsement of voluntary separation: "*so long as segregation provides facilitative conditions for the fostering of civic virtue*, integration is not an irreducible good."[109] But as I have shown, this condition can be met only because Merry reduces "civic virtue" to the point where it is basically indistinguishable from good neighborliness and has no particular relationship to the democratic state. It is, perhaps, true that if the ties linking democratic citizens extended no further than the neighborhood, this separatist conception of civic virtue would exhaust the relevant considerations of how neighbors ought to interact. But there is no non-naturalizing reason to elevate the neighborhood as the primary site of belonging, and there are strong reasons (grounded in the democratic ideal of self-rule on terms of equality) to resist this relocation of citizenship, since what binds citizens—and indeed, distinguishes them from mere denizens of the same place—is their association through the *state*, not the locality. The democratic state is the underlying association that links citizens together and gives rise to obligations among them: it demarcates the scope of civic virtue, lends substance to the actions that are to be performed, and denotes the persons obligated to perform them. We should hope that citizens are also good neighbors, but by subsuming citizenship into good neighborliness, localist critiques of integration abandon the conceptual resources necessary to explain how democratic ideals can be sustained on the scale of a state.

2b) *Broad Civic Identification Must Await Just Conditions.* The third major challenge to integration among contemporary philosophers guardedly concedes the importance of nationalized identification but insists that its cultivation must wait until fairer conditions emerge. This view has been espoused by Tommie Shelby and Sharon Stanley, both of whom are critical of Elizabeth Anderson's claim that "neither justice nor democracy can be realized if the self-segregated racial group is celebrated as a more worthy site of identity and emotional investment than the integrated 'us.'"[110] In response, Shelby argues that it is "entirely appropriate" for black Americans, as a stigmatized group, "to withhold some allegiance to the nation and to invest more in cultivating solidarity and mutual aid within the group, simply as a matter of self-defense and group survival," postponing "full identification with and loyalty to the nation" until they arise naturally, as a result of the broader nation's sustained "commitment to equal justice by removing the unfair burdens on the oppressed."[111] And while Stanley defends integration from one prominent criticism—arguing that it is "not *intrinsically* a project of compulsory assimilation"[112]—she nonetheless maintains, along with Shelby, that the integrationist vision endorsed by Anderson should be delayed until better conditions obtain. "To reject integration today is not to reject it tomorrow," writes Stanley. "It is simply to say 'not now, we are not ready yet.' Hope for integration resides in the 'yet' and the burden rests on whites to turn that endlessly deferred yet into a present reality."[113]

Shelby and Stanley's respective critiques both involve a kind of sequential reordering. Stanley writes that Anderson's call for multiracial fellow-feeling simply "begs the question of where this fellow feeling actually comes from,"[114] and she worries that "we may well be putting the cart before the horse" by asking Americans "to forge... bonds of [interracial] solidarity" when so many citizens still "have not had extensive experiences" with integrated settings.[115] Voicing a similar objection, Shelby writes:

> I believe that an integrationist ethos—a pervasive sense of interracial unity—would be a natural *by-product* of a just multiracial society of equals. While I doubt that residential integration is a necessary means to such a society, interracial unity would likely be a consequence of a just social structure and the manifest willingness of the citizenry to support and maintain it because it is just. Our emancipatory aim should be, therefore, to establish such a structure, not to artificially engineer multiracial or mixed-income neighborhoods in the name of national unity.[116]

These arguments advance a consequential reinterpretation of democratic solidarity. While solidarity is often understood affectively (as a form of positive fellow-feeling or "unity"), I have argued that from a democratic perspective, the importance of solidarity among citizens lies primarily in its ability to create the epistemic conditions of democracy. But Stanley and Shelby contend that solidarity is only a plausible sentiment or a justifiable demand *following* the achievement of democratic equality. This presents a dilemma: if solidarity among citizens is necessary to achieve democracy in the first place, then how can it be delayed until democratic equality has already been realized?

Stanley's account is especially sensitive to what she calls the apparent "temporal paradox" facing integration: "Each forward step, or each step toward greater integration, depends on a transformation of attitudes that would in fact derive from the forward step itself."[117] Put simply, she writes, "one needs integration for interracial solidarity, but one also needs interracial solidarity for integration."[118] As this formulation suggests, we may not be dealing with the cart and the horse so much as the chicken and the egg. This concern leads Stanley not to reject integration tout court but rather to treat it as a process in time. Instead of calling for a form of integration invested with nationwide solidarity, Stanley proposes that we understand integration as an ongoing process in which different solidarities are "constantly in flux for each citizen."[119] This endorsement of multiple, fluctuating solidarities is intended to correct what Stanley sees as an important mistake in Anderson's call for the *present-day* cultivation of multiracial solidarity among American citizens. Anderson sees such solidarity as a precondition of integrated equality, but Stanley—offering a rival interpretation of the empirical research cited by Anderson to demonstrate integration's benefits—counters that when "interracial solidarity" emerges in different settings, it is "because the settings are already integrated"; that is, solidarity "appears as the product, not the cause, of integration."[120] For these reasons, she concludes that Anderson's "ideal of national solidarity is ultimately imported from a speculative vision of integration as a fait accompli. Citizens are essentially asked to operate *as if* the nation were already integrated."[121] According to Stanley, in making this request, "Anderson falls prey to a mistake that Juliet Hooker identifies: 'To suggest that it is possible to determine a priori which kinds of solidarities will matter to individual persons and the order in which they will do so does not reflect how solidarity actually works.'"[122]

This conclusion—that Anderson's call for solidarity rests on a mistaken understanding of solidarity's nature—counters a conceptual claim about democracy with empirical claims about the theorist's inevitably limited knowledge of "how solidarity actually works" for any given individual. The empirical claims are convincing, so far as they go: there is no reason to think that theorists are in a privileged position to discern a priori which particular solidarities will actually matter to people or how they will rank them. And, of course, to insist on the importance of nationwide solidarity hardly demonstrates that it actually exists. Yet Anderson's call for multiracial national solidarity is a logical derivation from the distinctive conception of democracy that she develops, not an empirical claim about what solidarities Americans actually feel. Its endorsement of solidarity (of a certain kind, on a certain scale) follows from an underlying account of democracy (understood in a particular way). To show that the endorsement is mistaken, it would be necessary to demonstrate that solidarity does *not* follow from her underlying account of democracy or that the account of democracy is itself mistaken in some way.

The best way to evaluate Stanley's alternative vision, then, is to compare it along those same lines—as advancing a rival view of the relationship between solidarity (of a certain kind, on a certain scale) and democracy (understood in a particular way). In undertaking such a comparison, it is worth noting at the start that in some ways Stanley's account of democratic citizenship resembles Anderson's. It also asks of each citizen "the willing acceptance that one also belongs to a larger whole, to a democratic nation," where "responsible citizenship . . . requires one to develop an understanding of the perspectives of unfamiliar groups, rooted in their different historical experiences and the different structural positions they occupy in the greater society."[123] To some extent, these resemblances are unsurprising—since, to reiterate, a basic goal of Stanley's argument is not to reject integration outright; rather, it is to develop a model of integration that is sensitive to its temporal complexities and paradoxes and can therefore "withstand common critiques."[124] Nonetheless, as Stanley emphasizes at other points, there are important differences between Anderson's account of solidarity and her fluctuating, pluralized alternative, which she illustrates as follows:

> In this account, integration signifies the fact that we have multiple, complex loyalties, any of which can become active and guide our choices and political actions in appropriate circumstances... Therefore, we are capable of affirming multiple solidarities simultaneously. An individual may strongly identify as a black resident of a black neighborhood as she goes about her ordinary day-to-day affairs, but when she hears at a public meeting that a nearby, predominantly Latino neighborhood has suffered catastrophic flooding, her solidarity with the greater region can be activated.[125]

Although Stanley is no doubt correct that any given citizen has multiple solidarities whose salience varies by situation, this example nonetheless illustrates the limitations, rather than the advantages, of consecrating this fluctuating vision of solidarity and ceding a robust ideal of identification on the scale of the whole demos. Like Merry's endorsement of acts such as coaching and tree-planting, it suggests that democratic solidarity is, for the most part, encompassed by an ideal of good neighborliness—except when some unusual event activates it on a broader scale. This may capture how local solidarities often operate in practice, but it fails to capture key elements that distinguish the kind of relationship that exists *among citizens*. This leaves it unable to explain, even as an idealized account, how democratic equality might be achieved among compatriots whose relationship is characterized by high levels of separation.

One distinctive element of that relationship is that it originates and is circumscribed politically: it arises among a group of people because of their common citizenship. Yet the kind of solidarity activated by nearby flooding does not have this kind of political logic, either in its origins, its scope, or the details of its operation. Consider first that a catastrophic flood could easily generate feelings of solidarity in the absence of any political ties whatsoever. Because such events endanger and harm human beings in such a fundamental, universal way, they often activate a kind of global solidarity whose logic is humanitarian, not political, and which for that reason extends even to distant strangers.

The example in question, of course, imagines a *nearby* flood, not a distant one—activating a regional solidarity that temporarily takes precedence over everyday local solidarities. This suggests that the logic of the fellow-feeling is not primarily humanitarian but may instead be spatial: nearby residents are motivated by their proximity to the disaster. But a spatial logic of solidarity is also distinct from a political logic of solidarity. If spatial proximity explains the origins of the solidarity and the scope of its operation, then this example is not essentially different from the situation of a tourist who, while vacationing in a foreign country, rents a boat just before a catastrophic flood occurs. In such a situation, the tourist would likely feel solidarity with that country's citizens and be motivated to help them by virtue of proximity and ability: with access to a boat, the tourist can rescue people in danger.

But again, if proximity explains the origins of this fellow-feeling and the scope of its operation, we still lack an account of democratic solidarity—wherein the underlying relationship is defined politically, not spatially. An account of democratic solidarity should capture, for example, the willingness of citizens in (say) Maine and Hawaii, who reside thousands of miles away from each other, to pay into a common taxation system to support flooding relief if disaster afflicts either state. Is the response of black neighbors to flooding in the Latino neighborhood an example of spatial solidarity (like the tourist) or political solidarity (like the taxpayers)?

Stanley's account resists a purely spatial reading since it asks citizens to remember their shared political ties. But this attempt to forestall the collapse of solidarity into simple neighborly virtue confronts a serious problem in the example's distinction between a citizen's "ordinary day-to-day affairs," which take place in a more parochial spatial-psychological universe, and an unusual, catastrophic event like a flood, which "activates" our "solidarity with the greater region."[126] The problem is that a consequential, ongoing democratic life unfolds in "ordinary day-to-day affairs" too, and does not only become relevant in the occasional context of some exceptional disaster. Each citizen of a democratic state exercises power over, and bears political responsibility for, events that transpire outside their immediate community—through (for example) their voting behavior, news consumption, donations, activism, and participation in deliberation and other forms of political speech. It is a regular, not incidental or exceptional, feature of those actions that they reach beyond the immediate local community to encompass many others who are linked by institutional ties.

There is a cost to conflating spatial and political solidarity, for day-to-day parochialism can have damaging consequences for fellow-citizens beyond the parish. Citizens whose everyday focus extends only to their own neighborhood may develop a psychological insularity that matches their spatial separation, in which case they may—through no particular ill-will—ignore shared elements of political life that are within their scope of influence, and which therefore ought to be within their scope of everyday concern. Perhaps the risk of catastrophic flooding in the Latino neighborhood would have been more obvious to other citizens if they, too, lived in the same area close to the water. Perhaps other citizens, insensible to this risk beyond their immediate locality, opposed a candidate for statewide office who proposed new taxes to fund flood readiness. Perhaps they voted for a presidential candidate or supported a political party that wanted to slash spending on infrastructure and disaster response—thinking of their own possible financial gains, not the needs of other citizens over whom they exercise power. Perhaps their political choices never prioritized climate change because they live further inland, or at a higher elevation, and rarely have occasion to feel the effects of rising sea levels.

By the time the flood occurs, the activation of their broader solidarity is too late. Its after-the-fact emergence is a pale substitute for a broader, more ongoing form of identification that should have been guiding their political behavior all along—and which might have prevented, or at least mitigated, the disaster in response to which it is now activated. Like other localist conceptions of citizenship, then, this vision of fluctuating solidarities ultimately fails to see the whole democratic state. It does not capture the fact that democratic citizenship is an ongoing, politically defined relationship that stretches continuously over time, not a spatial relationship whose scope broadens only at discrete moments. In other words, it does not account for identification on the scale of the whole polity.

To correct for these shortcomings, we could amend the theory's account of solidarity—making it more prospective and more far-reaching. These amendments would reflect the view that identification among citizens is necessary to generate democratic decisions in the first place, and therefore must characterize their shared life not only at exceptional moments but on an ongoing basis under normal conditions as well. This point likewise applies to Shelby's suggestion that while an "integrationist ethos" might be a "*by-product* of a just multiracial society of equals," it is not a precondition of such a society. This claim overlooks two important points about solidaristic identification. First, identification with the larger citizenry need not entail feelings of warmth or affection; prominent black thinkers from Frederick Douglass to Ralph Ellison have stressed their deep identification with the United States precisely to advance searing critiques of it, as well as to ground the obligations that they believe their compatriots have toward black people as fellow-members. Second, identification is knowledge generating: it reveals the existence and nature of public problems, equipping citizens with the necessary information to democratically craft responses and rectify injustices.[127] Unless we presume that just policies could be formulated and implemented without such public processes of deliberation (broadly defined), then we have strong reasons to view those processes as a necessary condition of democratic repair. Integration, insofar as it promotes interaction and communication among citizens, is thus part of achieving the epistemic conditions of a democratic agenda of racial justice. This understanding of democracy's epistemic conditions indicates why black thinkers like Douglass saw separatism as no more than a temporary defensive strategy, to be adopted only in extreme situations. Even in 1889, during an especially bleak period of the United States' lynching crisis, Douglass argued that "circumstances should only be yielded to the least practicable extent," since "when we thus isolate ourselves we say to those around us, 'We have nothing in common with you,' and, very naturally, the reply of our neighbors is in the same tone and to the same effect." To avoid this outcome, Douglass counseled that "our policy should be to unite with the great mass of the American people in all their activities and resolve to fall or flourish with our common country."[128] This vision of solidarity points toward a possible ethos of identification that does not require citizens to overlook their oppression or develop sentiments of uncomplicated affection for their country.

In the next section, I offer a description of this ideal of identification—presenting it as the imperative to "think like a citizen." To think like a citizen, we need an account of democratic membership that recognizes shared membership in a state, not a locality, as a source of special responsibilities that stem from the valuable ideal of democratic self-rule.

Thinking Like a Citizen

In popular discourse, it is common to define democracy in terms of "free and fair elections"—a limited definition that reveals an emaciated, and excessively institutional, civic imagination. An election is a single act at a single moment in time, when voters choose among a specified range of alternatives. This moment of choice is preceded by a longer, more open-ended process, during which different interpretations of the demos's common life are put forth, different definitions of its problems are proposed, rival solutions are debated, coalitions are formed, opponents are rebutted or converted, and so on. Many students of democracy regard this antecedent process as the site of the action. To a committed democrat like John Dewey, majority rule was not defensible "just as majority rule"—its importance, rather, was linked to "antecedent debates, modification of views to meet the opinions of minorities, [and] the relative satisfaction given the latter by the fact that it has had a chance and that next time it may be successful in becoming a majority."[129] To that point, Dewey approvingly quoted New York Governor Samuel Tilden: "The means by which a majority comes to be a majority is the more important thing."[130]

For these processes to work, individuals must learn to think like citizens. This presumes that they have a more-or-less accurate sense of who their compatriots *are*. Otherwise, they cannot know whose views to consult, whose perspectives to prioritize, whom to engage in discussion, and so on. A demos that is stably bounded, and whose members engage in these processes of identification, forms an ongoing "We" that can be said to act from a collective perspective when shaping the conditions of its shared life.[131]

In reality, of course, citizens often fail to meet the standards to which this ideal of democracy holds them. If they are unwilling or unable to reflect critically on the status quo, their political imaginations will atrophy, and they will become passive and irresponsible as citizens. If they fail to consider other citizens' perspectives, they will mistake the views of one group for the views of the whole—or even, as the sinister phrase "real Americans" suggests, treat certain kinds of compatriots as presumptively illegitimate, as people whose perspectives should be rejected out of hand.

To use a term proposed by Danielle Allen, the goal of identification is better captured by the idea of civic "wholeness" than by the idea of national "unity." Wholeness, argues Allen, better captures an ideal of civic integrity for a diverse society and is capable of distinguishing integration from assimilation. Allen argues that "the seesawing back and forth of African American political ideology between assimilation and separatism is itself a product of our failure to address directly the question: what modes of citizenship can make a citizenry whole without covering up difference?"[132] She suggests this answer:

> To be the people as "whole," citizens ... must learn to see and hear what is political in the interactions they already have with their fellow citizens ... They are asked to see customers, employees, employers, attendants as citizens, and to look out for

how their participation in institutions—whether schools, churches, or businesses—implicates them in strangers' lives.[133]

On Allen's description, individuals come to see and hear like citizens when they recognize their encounters in the realms of economic exchange and civil society not as discrete, private, and sporadic but rather as patterned interactions located within webs of political belonging that "implicate" them in the lives of certain strangers. These strangers are our political co-members: "fellow citizens" in the "public sphere." Likening citizens to musicians who rely on eye contact to coordinate their individual playing in the collective performance of a song, Allen writes: "The people as a whole is constituted of a multitude of citizens exchanging glances while holding firmly to the legitimate institutions of collective decision making."[134]

Allen's references to churches, schools, and businesses may seem to echo Stanley's and Merry's prioritization of local ties, but her attribution of political significance to those ties cannot be accounted for purely by reference to what neighbors in some locality share *qua* neighbors. Neighborly relations are distinguished from civic relations by the fact of shared membership in a state. The key feature of such relationships is institutional, and so their scope is also circumscribed institutionally:

> And, happily, liberal institutions make it possible for us to interact with fellow citizens well beyond the limit of the "polis" ... liberalism allows us to extend political friendship beyond local and to national contexts. Wherever we move throughout our polity, we have opportunities to engage strangers in political friendship because strong institutional protections of rights free us to take risks on interactions that we could not otherwise afford. Nor, when we are active as political friends in our own polis, can we forget about the rest of the people with whom we share our polity.[135]

By tracing citizenship to institutional ties rather than local denizenship, this account preserves an emphasis on the necessity of identification on a scale that cuts across local, racialized boundaries.[136] In a racially divided democracy like the United States, members of the racial majority cannot help but make political decisions that affect the minority, even under conditions of voluntary separation. To the extent that separation grows more pervasive, collective decisions are likely to be less attentive, less informed, and less guided by shared deliberation and shared concern. The valorization of local ties over national ties cannot ultimately sustain the possibility of a democratic future in the United States. That ideal requires integration, and integration rests on a broader vision of shared peoplehood.

The Haverford Group and Paths Not Taken

In his statement after the May 1969 Haverford discussions, Robert C. Weaver, who had only a few months earlier concluded his tenure as the first secretary of housing and urban development, again raised the basic issue of conceptual clarity that had haunted discussions of separatism and integration since at least *Brown*. "I find that I have a degree of ambivalence about the subject," Weaver admitted, adding: "I am confident that part of my difficulty lies in the fact that many of the terms used in these discussions are rarely defined."[137]

The reappearance of this concern, at a conference of integrationists at the end of the 1960s, suggests that some of the basic questions raised in the immediate wake of *Brown* remained unresolved fifteen years later. It does not follow, however, that this was a period of intellectual stagnation. Quite the contrary: as the Haverford meeting's conveners realized, the ground had shifted in those intervening years. Racial egalitarians' belief in a common country—as a possible site of democracy, as a plausible locus of belonging—was in decline, and there was no clear consensus alternative to replace it. Weaver's comments reflect his concern that the ambivalence he felt was settling over the racial justice movement as a whole:

> Perhaps the most basic issue is that of goals. Do we want to establish a separate black society; and if so is it a permanent goal or a temporary arrangement which is achievable now and will be effective in ultimately facilitating black people's full participation in this nation? And if the latter position is espoused, is it viable, or does the acceptance of separation create institutional patterns and vested interests that give it permanence?[138]

This question, restating the basic dilemma of affiliation that is at the core of African American political thought, reflects the difficulty of framing political goals when the identity of the "We" is unclear. Who belongs to the collective that frames this future-oriented vision? Who sets its shared goals and directs present-day political strategy in light of those goals? Could black Americans remain separate in the present as a means to affiliation at some point in the future? Weaver's questions reflect an acute perception of the complications of sanctioning a mismatch between the scope of identification and the scope of citizenship. African Americans might establish a permanently separate society, or they might separate temporarily, with the ultimate goal of affiliating themselves with a multiracial demos at the appropriate time. But would this strategy disrupt their ability to work collectively toward that multiracial future or even ossify into an unintended form of quasi-membership?

Ultimately, if the goal is to live together as a multiracial, democratic people, then all these forms of separatism seem doomed to indefinitely postpone that future. For this reason, Anderson is correct to conclude that "the integrated 'us,' not the self-segregated racial group, is the critical agent of racial justice that most urgently awaits deeper and richer construction."[139] Anderson's suggestion that the integrated "We" is *not yet built* indicates that the integrative ideal of nationalized identification does not envision a simple "entry" of black Americans into white institutions and spaces; rather, it insists on the transformation of those spaces so that they are genuinely inclusive of all Americans. The ultimate path that such a transformation takes cannot be determined in advance. It can only emerge from the interaction of citizens on terms of equality. This idea was captured in a 1964 remark from James Baldwin: "This is why I say that in order for the Negro to become an American citizen, *all* American citizens will be forced to undergo a change, and all American institutions will be forced to undergo a change too. These institutions, which are established, can only begin to operate to free me and all other Americans by changing."[140]

Here, the theoretical premises of the Haverford Group are worth revisiting. I have already discussed how their sociocultural and historicized understanding of race made them skeptical of strongly identity-based claims for separatism. That same understanding also informed their emphasis on a form of identification that could promote a more egalitarian future.

The theme emerges repeatedly in their conversation and written statements. Resisting the implicitly ahistorical appeal of racial romanticism and framing the situation of African Americans as inextricably bound up with the United States itself, the Haverford discussants emphasized that African Americans had made the U.S., just as it had made them. Because hybridity already characterized American life, what blackness *meant* as a social, historical, and political reality simply could not be isolated from its embeddedness in the American whole. Neither could the United States' white majority understand itself without understanding how it had been formed by a racial minority, an understanding segregation had masked, and which voluntary separation would further inhibit. For that reason, William Hastie implored young activists "to think and act intelligently, aggressively, generously and compassionately, with a view to a *better total society*, not to think and act belligerently black with a view to a *separate society*."[141] And John Hope Franklin, a few weeks before joining the Haverford discussions, bluntly stated in a lecture: "What we have to say we have to say to the whole world and not to this little jim crow bunch of Negro kids."[142]

But no member of the Haverford Group was more explicit about the need to fuse the pursuit of democracy and racial justice to a positive vision of

American peoplehood than Ellison. Ellison maintained that Americans were already marked by a far greater degree of hybridity than they realized, and if they could but understand the substantial integration that already marked their cultural life, they would come to see the futility and self-denial of *political* segregation. As he asked during the Haverford meeting: "Where do we find elements of our spirit, our values, our traditions, our style in the larger American culture? What metamorphoses have our contributions undergone?"[143] In his introduction to the thirtieth anniversary edition of *Invisible Man*, Ellison described the "development of conscious, articulate citizens" as "an established goal of this democratic society" and the social equivalent of the novelist's aesthetic goal: the "creation of conscious, articulate characters."[144] Facing the project of "imposing meaning upon our disparate American experience," the novelist was helped by the fact that "human imagination is integrative—and the same is true of the centrifugal force that inspirits the democratic process."[145] Ellison gave these commitments lucid expression in a remark made during the Haverford discussions:

> Our situation cries out for new definitions—or at least for conscious intellectual restatement of those abiding attitudes and values which have been acted out, if not stated explicitly, by our people as they have repudiated theories of white superiority. It is our task to define who and what we are with as much intellectual precision as is possible. And since we are an inseparable part of the American nation and its culture, let us accept the obligation of defining it from the perspective of our own backgrounds and insist that its values be brought in line with our own group's aspirations and needs.[146]

This tendency to see the work of democracy as "defining" the people, in order that it might repudiate white supremacy and create citizens, places Ellison and his Haverford interlocutors in a tradition of democratic thinking that stretches back to Reconstruction. But that task of self-definition is only possible if citizens believe in the existence, or at least the possibility and desirability, of their shared peoplehood. As Jeffrey Stout has observed, separatist politics may be an understandable reaction "against an exclusionary definition of the democratic community," but this reaction tends to "obscure the relations of mutual dependence actually at work in democratic communities."[147] The abandonment of integrationist goals severed the once-twinned pursuits of racial justice and American democracy. The result was a fatal mismatch between the scope of egalitarians' imagined community and the scope of the democratic polity that fully and collectively bore responsibility for their situation.

There is no plausible path to democratic equality in a multiracial United States that does not involve integration. Yet the vision of peoplehood underlying the integrationist ideal has fallen from favor, and racial egalitarians today—skeptical of broad civic solidarity—defend the relocation of citizenship to the local level, effectively redrawing the demos along lines that do not match the actual scope of the citizenry. In contrast, the view defended by members of the Haverford Group generates a basis for inclusive, expansive identification of the sort that is necessary to achieve a genuine multiracial democracy. If American egalitarians are to renew a push for integrated racial equality, they will need to appeal to this broadened self-understanding to explain and motivate their program. In this way, the prospect of racial justice in the United States remains linked to the prospect of a broadly shared form of American peoplehood.

Chapter 5
Inequality, Citizenship, and the Permanent Tax Revolt

On December 6, 2011, President Barack Obama traveled to Osawatomie, Kansas. With a population of 4,447, the president's destination was chosen not for its size but for its symbolism. About a century before, Theodore Roosevelt had delivered a speech in the same town, on the same topic, and the forty-fourth president intended to draw explicit parallels with his predecessor. "In 1910, Teddy Roosevelt came here to Osawatomie and he laid out his vision for what he called a New Nationalism," explained Obama as he called for action on "the defining issue of our time." "This is a make-or-break moment for the middle class," he explained: "What's at stake is whether this will be a country where working people can earn enough to raise a family, build a modest savings, own a home, secure their retirement."[1]

Obama's ambitious "inequality speech" received a dyspeptic response from conservatives. The speech "was not given by the President of the United States," complained a writer in *The Wall Street Journal*; it "sounded like what you'd expect to hear in Caracas or Buenos Aires," with ominous overtones of left-wing populist authoritarianism. Accusing the president of singling out wealthy Americans "as basically enemies of 'the middle class,'" the writer mused: "If in fact there are categories of Americans he simply doesn't like, a second Obama term . . . could be a clinical exercise in hammering the people he singled out in this speech. Metaphorically speaking."[2] *National Review*, the flagship publication of the American right, published multiple denunciations of Obama's remarks. One *NR* writer deemed it a "speech of such fascinating awfulness archeologists of the future sifting through the rubble of our civilization will surely doubt whether it could really have been delivered by the chief executive of the global superpower in the year 2011."[3] In another piece, the magazine's editors chastised the speech for its allegedly misplaced priorities: "Americans are not suffering mainly from inequality. They are suffering from unemployment."[4] And in a third, a vice president at the Heritage Foundation claimed, in a more philosophical vein, that Obama had attacked the "principle that each has a right to the rewards of his own labor," imperiling the very idea that "makes possible a dynamic social order in which every member of society can work hard and advance based on individual talent and ability."[5] Obama's call for high earners to pay their "fair share" and his criticism of low taxes on the wealthy as the "height of unfairness"[6] portended nothing less than a radical restructuring of American life under the control of unaccountable government managers. "Obama's program is fundamentally about the rise of a new governing class that insists on enforcing political and economic 'fairness' rather than letting us govern ourselves," a program that would make the state "more undemocratic, and more potentially despotic, than ever."[7]

Such complaints echoed the reaction that had met Roosevelt in 1910. A *New York Times* editorial about Roosevelt's speech had similarly claimed that tasking the federal government with the pursuit of economic fairness was a step toward unaccountable despotism. Skeptical of what it called the speech's "spirit of universal Federal dominion," the *Times* insisted that constitutionally speaking, "the Federal Government may do only what it is specifically empowered to do," whereas Roosevelt promoted "the essential, inherent, besetting, and obsessing idea that the Federal Government shall take control of the daily life, the earnings, the property of every American citizen."[8] The newspaper recoiled at Roosevelt's argument for a progressive income tax, in which he drew a categorical distinction between the income of an average American and "the really big fortune, the swollen fortune" of a wealthy one. In such a distinction, the *Times* saw a clear threat to liberty: "Therefore the universal regulator at Washington should take steps to reduce 'big' or 'swollen' fortunes. This involves necessarily the discretion at Washington to decide what is big and must be cut down. It is discretion that none but an absolute ruler can possess."[9]

The *Times*'s feared "universal regulator" was, for *National Review*, a "new governing class"; its invocation of an "absolute ruler" became for *NR* a "potentially despotic" regime and for the *Journal* a Latin American–style dictatorship. In other words, both the president and his conservative detractors concurred that Obama was indeed resurrecting, for good or ill, the program of New Nationalism that Roosevelt had outlined a century earlier.[10]

However, a closer comparison reveals important differences between the two presidents' speeches. Although Obama invoked Roosevelt's program of New Nationalism and its call for "real democracy," his speech struck a far different tone, portraying Americans more as consumers than as citizens.[11] "America," the president declared, "was built on the idea of broad-based prosperity, of strong consumers all across the country."[12] He hastened to add that "inequality also distorts our democracy." But the speech's turn from economic to political questions was only a brief rhetorical pivot: after just three sentences on the theme of democracy, Obama informed his listeners that there is "an even more fundamental issue at stake. This kind of gaping inequality gives lie to the promise that's at the very heart of America: that this is a place where you can make it if you try. We tell people—we tell our kids—that in this country, even if you're born with nothing, work hard and you can get into the middle class."[13]

By contrast, Roosevelt's speech had made no suggestion that obstacles to a middle-class consumer lifestyle were an "even more fundamental issue" than inequality's distortion of democracy. Quite the opposite: Roosevelt had endorsed "practical equality of opportunity for all citizens" for its ability to advance "two great results": not only affording "every man . . . a fair chance to make of himself all that in him lies," but also ensuring "that the commonwealth will get from every citizen the highest service of which he is capable."[14] By articulating his critique of inequality in terms of a New Nationalism, Roosevelt intended not only to promote a scope of concern that superseded what he called "sectional or personal advantage," but he also sought to cast the threat of growing inequality as a problem with economic *and* civic dimensions of equal importance. "Ruin in its worst form is inevitable," he warned, "if our national life brings us nothing better than swollen fortunes for the few and the triumph in both politics and business of a sordid and selfish materialism . . . The material progress and prosperity of a nation are desirable chiefly so long as they lead to the moral and material welfare of all good citizens."[15]

In the century separating Roosevelt from Obama, egalitarians initially succeeded in making the United States a more equal democracy, but over time, they grew far less inclined to think and speak about distribution in these strongly political terms. By the time inequality had begun to expand in the late 1970s, they had largely abandoned a democratic approach to political economy. This subtle transformation essentially surrendered the contested political economy of citizenship to conservatives, who organized with massive success around what became the defining policy ambition of the new Gilded Age: opposition to taxation.

The Permanent Tax Revolt

Antitax ideology is a defining and exceptional feature of American conservatism. As Fred Block observes, its predominance on the American right "diverges sharply from hundreds of years of political history in which durable ruling regimes in all parts of the world have increased the capacity of government by strengthening the state's fiscal base."[16] Antitax sentiment is not merely one policy stance among many;[17] it is, in the words of one historian, "an ideological crusade" through which "the conservative movement transformed a specific economic prescription into an overarching theory of government."[18]

Antitax activism is, to understate the matter considerably, not a new phenomenon in American political history. But its takeover of a political party and near-hegemonic dominance of popular understandings of freedom are both relatively recent developments, each of which is intimately bound up with the midcentury rise of the conservative movement. Jennifer Burns has noted that "in the early 1950s, conservatism had yet to harden into a clearly defined ideology,"[19] but that "by the 1960s . . . conservatives had managed to redefine the word so that it referred almost solely to traditionalists comfortable with the despised Manchester economics. A conservative was now someone who called for both an unfettered free market and a return to tradition, however bizarre such a position seemed to liberals."[20] That combination has proved durable. One historian of fiscal policymaking deems the tax revolt "the third great transformation in American public finance," ranking in importance alongside the early twentieth-century development of the fiscal state and the World War II–era expansion of a "mass tax" to millions of new households.[21]

Like these earlier transformations, the tax revolt was inspired and publicly legitimated by a set of guiding ideas. These ideas are not solely, or perhaps not even primarily, a set of empirical propositions about economic growth, and economic interests alone cannot explain the intensity of the American right's focus on tax cutting. As Block has argued, that focus arose as an "ideological response" to events, one that exhibited a familiar "cultural dynamic" witnessed in an earlier surge of laissez-faire thought during the Industrial Revolution.[22]

Chief among the guiding ideas of the tax revolt is a narrative of citizenship that is largely left unchallenged in contemporary American political discourse. In this narrative, the virtuous citizen is an individualistic creator of wealth whose freedom is threatened by majoritarian tyranny in the form of illegitimate claims on his earnings voiced by undeserving, alien others. Through this potent idea, American conservatives have redefined and monopolized the concept of freedom in American political discourse,[23] linking it to antistatist and antidemocratic policies, and going so far as to associate their opponents' agenda with slavery.[24] This conception of citizenship underwrites the political economy of inequality, granting it normative legitimacy and blocking policies that would seek to mitigate it. It unites the distinctive themes of antitax politics: individualism and antigovernment sentiment; skepticism about solidarity and majority rule; and the naturalism of market economies. Perhaps most radically, this individualistic view of citizenship comes close to denying the coherence of collective self-rule as a conception of political freedom, at least as it relates to economic matters. In this way, the tax revolt's conception of citizenship directly challenges the importance of identification. Informed by a deep skepticism of the notion that a demos could make itself free by controlling the conditions of its shared life, the permanent tax revolt is distinguished by an extreme and defiant individualism—a rejection of the idea that democratic politics emerges from, and is sustained by, an intersubjective understanding among citizens that they are connected through membership in the polity to each other.

An alternative to this view must be able to explain why the fact of shared democratic citizenship is relevant to political economy, and why it raises specifically egalitarian demands. Not all theorists agree on the primacy of equality: some, following a position originally developed by Derek Parfit, take the "prioritarian" view that distributions should prioritize the worst off because they are worst off in an *absolute* sense and will thus benefit the most from any gains; their relative well-being compared to other people is not morally important in itself.[25] In defending the priority view, Parfit claimed that it avoids certain perverse implications that seem to follow from egalitarianism's focus on relative well-being—such as the idea that benefiting the worst off would be less morally urgent if there were no people who were better off.[26] More seriously, Parfit also saw the prioritarian view as immune to the "Levelling-Down" objection that he attributed to some formulations of egalitarianism—that greater equality is good even if it is "worse for some people, and better for no one." (As illustrations of such undesirable forms of equality, Parfit imagined a natural disaster that struck only the wealthy without benefiting the poor, or a policy of removing the eyes of the sighted, leading to a world where everyone is equally blind).[27] Other skeptics of egalitarianism take a somewhat different view, arguing that what matters is for everyone to enjoy *sufficient* resources and that beyond that threshold of sufficiency, there is no reason to keep redistributing in the pursuit of greater equality. As Harry Frankfurt argued in defense of the sufficientarian view: "From the point of view of morality, it is not important that everyone should have *the same*. What is morally important is that each should have *enough*. If everyone had enough money, it would be of no special or deliberate concern whether some people had more money than others."[28]

Notably, these rejections of egalitarianism also evince little interest in the relevance of relationships such as shared citizenship. If a sufficientarian were to examine a democratic society with a generous universal basic income, they might well conclude that there is little to analyze from the perspective of distributive justice. And Parfit observes that the priority view "naturally has universal scope": "If it is more important to benefit one of two people, because this person is worse off, it is irrelevant whether these people are in the same community, or are aware of each other's existence. The greater urgency of benefiting this person does not depend on her *relation* to the other person. It depends only on her lower absolute level."[29]

In contrast, the most persuasive egalitarian rebuttal to these views draws on a rich account of social relations. On a "relational" approach, as Elizabeth Anderson explains, equality is not solely, or even primarily, a *distributive* question—as if "there exists a single good that egalitarians should want to see equally distributed."[30] Rather, relational egalitarians "take the object of evaluation to be not simply a pattern of distribution but a system of social relations that, among other things, results in a distributive pattern";[31] therefore, "a distribution is objectionable from an egalitarian point of view if it causes, embodies, or is a specific consequence of unjust social hierarchy."[32] This analytical focus on a "system of social relations" yields a clearer argument for equality's distinctive importance while addressing some important questions about egalitarianism's scope.

Political philosophers have long been concerned with the corrupting effects of inequality on social relations. As T. M. Scanlon has observed, these corrupting effects are numerous and diverse. Among other things, inequality induces feelings of shame or inferiority among some and feelings of superiority among others; it enables some people to exercise political and economic domination over others; and it undermines the fairness of social institutions.[33] Because these various harms could arise even when all citizens have reached a threshold of sufficiency, an ideal of equal social relations generates reasons to reach a sufficientarian floor, understood in distributive terms, but also to go beyond it.[34] As David Rondel observes, "there is nothing in egalitarianism that forbids acceptance of the moral platitude expressed in sufficientarianism's positive thesis, *viz.*, it is morally important that everyone have enough."[35] Similarly, egalitarianism is capable of incorporating prioritarian concerns while going further when that framework proves incapable of accounting for other objectionable features of inequality. As Martin O'Neill has noted, while "most writers ... have seen prioritarianism as a rival distributive view to egalitarianism," to cast them as "straightforward adversaries is to mischaracterize the conceptual terrain," since "the Priority View, construed as an axiological claim about the diminishing marginal moral significance of gains in well-being, does not conflict with" the most compelling versions of egalitarianism. Therefore, "we should be both egalitarians *and* prioritarians, and do not need to choose between the two sorts of views."[36]

A focus on social relations not only clarifies what is distinctively valuable about equality but also indicates why egalitarian ideals make especially strong demands in the context of shared democratic citizenship. Social hierarchies, feelings of superiority and inferiority, political domination, unfair social institutions, and other effects of inequality strike directly at the ideal of collective self-rule since their effect is to subordinate one part of the citizenry to another, rendering the subordinate group less free. O'Neill observes that while adherents of a relational framework will be committed to endorse certain global egalitarian obligations, it is also the case that "the degree to which distributive inequalities will manifest these forms of [social] badness will depend to some large degree on the nature and intimacy of the social relations that exist between the individuals in question." Relational egalitarianism, then, can incorporate the most appealing elements of cosmopolitan, sufficientarian, and prioritarian views while retaining—in a way that those other positions, to varying degrees, cannot—the ability to explain "why the demands of equality will be especially salient within the bounds of particular nation states, where social relations are, in the typical case, more intimate."[37]

This way of thinking about equality—as an ideal of social relations, particularly democratic citizenship—illuminates what is lost when conceptions of citizenship become dominated by an extreme individualism that obscures the embedded, artificial, and political nature of markets. The success of the new right in redefining citizenship along such individualist and market-naturalist terms, terms amenable to the permanent tax revolt and the age of inequality, must be understood in the context of a broader set of midcentury shifts in thinking about American peoplehood. As fiscal historian Ajay Mehrotra has written, the 1970s witnessed a "dissolution of society as a national community," and this dissolution "was expressed in the anti-tax policies and anti-statist ideology that came to rule the times."[38] According to this way of thinking, the broader society had few legitimate interests in the highly personal matters of production, wealth, and distribution. Versions of this claim had long been conservative orthodoxy, but in the wake of the decline of a tradition that stressed Americans' shared membership in an expansively defined, nationally scaled demos, they transformed into a new "common sense."[39] By the time the age of inequality was underway in the 1980s, Americans' newly dominant social self-conception reflected, as Daniel Rodgers writes, "a disaggregation of society and its troubling collective presence and demands into an array of consenting, voluntarily acting individual pieces."[40]

Like the politics of immigration and race, the politics of taxation and inequality are profoundly shaped by whether Americans see themselves as fellow-members of a shared political association. Inequality is a political problem not only because it is generated by political choices but also because in extreme cases, it replaces equal relations with hierarchical ones, transforming democracy into oligarchy. So long as market naturalism dominates the public imagination, the economy will be seen as closed off from legitimate democratic debate and contestation; so long as reigning conceptions of citizenship emphasize individualism and consumerism, it will be difficult to see how inequality leads to unjust social relations and corrodes democracy. The resources to contest our present political vocabulary were latent in the democratic thinking and activism of earlier reformers. But these resources were tied to an enduringly controversial understanding of membership that has sharply declined in popularity since the end of the Second Reconstruction.

The timing of the tax revolt's emergence helps explain why these questions of membership have long complicated the pursuit of egalitarianism in the United States. It was not until the 1960s that the balance of power within the Republican Party began to decisively shift toward individualist conservatives whose market naturalism informed a deep skepticism of civic-associative duties and a celebration of tax cutting as synonymous with freedom. The libertarian faction's ascent coincided with a marked intensification of the federal government's pursuit of racial equality through such steps as the *Brown* decision of 1954 and the federalization of the Arkansas National Guard during the desegregation of Little Rock's Central High School in 1957. In many cases, the desire to preserve racial hierarchy directly motivated the rejection of public amenities. When, in 1958, black residents of Montgomery, Alabama, filed a lawsuit seeking to integrate the city's public parks, officials responded by closing the entire system. The shuttered facilities included the majestic Oak Park, which contained the city's largest public pool—a Works Progress Administration (WPA) project from the 1930s—and a zoo. In response to the black citizens' effort to integrate the park, an editorial in *The Montgomery Advertiser* warned:

> A park is not a bus system or a school. It is something that can be disposed with. Oak Park might simply be closed. Certainly it must be obvious that before the races are mixed in Oak Park that the squirrels would be trapped and set free in Catoma swamp, the roses and azaleas would be ploughed up, the ancient oaks and pines would be cut and sold for timber. An official who saw it otherwise could not survive in Montgomery politics.[41]

The editorial was prescient: Oak Park's pool was drained and filled in, and the zoo animals were sold off. Rather than comply with desegregation mandates, Montgomery sold (or simply gave away) much of the system and kept the remaining facilities closed until the mid-1960s. As Heather McGhee has noted, this decision to abandon public amenities in the name of segregation and white supremacy was replicated in many communities across the United States.[42]

Montgomery's decision to shutter, rather than integrate, its WPA-built pool poignantly symbolizes the emerging cracks in the New Deal coalition, driven by what Thomas and Mary Edsall have called the "embourgeoisiement" of white voters "who had previously seen their interests as aligned with a downwardly-redistributive federal government."[43] As Ira Katznelson has shown, racial conservatives had been reliable members of the New Deal coalition in previous decades, supporting its interventionist economic policies so long as the boundaries of distribution observed strict racial limits. Among FDR's Southern allies in Congress, support for the New Deal was "premised on" the security of Jim Crow:[44] America's welfare state was safe, so long as it was limited to white citizens.[45] But this coalition did not last, as Southern Democrats eventually began to worry that their party was being overtaken by racial egalitarians who would extend the New Deal across the boundaries they had worked so hard to maintain. As early as the late 1940s, prescient Southerners were predicting that in the name of racial hierarchy, the white South would eventually find itself partnering with conservative Republicans, despite the obvious ideological mismatch.[46]

The political logic underlying this prediction implied that intraparty tensions might be partly smoothed over and the coming fracture of the coalition delayed, so long as Democratic support for civil rights remained relatively constrained and the economy continued to deliver broad-based prosperity. But these conditions snapped almost simultaneously: in 1964 and 1965, President Johnson signed landmark civil and voting rights legislation, and in 1966 the U.S. experienced the first credit crunch of the postwar era.[47] By the mid-1960s, worsening macroeconomic conditions were making former New Deal Democrats more receptive to racialized fears that Democrats would "raise taxes from the largely white lower-middle and middle classes in order to direct benefits towards the disproportionately black and Hispanic poor—benefits often seen as wastefully spent."[48] Similar racialized perceptions continue to influence white Americans' views on a range of distributive issues, from welfare to healthcare to taxation.[49]

By the time of Ronald Reagan's 1980 presidential victory, showdowns like the one in Montgomery, which had prompted the city to trumpet its intransigence toward "race mixing," belonged to a different (although not very distant) era. Although overt segregation was no longer legal, the intervening years had shown that many of its goals could be achieved through subtler means—including by what Kevin Kruse calls "suburban secession," which transformed national politics in the 1970s.[50] Aided by a string of sympathetic Supreme Court decisions that reinforced jurisdictional boundaries insulating suburbs from cities, white residents of the suburbs were empowered, as K. Sabeel Rahman notes, to opt for "withdrawal and secession in response to mandates to provide racially desegregated access to local public goods."[51] By thus "manipulating the terms of access" to goods like healthcare, housing, and water, it became possible to quietly "construct exclusion or inclusion—and in so doing, effectively *construct citizenship*"; to "implicitly demarcate the boundaries of the polity, the scope of who belongs, and the privileges and substantive goods such membership affords."[52] As Kruse observes, the political worldview associated with suburban secession was marked by "a convenient, collective amnesia about the nation's troubling history of residential apartheid, school segregation, and economic discrimination"; suburbanites simply "came to see their isolation as natural and innocuous."[53]

Conservative analysts of Reagan's ascent took a different view. By the mid-1980s, wrote William Schambra, it was "perhaps inevitable that the American people should have turned to . . . small, participatory groups such as family, neighborhood, and ethnic and voluntary associations," which "*are*, after all, more 'naturally' communities."[54] In contrast, "the idea of national community," which had "explained and provided the moral underpinnings" for generations of progressive reformers, "had been in decline for a decade and a half,"[55] and as a result, its "programmatic superstructure—a massive, centralized federal government—was left in a peculiarly exposed and precarious position."[56] Reagan proved to be an ideal figure to exploit this weakness and to unite economic and racial conservatives who both opposed the egalitarian goals and interventionist methods of the New Deal and Great Society. As a political leader, he ended the ideological hegemony of these reform movements by popularizing an antithetical set of ideas: government was inimical to freedom, capitalism was a natural (and therefore normatively sanctioned) phenomenon, and the ideal American citizen was an individualistic wealth creator badly in need of tax relief to better secure the blessings of liberty. As president, his signature domestic legacy consisted of tax cuts that, as Eric Foner has written, resulted in "a massive shift of wealth from poorer to wealthier Americans." In that time, Foner argues, "nothing did more to prevent a revitalized sense of common national purpose more than the widening gap between rich and poor."[57] But if Reagan's intellectual interpreters were to be believed, this common national purpose had always been a liberal fiction; Americans simply did not see their communal ties so expansively. Or, as Reagan put it during his 1980 campaign kickoff speech in Neshoba County, Mississippi, where three civil rights workers had been murdered during Freedom Summer in 1964: "I believe in state's rights."[58]

These antigovernment and individualist themes powered a conception of American citizenship so successful that even today, despite an apparent normative consensus against inequality,[59] national political debate seems only fitfully able to imagine alternatives to the status quo.[60] As Jacob Hacker and Paul Pierson note, a widespread "amnesia" flourished during the period of market fundamentalism that followed the downfall of mixed-economy liberalism in the 1970s. Of course, the broad growth of antigovernment sentiment in that era "did not go unnoticed or occur without pushback," but those who resisted it nonetheless "found themselves caught in what communications experts call a 'spiral of silence'": alternative ideas and their associated labels were gradually pushed out of mainstream discourse.[61] This process owed much to the success of policies that dismantled the shared spaces and common experiences that underwrite a sense of identification among citizens. The result was, to use Wendy Brown's term, "an important remaking of the demos," in which "assaults on collective consciousness and action" lead not only to "the erosion of popular power, but its elimination from a democratic political imaginary"—as well as the elimination of those "forms of identity" that correspond to that imaginary.[62] This gives reason to think that the intermittent, circumscribed appeals to solidarity in Obama's "inequality speech" reflected not only the absence of a genuinely political critique of inequality among liberal elites, but also the absence of receptive listeners to that critique. In other words, even if the president had made a strong appeal to Americans' mutual obligations, their shared circumstances, and their common fate, he would have been invoking things that were increasingly alien to his audience.

An End of History for Economics

At the time of the new right's rise to prominence, it was nearly commonplace among analysts of American politics to assume that conservatives simply had to make peace with the national state represented by the New Deal. It is clear in retrospect, however, that the New Deal order was less stable than it appeared at midcentury. In fact, its fall in the late 1960s coincided with the end of an anomalous era in American economic history. With the entry of the U.S. into World War II, the share of income held by the top decile of Americans (and, within that group, the top 1 percent in particular) had suddenly and sharply plummeted, falling from interwar highs of about 45 percent to almost 30 percent.[63] There is some reason to think that this shock to the incomes of the well-off might have lasted only as long as the fighting. After all, their share of income had risen in the years between the Treaty of Versailles and the Great Depression,[64] and a return to prewar wage structures had arrived quickly following the end of World War I.[65]

Yet after 1945, the top decile's share did not rebound to its prewar highs. Instead, it hardly budged for three decades, a period during which wages also became substantially more equal. As two economists summarize the era: "When the United States emerged from war and depression, it had not only a considerably lower rate of unemployment, it also had a wage structure more egalitarian than at any time since. Further, the new wage structure remained somewhat intact for several decades."[66] Economists have termed this war-era increase in wage equality the "Great Compression,"[67] and the economy it created persisted until the 1970s. The era's egalitarian prosperity was modeled in the Nobel Prize–winning economist Simon Kuznets's inverted U-shaped curve of industrialization and inequality. In the mid-1950s, Kuznets proposed that while inequality would increase in the early stages of industrialization (as it had in the Gilded Age United States), it would eventually dissipate—resulting in the happy combination of growth and increasing equality that Americans enjoyed at the time. Kuznets admitted that his theory was highly speculative and perhaps influenced by wishful thinking,[68] but that did not deter its popularity as an explanation of the country's economic boom.

Indeed, so powerful was this era's effect on the political imagination that it briefly became possible to think that the major issues of organizing the political economy of an industrialized mass democracy had been solved. The problems posed by a mature economy's low growth rate, which had so concerned the liberal and left intellectuals of the early New Deal era,[69] seemed to disappear amid the egalitarian boom of the postwar decades.[70] Faith in the expertise of liberal economists was, not coincidentally, at an all-time high.[71] As Arthur Schlesinger reflected later in the 1960s, this optimism informed the supposedly post-political perspective that distinguished economic policymaking in the Kennedy administration:

> The ideological debates of the past began to give way to a new agreement on the practicalities of managing a modern economy. There thus developed in the Kennedy years a national accord on economic policy—a new consensus which gave

hope of harnessing government, business, and labor in rational partnership for a steadily expanding American economy.[72]

This way of framing debates (or, rather, the end of debate) in political economy was not something liberals came to recognize only in retrospect; President Kennedy himself had given influential and crisp expression to the post-ideological impulse at the time. "What is at stake in our economic decisions today," Kennedy declared in 1962, "is not some grand warfare of rival ideologies which will sweep the country with passion, but the practical management of a modern economy. What we need is not labels and cliches but more basic discussion of the sophisticated and technical questions involved in keeping a great economic machinery moving ahead... political labels and ideological approaches are irrelevant to the solution."[73] Giving voice to the confidence born of the postwar boom, Kennedy announced that economics had entered a new era:

> I am suggesting that the problems of fiscal and monetary policies in the sixties as opposed to the kinds of problems we faced in the thirties demand subtle challenges for which technical answers, not political answers, must be provided... governments, and many of them are conservative governments, [are] prepared to face technical problems without ideological preconceptions, [and] can coordinate the elements of a national economy and bring about growth and prosperity—a decade of it.[74]

This faith in growth and skepticism toward anything that resembled divisive class politics also reflected the pressures of the Cold War, which made liberals reluctant to discuss political economy using the terms they had employed only a few decades prior. For comparison, consider President Franklin Roosevelt's 1936 renomination speech, which illustrates Kennedy's distinction between political and technical approaches to economic questions:

> These economic royalists complain that we seek to overthrow the institutions of America. What they really complain of is that we seek to take away their power. *Our allegiance to American institutions requires the overthrow of this kind of power.* In vain they seek to hide behind the Flag and the Constitution. In their blindness they forget what the Flag and the Constitution stand for. Now, as always, they stand for democracy, not tyranny; for freedom, not subjection; and against a dictatorship by mob rule and the over-privileged alike.[75]

Here, there is no suggestion that growth and prosperity are the sole questions of political economy. Roosevelt foregrounds the distribution of power and, far from predicting the rise of a post-ideological consensus, frames opposition to "economic royalism" as an ongoing imperative of American democracy. Although this way of approaching matters of political economy draws on powerful rhetorical and intellectual traditions, its popularity among liberal politicians was ultimately short-lived. As Gary Gerstle notes, "in the hands of anti-Communist crusaders," overtly politicized rhetoric eventually "became a tool for narrowing the political and ideological boundaries of the American nation ... By the mid-1950s, the opportunity to use the language of civic nationalism to advance a radical economic program—so prominent a feature of Progressive and New Deal reform—had largely vanished."[76]

Ironically, the egalitarian prosperity created by these reform movements helped produce the attitude that hastened their decline and created an opening for a conservative alternative. By the early 1960s, the distinctive feature in the discourse of liberal political economy was, to be specific, not its faith in expertise per se (which had a lineage tracing back to the Progressives) but rather its confidence in the post-ideological character of the issues that economic policy would address.[77] By the 1960s, the divisive arguments that have historically accompanied attempts to bring the market in line with democratic aspirations no longer seemed necessary. The pie was growing rapidly, and the only remaining task was to set more places at the table. As William Forbath and Joseph Fishkin observe, "the Civil Rights Revolution and Great Society unfolded in an unprecedented moment of broadly shared prosperity," when "America appeared to be becoming the kind of middle-class nation past generations of reformers dreamed about—or so liberals believed at the time." This made it possible for the designers of the War on Poverty to argue that they could achieve their policy goals through growth alone: "no tax hikes would be necessary, no controversial redistribution, no structural changes in the political economy."[78] Harold Lasswell's "who gets what, when, and how" can seem merely a matter of administration when there is plenty go around; only in a context of scarcity does the political character of these questions become fully apparent.[79]

The perspective derived from theorists of democratic solidarity was thus gradually displaced from discussions of political economy. In intellectual circles, this trend could be detected in the reaction to Rawls's *A Theory of Justice*, the definitive philosophical statement of postwar redistributionist liberalism. As one study has noted, *Theory* "did not appear until the disintegration of the liberal consensus was well under way. During the most opportune moment for consensus thinkers to have aggressively developed their ideas on political economy—the two decades immediately following World War II—they had failed to do so. By the time such a statement arrived, the nation's political and intellectual tide was turning toward conservatism."[80] But the moment of *Theory*'s arrival in 1971 was not only distinguished by ascendant conservatism; it was also, and no less importantly, a time of changing attitudes toward bounded solidarity on the American left. After all, one of the earliest critical reactions among sympathetic liberal readers was to globalize Rawls's argument: Why, they asked, should it apply only to societies conceived as closed systems, as he had stipulated?[81] Was not national membership, as Rawls might put it, so arbitrary from a moral point of view?

The reaction among philosophers mirrored broader trends in the 1970s, as American egalitarians came to abandon the invocations of shared peoplehood that had been central to the reforms of Reconstruction, the Progressive era, the New Deal, and the early postwar years.[82] The embittering political divisions of the late 1960s had made the concept of the national commonweal seem elusive, and the emergent critique of corporate liberalism, combined with the deepening crisis of the Vietnam War, made an institutional reliance on the federal government seem naïve, if not directly opposed to basic left-wing goals. As Jennifer Burns notes, liberal thinkers had, for a brief moment in the 1950s, evoked the "national good . . . in response to resurgent conservatism," but "after a brief moment of popularity, it was rarely articulated again."

> At midcentury, liberals spoke in a confident, sure voice about the interests of the nation as a whole. They confidently criticized the behavior of capitalists without impugning capitalism, and their tone was steady, not defensive. Since then, these attitudes have been mocked from both the right and the left as complacent centralism and a false consensus that papered over the realities of American life. But without a robust sense of the public good, liberalism has little to do but carp at business. Surely, such carping has its uses, for as a dominant feature of American life and a thoroughly human institution, business will always behave in ways that call for criticism and correction. But liberals also need to offer a positive idea of what America can do and be. In the 1950s, as they fought back against the first surge of conservatism, liberals articulated such a vision.[83]

The faltering of this vision in subsequent years made it more difficult to popularize a genuine alternative to conservative ideas while enhancing the appeal of notionally post-ideological arguments centered on economic growth. This embrace of putatively disinterested technocracy, however, was based on mistaken predictions about the future of American political economy. As egalitarians increasingly abandoned their conceptual anchoring in a broad vision of shared peoplehood, both economic crisis and ideological revolt were drawing nearer—developments that they had largely failed to anticipate and which they were ill-prepared to address. As a result, when archaic economic concepts roared back against the stumbling Keynesian macroeconomic paradigm, their proponents found the conceptual terrain unoccupied.[84] Because economic liberalism had been guided, as K. Sabeel Rahman writes, by a model of "market-optimizing, technocratic regulation," it proved "troublingly vulnerable to laissez faire critiques" that questioned "the efficacy and accountability of expertise."[85] Technocracy's legitimacy rested not on a normative vision of the kind of political economy proper to a democracy but on the supposed ability of experts to deliver economic growth. All that was required was an economic downturn to undermine the authority of the technocrats—and to make it appear that rival, free-market approaches were superior on the technocrats' own growth-centric terms.

When the downturn came, the revival of free-market discourse would not only dethrone the technocrats, but it would also come to dominate social thinking in general. And the *kind* of market that emerged in the era's prominent metaphors and conceptual frames was not the institutionally thick, historical, and sociological realm imagined by mainstream macroeconomists at midcentury. Rather, as Daniel Rodgers has demonstrated, the novel feature of post-stagflation market metaphors "was their detachment from history and institutions and from questions of power ... To imagine the market now was to imagine a socially detached array of economic actors, free to choose and optimize, unconstrained by power or inequalities, governed not by their common deliberative action but only by the impersonal laws of the market."[86] The task of resisting economic royalty had given way to the task of freeing socially detached individuals from the state's imposition of inefficient, unjust burdens, especially taxation. Political economy had been reshaped to fit a civic vision stripped of identification.

Taxation, Citizenship, and the New Right

On the eve of the GOP's 1964 Convention, William F. Buckley Jr. reminded the readers of *Newsday* what "Establishment" opinion had made of Barry Goldwater, the conservative Republican senator who was about to secure the party's nomination. Goldwater made Walter Lippmann "hysterical"; Murray Kempton had issued a "burst of frenzy" against him; and before his successful nomination push, Joseph Alsop had dismissed him entirely: "No serious Republican politician, even the most Neanderthal type, any longer takes Goldwater seriously."[87]

Buckley's relish in recounting these dismissals reflected his feeling of vindication. Less than a decade before, the founding of his *National Review* had been greeted with similar scorn from liberal writers whose respect was reserved (with the occasionally patronizing charity of the dominant) for the "New Conservatives," like Peter Viereck and Clinton Rossiter, whom Buckley's magazine would soon help displace.[88] In their battle to define conservatism in more sharply ideological terms, Buckley and others associated with *National Review* would focus much of their critique on these traditionalists who were, in their view, far too accommodating of the New Deal state—who had earned liberals' respect at the cost of ideological capitulation. The "fusionist" approach pioneered by *National Review* blended conservative traditionalism with a strident championing of free-market economics.

In the 1964 presidential election, Goldwater became the first conservative to popularize that fusionist message on a national scale. Goldwater shared some of Buckley's literary and intellectual ambitions: just four years earlier, he had published a bestselling ideological manifesto, *The Conscience of a Conservative* (aided by his ghostwriter L. Brent Bozell Jr., a *National Review* editor and, later, Buckley's brother-in-law). Along with the founding of *National Review* in 1955, the publication of *Conscience* represents a seminal moment in the transformation of American conservatism.

Each of *Conscience*'s chapters covered a topic of special importance to this emerging movement, including states' rights, civil rights, education, the USSR, and "Taxes and Spending." In that latter chapter, Goldwater gave influential expression to the conservative movement's understanding of the relationship between the individual and the political community. At a moment when liberal elites were publicly declaring that economic issues no longer had any political dimensions, Goldwater offered a dramatically different perspective. "We have been led to look upon taxation as merely a problem of public financing: How much money does the government need?," he wrote. "We have been led to discount, and often to forget altogether, the bearing of taxation on the problem of individual freedom."[89]

The individualistic vision that informs Goldwater's political economy rejects the possibility that a demos could legitimately intervene with market outputs to combat economic inequality. While conceding that government "has *some* claim on our wealth,"[90] Goldwater argued that the Constitution strictly limits "the federal government's total tax bill" to the cost of exercising its "*delegated* powers,"[91] and that any taxes collected to fund programs not explicitly authorized by the Constitution "*exceed* the government's rightful claim on our wealth."[92] Claiming that the public's vigilance against high taxes had been dampened by the widespread assumption that citizens are, "in the nature of things, obliged to accommodate" whatever level of revenue the government seeks to collect, Goldwater countered: "The 'nature of things,' I submit, is quite different. Government does *not* have an unlimited claim on the earnings of individuals. One of the foremost precepts of the natural law is man's right to the possession and the use of his property."[93] "Property and freedom," asserted Goldwater, "are inseparable: to the extent government takes the one in the form of taxes, it intrudes on the other."[94] Offering the example of a person who pays 32 percent of his income in taxes, he concluded that such a person is "working one-third of the time for government: a third of what he produces is not available for his own use but is confiscated and used by others who have not earned it."[95] For Goldwater, the individual's natural right to property not only restricted the amount of revenue the government could justly collect but also dictated the distribution of its taxation scheme:

> The distribution of the government's claim is the next part of the definition. What is a "fair share"? I believe that the requirements of justice here are perfectly clear: *government has a right to claim an equal percentage of each man's wealth, and no more* . . . I believe it is contrary to the natural right to property to which we have just alluded—and is therefore immoral—to deny to the man whose labor has produced more abundant fruit than that of his neighbor the opportunity of enjoying the abundance he has created.[96]

Dismissing progressive taxation as "confiscatory," he continued:

> Its effect, and to a large extent its aim, is to bring all men down to a common level. Many of the leading proponents of the graduated tax frankly admit that their purpose is to redistribute the nation's wealth. Their aim is an egalitarian society—an objective that does violence both to the charter of the Republic and the laws of Nature. We are all equal in the eyes of God but we are equal *in no other respect*. Artificial devices for enforcing equality among unequal men must be rejected if we would restore that charter and honor those laws.[97]

Goldwater's flat denial that "the charter of the Republic" could legitimately be tasked with egalitarian goals is notable because, by the time *Conscience* was published, nearly half a century had passed since the 16th Amendment granted Congress the power to levy income taxes. The adoption of that amendment was driven by worries about the growing power of corporations and wealthy individuals, as well as by objections to the regressive character of the prevailing consumption tax regime. "Instead of relying exclusively on consumption taxes that fell most heavily on ordinary people," write Joseph

Fishkin and William Forbath, "the Populists and later the Progressives wanted a federal income tax that would fall most heavily on the enormous new fortunes of the era."[98] They ended up supporting a constitutional amendment after a conservative Supreme Court, in a highly controversial ruling, struck down an income tax that Congress had passed in 1894. The egalitarian purposes of the 16th Amendment indicate why Goldwater found it necessary to augment constitutionalist arguments with extraconstitutional appeals to the naturalness of markets and of property rights.

Goldwater maintained that all forms of production were "*best controlled by the natural operation of the free market.*"[99] This view of markets as natural, spontaneous, and uncoerced—free in their operations and fair in their outcomes—informed his rejection of progressive taxes and redistribution. For Goldwater, such practices violated what Ian Shapiro has called the "workmanship ideal": the Lockean idea that work mixed with justly acquired resources confers legitimate ownership over the resulting product.[100] This preindustrial ideal does not translate smoothly to contemporary economic conditions. Among other things, it assumes that for any given piece of property, both the identity of the laborer who produced it and the origin of the resources involved are relatively straightforward, assumptions that poorly reflect the reality of complex, industrialized economies.[101] While sophisticated reformulations of the workmanship ideal might be able to rescue this Lockean notion for modern applications, Goldwater simply abstracted away from such problems—and in so doing, marshaled all the intuitive moral force of the idea by omitting from view the whole nexus of social, legal, and political relations in which markets are embedded. In this way, he helped create a template for the politics of permanent tax revolt, in which earnings seem to emerge from a natural realm untouched by politics and law. On this view, the individual exists in a market order that is apolitical and free of coercion until the point of redistribution, when covetous others, claiming to act on behalf of the majority or the common good, enter the picture and artificially interfere.

From these ingredients, the new right developed a theory of citizenship that denies the legitimacy of democratically authorized redistribution. Robin Einhorn notes that this narrative of American taxation "leaves out a lot," not least "the little matter of democracy": "This story casts 'the government' of the United States as an autonomous entity . . . In the radical libertarian world of this story, it is inconceivable that Americans might have wanted (and might still want) to use their (our) government to provide certain services, voting for candidates who promised to deliver them."[102] But if "Americans" as a whole are absent from the market processes that produce earnings in the first place, then they can have no warrant to interfere with those processes. As Goldwater wrote, taxation bears on the question of *individual* freedom, not the question of collective freedom. This view's deep suspicion of majoritarian politics and egalitarianism sets it against nationally scaled conceptions of peoplehood,[103] since the demos that would presume to redistribute is a pernicious fiction. It is not the agent of collective sovereignty to which each individual belongs but rather a mere aggregate of alien others illegitimately trying to seize something to which it has no claim. As Wendy Brown notes, this view implies a fundamental rethinking of public amenities, the public sector, and indeed the very notion of what it means to belong to the public:

> The market metrics contouring every dimension of human conduct and institutions make it daily more difficult to explain why universities, libraries, parks and natural reserves[,] city services and elementary schools, even roads and sidewalks, are or should be publicly accessible and publicly provisioned. Why should the public fund and administer them? Why should everyone have free access to them? Why shouldn't their cost be borne only by those who "consume" them? It is already a symptom of the vanishing value and lexicon for public things that such questions today are generally converted to a different one, namely, the role of government versus the private sector for the provision of goods and services. In this conversion, government is not identified with the public, but only as an alternate market actor. Citizens, meanwhile, are rendered as investors or consumers, not as members of a democratic polity who share power and certain common goods, spaces, and experiences.[104]

In this way, solidaristic identification is jettisoned from the conservative movement's vision of citizenship. In denying the demos any meaningful role in economic life, the permanent tax revolt suggests that the larger collective theorized by generations of democratic thinkers does not exist.

Inequality, Understood Politically: Beyond Need and Desert

Market naturalism, which furnishes a simple, seemingly commonsense way of thinking about economics, has powerful effects on normative beliefs about inequality. Depicting a world of spontaneous, voluntary, efficient, and potentially frictionless exchange, it implies that inequality, in most of its manifestations, is exempt from criticism—either because it is natural or because it is the result of voluntary actions that, it can safely be assumed, benefit all parties (because they agreed to them). Milton Friedman's defense of "competitive capitalism" rests on this latter idea: "The possibility of co-ordination through voluntary co-operation rests on the elementary—yet frequently denied—proposition that both parties to an economic transaction benefit from it, *provided the transaction is bi-laterally voluntary and informed.*[105] A broad interpretation of what constitutes sufficient voluntarism and information, combined with the assumption that these conditions generally obtain, underwrites the belief that market transactions are definitionally free, and that they are unfree only to the extent that they are subject to external interference.

Yet as a growing body of literature has demonstrated, this is an untenably depoliticized and ahistorical understanding of actually-existing markets,[106] and it occludes our ability to understand the actual origins and effects of growing inequality. As Larry Bartels has argued, "interpretations of economic inequality are politically consequential because they shape political responses to inequality."[107] This link between a descriptive evaluation and a normative response—between a diagnosis and prescription—is evident in the divergent ways that observers of inequality understand and respond to it. If high levels of economic inequality are natural (a matter of differential returns to individuals' different endowments of talent and intelligence), or a reflection of just deserts (rewarding harder work with higher returns), or otherwise uncontrollable (because they result from powerful market forces), they may be undesirable or impossible to effectively counteract. At best, post hoc redistributive schemes might be able to partly compensate those lacking in talent, intelligence, work ethic, or in-demand skills. But defenders of market naturalism have raised a range of objections to such policies. Following Hirschman's three modes of reactionary rhetoric, redistribution is often portrayed either as futile, or as perverse (rewarding laziness, stupidity, or obsolescence), or as jeopardizing social values such as just deserts, returns to hard work, economic freedom, and so on.[108]

Such objections carry much less force if we drop these naturalistic empirical assumptions and begin instead with the presumption that the inequality that marks contemporary capitalist economies is—because it derives from artificially constructed markets—produced and reproduced politically. Ignoring the political character of market exchange creates the impression that political questions arise only *after* the market has done its work, when the state intervenes to artificially redistribute what the market has naturally distributed. This alluring misconception derives its potency from some of the basic conceptual oppositions and biases around which modern thinking is arranged—particularly the normative priority awarded to the natural over the artificial.[109] As the creator and enforcer of the laws that make market exchange possible, however, the state is always already part of economic life: the agent not only of redistribution but also of predistribution.[110]

Treating the market as a political artifice, rather than as the spontaneous result of individuals' isolated labor and natural propensity to exchange, directly counters the market naturalism that grounds antitax politics and the new right's view of citizenship. Yet since the 1960s, inequality has become depoliticized in public debate even as it has become a greater force in American politics.[111] This is apparent in the tendency of public debate to approach the topic of inequality through two frameworks that occlude its political dimensions: desert and need. Desert is often, but not exclusively, invoked by conservative defenders of the status quo, who claim that market outcomes, even unequal ones, are fair because they represent just returns to work. As one of Obama's critics in *National Review* argued, echoing Goldwater, a "dynamic social order" depends on the "principle that each has a right to the rewards of his own labor." In the view of the American right, it was the rejection of this principle—the belief that "government could engineer a better society, rather than simply leaving the people free to create one"—that led to the embrace of "progressive taxation, economic regulations, and extensive social-welfare programs,"[112] technologies that obstruct spontaneous market dynamism and undermine property rights (and therefore freedom).

"Need" appeals to the principle of sufficiency: instead of trying to specify some ideal pattern of distribution amid contentious disagreements, or pursuing the controversial goal of a ceiling on top incomes, need simply insists on ensuring that everyone has enough for survival, or (more ambitiously) a minimally decent life—something any reasonable person could endorse. Yet the broad assent sought by this sufficientarian principle comes with a number of downsides. Consider the call in Obama's Osawatomie speech to ensure that "working people can earn *enough* to raise a family, build a modest savings, own a home, [and] secure their retirement."[113] First, the list of basic necessities in the passage are all self-regarding: they capture individuals' aspirations for their own lives, such as purchasing a home and saving for retirement, but say nothing about their relations with others in their society. Additionally, the argument's appeal to sufficiency is vulnerable to a kind of pyrrhic agreement: those who grant the point may do so in a restrictive, but not necessarily implausible, way. For while some elements of Obama's list, such as minimal financial security, are close to necessities (if not quite as fundamental as food, shelter, and clothing), others, such as the ability to own a home, are culturally conditioned signifiers of middle-class stability; the notion that they should be regarded as *needs* stretches the principle beyond what it can uncontroversially accommodate. The inclusion of these other elements exposes the argument to precisely the kind of political contestation it is designed to avoid. Its broad appeal can be preserved only by conceding, at least partially, *National Review*'s rejoinder that Americans' real problem was unemployment, not inequality—in other words, not the relative disadvantage of middle- and lower-income Americans in a society increasingly divided by class, but the absolute deprivation of Americans who have no source of income or who cannot afford even a minimally decent life.

Moreover, once it is granted (even implicitly) that the core problem is not really inequality but rather insufficiency, critics can further restrict the implications of this conclusion by arguing that *American* poverty is rarely characterized by deprivation. This was the position taken by a 2011 Heritage Foundation report that typified the conservative response to Obama. The report argued that "if poverty means lacking nutritious food, adequate warm housing, and clothing for a family, relatively few of the more than 30 million people identified as being 'in poverty' by the Census Bureau could be characterized as poor."[114] Heritage noted that the vast majority of U.S. households defined as "poor" have amenities such as refrigerators, televisions, ovens, microwaves, and air conditioning.[115] Taking ownership of such consumer appliances to be indicative of the absence of *true* need (in the sense suggested by a straightforward interpretation of the principle), the writers argued that to label such Americans as impoverished was "a public relations Trojan horse, smuggling in a 'spread-the-wealth' agenda under the ruse of fighting significant material deprivation."[116] This kind of political misdirection, they claimed, is necessary because "the American voter is unwilling to support massive welfare increases, soaring deficits, and tax increases just to equalize incomes."[117] I leave aside the many empirical objections raised by critics about the report's statistics, conclusions, and focus on cheap consumer goods rather than the rising cost of necessities such as healthcare, education, and housing.[118] For our purposes, what is revealing about Heritage's response is that it superficially concedes the point: inequality *would* demand action, if what we really mean by inequality is a state of deprivation. The sufficientarian normative principle can be endorsed without necessarily conceding anything else; all that is in dispute is the empirical question of whether genuine deprivation has occurred.

This view is also compatible with regarding any ameliorative steps beyond the relief of deprivation as otiose, even petty. As Heritage characterized a more ambitious egalitarian agenda: voters will not "support massive welfare increases, soaring deficits, and tax increases *just to equalize incomes*."[119] At least two key ideas are implicit here—not only that, for egalitarians, equal incomes are a goal in themselves but also that only post hoc redistribution (welfare and tax increases) can achieve that goal. Here, the powerful influence of market naturalism is on display: inequality is fair; equality can be achieved only by after-the-fact interference with the work of the invisible hand; and the entire political collective that structures the "initial" distribution is analytically absent.

American history has witnessed sporadic attempts to articulate accounts of peoplehood that could guide a democratic political economy, but such attempts, from the Jacksonian era through the Gilded Age through the New Deal, have consistently been marred by the exclusion of certain groups (especially women and nonwhite men) from the imagined civic-distributive community. Liberalism's belated inclusion of these historically excluded groups coincided with its abandonment of a more political critique of inequality. The timing was consequential. As Fishkin and Forbath note, it was possible to believe during the midcentury "great compression" that "the threat of oligarchy had receded . . . that America had built the political economy of a middle-class democracy and that the work that remained was to dismantle the racial and gender exclusions that severely limited access to the rich opportunities this economy offered—and to full citizenship in the American polity."[120] But the threat of oligarchy returned in short order. The prosperous middle-class democracy that the New Deal had helped build would soon buckle under the combined weight of conservative policy changes and external economic pressures, and so the politics of distribution would not simply dissolve amid widespread growth.

As this history suggests, the project of combating inequality cannot rely on sheer growth to compensate for political work that has been left undone. Even if economic growth were manageable and predictable, growth does not answer questions about who belongs to the demos, and what they are owed by virtue of their membership in it. It is unlikely that any critique of inequality can get off the ground unless it supplies a narrative of this sort.

Today, American debates over inequality reflect the absence of this vision of peoplehood; in its place, the individualism and market naturalism popularized by figures like Goldwater have become a kind of commonsense doctrine for much of the country—part of the invisible backdrop of public discussion, and to that extent inoculated from critical scrutiny. In this way, a country whose democracy is endangered by extreme inequality can believe that it is becoming freer whenever it declines to combat that inequality. As Ronald Reagan declared in 1985: "My friends, history is clear: Lower tax rates mean greater freedom, and whenever we lower the tax rates, our entire nation is better off."[121]

A response to the crisis of inequality begins with understanding how alternatives to this worldview were pushed aside, and why democracy requires not merely the relief of deprivation but the pursuit of equality as well. The possibility of a democratic political economy depends on citizens understanding themselves not as atomistic individuals engaged in apolitical forms of production but as fellow-members of a demos that creates and governs markets and which aims at self-rule on terms of equality. This dormant ideal offers an alternative to the vision of citizenship advanced by the permanent tax revolt. In this way, it satisfies a requirement succinctly summarized by Mark Blyth: "To beat an idea, one needs another."[122] Or, as none other than Milton Friedman observed in 1962: when a crisis occurs, "the actions that are taken depend on the ideas that are lying around." [123]

Conclusion

Reconstruction Revisited

From the vantage point of 1871, it was impossible for Walt Whitman to summon unalloyed optimism about American democracy. In the wake of Union victory and Lincoln's assassination, its combination of triumph and tragedy led him to write of "America, filling the present with greatest deeds and problems" and to demand of his reader:

> Did you, too, O friend, suppose democracy was only for elections, for politics, and for a party name? I say democracy is only of use there that it may pass on and come to its flower and fruits in manners, in the highest forms of interaction between men, and their beliefs—in religion, literature, colleges, and schools—democracy in all public and private life.[2]

Whitman's attempt to explain the flowering of this ethos reached beyond institutions and laws:

> For not only is it not enough that the new blood, new frame of democracy shall be vivified and held together merely by political means, superficial suffrage, legislation, &c., but it is clear to me that, unless it goes deeper, gets at least as firm and as warm a hold in men's hearts, emotions and belief, as, in their days, feudalism or ecclesiasticism, and inaugurates its own perennial sources, welling from the centre forever, its strength will be defective, its growth doubtful, and its main charm wanting.[3]

What could serve as these perennial sources of democratic attachment? Whitman imagined "two or three really original American poets, (perhaps artists or lecturers) . . . fusing contributions, races, far localities, &c.," and providing "more compaction and more moral identity, (the quality to-day most needed,) to these States, than all its Constitutions, legislative and judicial ties, and all its hitherto political, warlike, or materialistic experiences."[4] Such "national expressers, comprehending and effusing for the men and women of the States, what is universal, native, common to all, inland and seaboard, northern and southern," would prevent the ossification of "conflicting and irreconcilable interiors."[5] For as Whitman admitted,

> the lack of a common skeleton, knitting all close, continually haunts me ... the true nationality of the States, the genuine union, when we come to a mortal crisis, is, and is to be, after all, neither the written law, nor, (as is generally supposed,) either self-interest, or common pecuniary or material objects—but the fervid and tremendous IDEA, melting everything else with resistless heat, and solving all lesser and definite distinctions in vast, indefinite, spiritual, emotional power.[6]

A century later, democratic thinkers of the Second Reconstruction confronted a similar combination of triumph and tragedy. Experiencing once again the impossibility of summoning unalloyed optimism in the face of the "greatest deeds and problems" filling the present, these thinkers voiced renewed hopes for an expansive sense of peoplehood that might help realize democratic ideals. In a 1972 remark reminiscent of Whitman's call for "national expressers," Ralph Ellison speculated that "in speaking, describing, and bringing together the diversity of the experience that was occurring throughout this vast nation," Americans might "discover ourselves and perhaps create new hope for mankind."[7]

Of course, the other side of this hope was the fear that without a "common skeleton," Americans would prove unable to respond to "a mortal crisis." James Baldwin's reflections from 1972 call to mind that other side of Whitman's vision. In the wake of Martin Luther King Jr.'s assassination, Baldwin wrote that he had been forced to acknowledge the "act of faith demanded by all those marches and petitions": that the citizens to whom civil rights activists directed their appeals could still be addressed "as the miracles they are," despite the "disasters they've become."

> One could scarcely be deluded by Americans anymore, one scarcely dared expect anything from the great, vast, blank generality; and yet one was compelled to demand of Americans—and for their sakes, after all—a generosity, a clarity, and a nobility which they did not dream of demanding of themselves. Part of the error was irreducible, in that the marchers and petitioners were forced to suppose the existence of an entity which, when the chips were down, could not be located—*i.e.*, there *are* no American people yet ... .[8]

The problem that Baldwin identified during the Second Reconstruction was, then, not fundamentally different from the problem that Whitman and Charles Sumner had identified during the First Reconstruction. The fact that civil rights marchers had no choice but to "suppose the existence" of the American people to whom they appealed showed that that the country still had not answered Sumner's apprehensive question of 1867: "Are we a nation?" Nor had it yet vindicated Sumner's hope that, with the spread of genuine equality, "we may be in reality as in name, a Nation."[9]

Taking stock of the crises facing American democracy in the twenty-first century, observers have sometimes invoked the reforms of the 1860s and the 1960s, calling for a "Third Reconstruction."[10] Yet as this historical allusion suggests, there is another possibility. The democratic thinkers of the First Reconstruction did not have an uncontested claim to the meaning of American peoplehood. Sumner had declared in 1867 that determining "the 'qualification' of a voter" based on "color, whether of the hair or of the skin," or "any other unchangeable circumstance of natural condition," was "preposterous"—"shocking to the moral sense"; and that Americans' failure to guarantee equal political rights for all citizens represented a "pitiable failure to perform a National duty."[11] But scarcely a decade earlier, in his debates with Lincoln, Stephen A. Douglas had given a popular defense of the opposite view: "I hold that this Government was made on the white basis; made by the white men, for the benefit of white men and their posterity forever, and should be administered by white men and none others."[12] In the 1870s, white "redeemers," acting in the spirit of Douglas's vision, ended the First Reconstruction.

Today, the successors of this movement are in increasingly open rebellion against the Second Reconstruction. When white supremacists gathered for a "Unite the Right" rally in Charlottesville, Virginia, in 2017 to oppose the removal of a statue of Robert E. Lee, their chants made their deeper motivations plain: "You will not replace us," and "Jews will not replace us."[13] The insurrectionists who stormed the U.S. Capitol on January 6, 2021, included several of the same people who had marched in Charlottesville just a few years before.[14]

The revanchist political ambitions of these figures, and their willingness to resort to violence, have led some scholars to label them the "New Redeemers."[15] This designation astutely calls attention to important historical parallels. While no single political movement likely has the power to arrest demographic change, determined factions—often claiming to embody the genuine American people—have long proven able to subvert the rise of a multiracial democracy through other means. As political scientists are at pains to remind Americans, their democracy is much younger than they tend to think. Understood as the universal extension of civil rights coupled with (nearly) universal suffrage, American democracy, even in this barest formal sense, dates only to 1965.[16] With the meaning of American peoplehood radically up for grabs, our next era could be one of reaction or reconstitution. Rather than approaching a Third Reconstruction, we may well be living through a Second Redemption.[17]

Against Fatalism

In 2018, the political scientists Steven Levitsky and Daniel Ziblatt reached the bestseller list with the starkly titled *How Democracies Die*. The book opens with the scholars' candid admission of astonishment at finding themselves studying their home country. Since 2016, they wrote, they had become sensitive to the emergence, in the United States, of the same "precursors of democratic crisis" they had studied in the histories of Europe and Latin America.[18] They argued that although the 2016 election was a clear sign that American democracy was entering newly dangerous territory, a path had been cleared by the "erosion of our democratic norms" since the 1980s. In particular, Levitsky and Ziblatt stressed the importance of two key norms: political parties' "mutual toleration . . . [of] one another as legitimate rivals," and the observation by politicians of "forbearance . . . in deploying their institutional prerogatives."[19]

Levitsky and Ziblatt's emphasis on norms was an influential contribution to post-2016 conversations about democratic decline, since it helped explain the United States' descent into what Jack Balkin calls "constitutional rot"—a state of pronounced decay characterized by the erosion of certain values, informal practices, and unwritten rules, which is not directly (or solely) traceable to changes in the letter of the law.[20] Yet critics argued that Levitsky and Ziblatt's attribution of democratic decline to norm erosion sometimes conflated political stability with fidelity to substantive democratic values, and even betrayed a (less than fully articulated) prioritization of the former. For example, Levitsky and Ziblatt identified the 1850s as an era when "polarization over slavery undermined America's democratic norms," leading to the collapse of long-standing practices of compromise and forbearance and inaugurating a "death spiral" that would end in civil war.[21] As Corey Robin objected, however, this example implies that the struggle over slavery ended up destroying American democracy, when the reality is just the opposite. The norms that had maintained relative stability in the antebellum United States were frequently norms of deference to the Slave Power. As Robin put it: "When you set up 'norms' as your standard, without evaluating their specific democratic valence in each instance, the projects to which they are attached, how could you know whether a norm contributes to democracy, in the substantive or procedural sense, or detracts from it? How could you know whether the erosion is good or bad, democratic or antidemocratic?"[22] Similarly, Jedediah Britton-Purdy concurred that "if you started out by supporting strong egalitarian democracy rather than 'norms,' you would have a clearer compass," adding: "Norms are like the statues of dead leaders: you can't know whether you are for or against them without knowing which values they support."[23]

To be fair, Levitsky and Ziblatt did allow that some norms are trivial and that in certain cases norm breaking can be "inevitable—even desirable."[24] But critics were right to detect ambiguities in both their argument and in some of their chosen examples. If left unclarified, these ambiguities risk inviting the dubious conclusion that democracy's defenders are sometimes bound to uphold conventions simply because they are conventional.[25]

The account of solidarity defended in this book offers a framework for a more fine-grained analysis, of the sort encouraged by Levitsky and Ziblatt's critics. It may be true that norms promote political stability, but whether they promote democracy *specifically* depends on whether they encourage citizens' intersubjective recognition of their common membership, the attendant obligations of that common membership, and their shared future together. Norms that fulfill these functions deserve our support; norms that do not, or which do so less effectively than would some alternative set of social practices, may be reasonably reformed or jettisoned. This way of evaluating norms avoids smuggling in an implicit prioritization of stability over democracy, and it avoids committing us to the view that there is anything *inherently* objectionable about the erosion of norms (or anything inherently valuable about their protection). Not only that, this approach also better captures the core concern raised by Levitsky and Ziblatt, which after all is the trend of norm erosion that has arisen *in response to attempts to democratize the United States* and which threatens to further disrupt that project. As they put it: "America's efforts to achieve racial equality as our society grows increasingly diverse have fueled an insidious reaction and intensifying polarization. And if one thing is clear from studying breakdowns through history, it's that extreme polarization can kill democracies."[26] In effect, Ziblatt and Levitsky were arguing that America, facing the choice between racial hierarchy and democracy, was in danger of opting for the former. As I have argued here, such a choice would not be unprecedented.

I use the language of "choice" intentionally, since how citizens imagine their polity *is* a choice—even if, as Rogers Smith has noted, our ordinary use of language often obscures that fact. As Smith writes, political communities are "endlessly contested and contesting human creations that dramatically and often coercively affect how people live," yet our "standard analogies" for them "are all 'de-politicizing' devices. They direct us to associations we do not ordinarily think of as chiefly political."[27] The metaphor of a "family," for example, obscures the artificial character of political peoplehood since it "to many people suggests an association that is both benign and natural."[28] Common invocations of American peoplehood often function in much the same way: to soothe and sedate citizens. Yet many democratic thinkers, in looking to American history for a useful civic vocabulary, engaged in a form of argument designed to shake citizens out of such dull complacency. In a rhetorical technique that is now often dismissed as naïve triumphalism, they put superficially revered elements of American political culture to a radical use. To many white listeners, Lincoln's mobilization of the Declaration to argue for a more egalitarian remaking of the polity was anathema—just as it was a century later, when Martin Luther King Jr. invoked the Declaration as a promissory note, yet to be paid. It is easy to invoke the icons of Americana in favor of the status quo, but this usage ignores the radical potential that often lies latent within the claims that they make. Taking those claims seriously has always been controversial.

For this reason, it is a mistake to turn longingly toward the ideal of American peoplehood, as so many Americans do, in search of comforting "unity" in an embittered political era. Democratic peoplehood is not a salve. Its pursuit tasks citizens with difficult work and confronts us with the bracing realization that democracy cannot run on autopilot. As long as there are democratic states, citizens will exercise power over each other's lives. But whether that power is exercised in egalitarian and reciprocal fashion depends, in large part, on whether citizens learn to see each other as fellow members of a democratic people.[29]

To become a demos in that sense, Americans must cultivate inclusive forms of identification—they must become the people whose contours, at earlier, critical junctures in American history, have come fleetingly into view. As James Baldwin observed in the passage quoted earlier, the American egalitarians who would exhort their compatriots to form a true demos must embrace a paradox: they are addressing the very entity they hope to bring into being. Today, as in his time, that entity is only potentially real. "There *are* no American people," wrote Baldwin, before adding a crucial qualifier: "yet."

Notes

Introduction

1. David Herbert Donald, *Charles Sumner and the Coming of the Civil War* (Naperville, IL: Sourcebooks, 2009), 246–48.
2. Williamjames Hull Hoffer, *The Caning of Charles Sumner: Honor, Idealism, and the Origins of the Civil War* (Baltimore: Johns Hopkins University Press, 2010), 92; see also Donald, *Charles Sumner and the Coming of the Civil War*, 251–57.
3. Charles Sumner, "'Are We a Nation?,' (Address Before the New York Young Men's Republican Union at the Cooper Institute, November 19, 1867)" 35, https://ia902302.us.archive.org/16/items/arewenationaddre00sumn/arewenationaddre00sumn.pdf. Emphasis in original.
4. Sumner, 34.
5. Charles Sumner, "The True Principles of Reconstruction. Illegality of Existing Governments in the Rebel States. Resolutions and Remarks in the Senate, December 5, 1866," in *The Works of Charles Sumner* (hereafter *WCS*), vol. 11 (Boston: Lee and Shepard, 1875), 45. Sumner's invocation of the Declaration's dual principles of equality and consent is a recurring theme in his speeches and writings. Other examples include Charles Sumner, "Guaranty of Republican Governments in the Rebel States. Resolutions in the Senate, February 25, 1865," in *WCS*, vol. 9 (Boston: Lee and Shepard, 1874), 329; Charles Sumner, "Admission of Mississippi to Representation in Congress. Speech in the Senate, February 17, 1870," in *WCS*, vol. 13 (Boston: Lee and Shepard, 1880), 333.
6. Charles Sumner, "Promises of the Declaration of Independence, and Abraham Lincoln. Eulogy on Abraham Lincoln, before the Municipal Authorities of the City of Boston, June 1, 1865," in *WCS*, vol. 9 (Boston: Lee and Shepard, 1874), 380.
7. Charles Sumner, "The Equal Rights of All: The Great Guaranty and Present Necessity, for the Sake of Security, and to Maintain a Republican Government. Speech in the Senate, on the Proposed Amendment of the Constitution Fixing the Basis of Representation, February 5 and 6, 1866," in *WCS*, vol. 10 (Boston: Lee and Shepard, 1876), 179.
8. Sumner, 197. Emphasis in original.
9. Sumner, 177. Emphasis in original.
10. Sumner, "'Are We a Nation?,'" 33.
11. Sumner, 30.
12. Sumner, 30.
13. Sumner, 36.
14. Sumner, 11.
15. Sumner, 3.
16. On the Reconstruction-era mobilization of arguments for *national* political and civil equality, and the scramble by opponents to reassert the "state-centered as well as racist views that republican rhetoric had long served," see Rogers M. Smith, *Civic Ideals: Conflicting Visions of Citizenship in U.S. History* (New Haven: Yale University Press, 1997), 296.

17. Sumner, "'Are We a Nation?,'" 33.
18. Sumner, 34. Emphasis in original.
19. Maria Cramer, "The Confederate Flag Inside the Capitol a 'Jarring and Disheartening' Sight," *The New York Times*, January 11, 2021, sec. U.S.; Rachel Weiner, "Man Carrying Confederate Flag in Capitol on Jan. 6 Sentenced to 3 Years," *The Washington Post*, February 10, 2023, https://www.washingtonpost.com/dc-md-va/2023/02/09/kevin-seefried-confederate-capitol/.
20. Glenn Ellmers, "'Conservatism' Is No Longer Enough," *The American Mind*, March 24, 2021, https://americanmind.org/salvo/why-the-claremont-institute-is-not-conservative-and-you-shouldnt-be-either/.
21. Sumner, "'Are We a Nation?,'" 15.
22. Elizabeth S. Anderson, "Democracy: Instrumental vs. Non-Instrumental Value," in *Contemporary Debates in Political Philosophy*, ed. Thomas Christiano and John Christman (Chichester, West Sussex, U.K.: Wiley-Blackwell, 2009), 215.
23. For a more detailed elaboration of this view, see Nathan Pippenger, "Listening to Strangers, or: Three Arguments for Bounded Solidarity," *American Journal of Political Science* 67, no. 3 (July 2023): 764–75, https://doi.org/10.1111/ajps.12671.s.
24. Frederick Douglass, "What to the Slave Is the Fourth of July?: An Address Delivered in Rochester, New York, on 5 July, 1852," in *The Frederick Douglass Papers*, ed. John W. Blassingame, vol. 2: 1847–54, Frederick Douglass Papers, Series One: Speeches, Debates, and Interviews (New Haven: Yale University Press, 1982), 368.
25. Consider Seyla Benhabib's description of Michael Walzer's interpretive method, in which "available and shared definitions and understandings of social meaning have to be" the "starting point" for "refining, systematizing, making coherent, criticizing and replacing by a 'better' understanding the common views of these issues." See Seyla Benhabib, *Situating the Self: Gender, Community, and Postmodernism in Contemporary Ethics* (New York: Routledge, 1992), 79–80.

Chapter 1

1. Wendy Brown, "We Are All Democrats Now...," in *Democracy in What State?* (New York: Columbia University Press, 2011), 50-52.
2. Charles Taylor, "Democratic Exclusion (and Its Remedies?)," in his *Dilemmas and Connections: Selected Essays* (Cambridge, MA: Belknap Press of Harvard University Press, 2011), 129.
3. Taylor, 129.
4. Anderson, Elizabeth S. "Democracy: Instrumental vs. Non-Instrumental Value," in *Contemporary Debates in Political Philosophy*, ed. Thomas Christiano and John Christman (Chichester, West Sussex, U.K.: Wiley-Blackwell, 2009), 214.
5. Anderson, 215. Emphasis in original.
6. Anderson, 216. Emphasis in original.
7. Anderson, 217.
8. Anderson, 218. Emphasis in original.
9. Anderson, 220.
10. Jürgen Habermas, "Three Normative Models of Democracy," *Constellations* 1, no. 1 (Dec. 1994): 3, https://doi.org/10.1111/j.1467-8675.1994.tb00001.x.

11. John Dewey, *The Public and Its Problems: An Essay in Political Inquiry*, ed. Melvin L. Rogers (Athens, OH: Swallow Press, 2016), 224.
12. Elizabeth S. Anderson, *The Imperative of Integration* (Princeton: Princeton University Press, 2010), 184.
13. Although I don't use the term "identification" precisely the way that Rogers Brubaker and Frederick Cooper do, my choice of "identification" over "identity" is partly informed by their warning of the reifying and essentializing errors that the latter term invites. Identification is an ongoing, perpetually revisable process among a group of people, not a static state of commonality. See Rogers Brubaker and Frederick Cooper, "Beyond 'Identity,'" *Theory and Society* 29, no. 1 (Feb. 2000): 1–47.
14. On the situation of meanings in discourses and traditions, see Mark Bevir and R. A. W. Rhodes, "Interpretation and Its Others," *Australian Journal of Political Science* 40, no. 2 (June 2005): 172–73.
15. Hanna Pitkin, "The Idea of a Constitution," *Journal of Legal Education* 37, no. 2 (1987): 167. Emphasis in original.
16. Pitkin, 168.
17. Pitkin, 168–69.
18. Pitkin, 169.
19. John Rawls, *A Theory of Justice* (Cambridge, MA: Belknap Press of Harvard University Press, 1971), 7.
20. They continue: "The net result was, for many commentators, a sort of internal inconsistency in Rawls's theory; if Rawls was to regard income inequality above that permitted by the difference principle as unjust, he should do so in a thoroughgoing way, and condemn the inequalities between the wealthy and the impoverished internationally (see Pogge 1989, 1992, 1994; Beitz 1973, 1979, 1983; Scanlon 1973). Rawls can, on this account, be taken as the originator of the modern dialogue on global distributive justice—not because he was the first to speak out against international inequality, but because he did not do so." Michael Blake and Patrick Taylor Smith, "International Distributive Justice," in *The Stanford Encyclopedia of Philosophy*, ed. Edward N. Zalta, 2015, http://plato.stanford.edu/archives/spr2015/entries/international-justice/.
21. Michael Walzer, *Spheres of Justice: A Defense of Pluralism and Equality* (New York: Basic Books, 1983), 5–6.
22. Walzer, 6.
23. Walzer, 8.
24. Walzer, 8.
25. Danielle S. Allen, *Talking to Strangers: Anxieties of Citizenship Since Brown v. Board of Education* (Chicago: University of Chicago Press, 2004), 27.
26. Allen, 29.
27. David Miller, *On Nationality* (Oxford: Oxford University Press, 1995), 98.
28. Miller, 158.
29. Miller, 68. Miller clarifies that a public culture is not the same as an ethnic identity and that multiethnic nations exist. See Miller, 21, 25.
30. Miller, 69.
31. Miller, 69.
32. Miller, 71–72.
33. Anna Stilz, *Liberal Loyalty: Freedom, Obligation, and the State* (Princeton: Princeton University Press, 2009), 146.

34. Stilz, 146.
35. Miller, *On Nationality*, 72–73.
36. A defense of this form of boundedness can be found in Sarah Song, "The Boundary Problem in Democratic Theory: Why the Demos Should Be Bounded by the State," *International Theory* 4, no. 1 (Mar. 2012): 39–68, https://doi.org/10.1017/S1752971911000248.
37. Abraham Lincoln, "Gettysburg Address," November 19, 1863, Avalon Project, Yale University, http://avalon.law.yale.edu/19th_century/gettyb.asp.
38. Sumner, "'Are We a Nation?' (Address Before the New York Young Men's Republican Union at the Cooper Institute, November 19, 1867)," 5.
39. Sumner, 5–6.
40. Frederick Douglass, "The Nation's Problem: An Address Delivered in Washington, D.C., on 16 April 1889," in *The Frederick Douglass Papers*, ed. John W. Blassingame and John R. McKivigan, vol. 5: *1881–95*, Frederick Douglass Papers, Series One: Speeches, Debates, and Interviews (New Haven: Yale University Press, 1992), 415. Emphases added.
41. I describe this problem at greater length in Nathan Pippenger, "Contested Past, Contested Future: Identity Politics and Liberal Democracy," *Ethics & International Affairs* 37, no. 4 (Winter 2023): 391–400, https://doi.org/10.1017/S0892679423000382.
42. Jan-Werner Müller, *Constitutional Patriotism* (Princeton: Princeton University Press, 2007), 1.
43. Jürgen Habermas, "Appendix II: Citizenship and National Identity (1990)," in *Between Facts and Norms: Contributions to a Discourse Theory of Law and Democracy*, trans. William Rehg (Cambridge, MA: The MIT Press, 1996), 495.
44. Habermas, 495.
45. Habermas wrote in 2001 that "at present, legitimacy flows more or less through the channels of democratic institutions and procedures within each nation-state," which "falls short of what is needed for the kind of supranational and transnational decision-making that has long since developed within the institutional framework of the Union and its huge network of committees." In his view, the history of European state-building does not refute, but rather supports, this supranational aspiration: "If the emergence of national consciousness involved a painful process of abstraction, leading from local and dynastic identities to national and democratic ones, why . . . should this generation of a highly artificial kind of civic solidarity—a 'solidarity among strangers'—be doomed to come to a final halt just at the borders of our classical nation-states?" Jürgen Habermas, "Why Europe Needs a Constitution," *New Left Review* 2, no. 11 (Oct. 2001): 14, 16.
46. Habermas, "Appendix II," 507. Emphasis in original.
47. For a related objection, focusing on the relationship between language and politics, and the role of language in shaping both individual identity and broader ethical-cultural forms of life, see Sarah Song, "Three Models of Civic Solidarity," in *Citizenship, Borders, and Human Needs*, ed. Rogers M. Smith (Philadelphia: University of Pennsylvania Press, 2011), 198.
48. Walt Whitman, "Democratic Vistas," in *Complete Poetry and Selected Prose*, ed. James E. Miller, Jr., Riverside Editions (Boston: Houghton Mifflin, 1959), 459–60.
49. Habermas, "Appendix II," 500.
50. For an overview of this ubiquitous and malleable term, see Eric Foner, *The Story of American Freedom* (New York: W. W. Norton, 1998).
51. Wendell Phillips denounced the Constitution as a "pro-slavery compact" that the "Nation at large" had "entered into . . . willingly and with open eyes." See Wendell Phillips, *The*

Constitution a Pro-Slavery Compact; or, Extracts from the Madison Papers, Etc., 2nd ed. (New York: American Anti-Slavery Society, 1845), v–vi. William Lloyd Garrison, who famously dubbed the Constitution "a covenant with death and an agreement with hell," marked the 4th of July in 1854 with a public burning of the document. See William Lloyd Garrison, *The Letters of William Lloyd Garrison*, vol. 5: *Let the Oppressed Go Free (1861–1867)*, ed. Walter M. Merrill (Cambridge, MA: Belknap Press of Harvard University Press, 1979), 131–32. Frederick Douglass, however, insisted that slavery's opponents should embrace the Constitution as a "glorious liberty document." Two years before Garrison's public burning of the "covenant with death," Douglass declared: "Take the constitution according to its plain reading, and I defy the presentation of a single pro-slavery clause in it. On the other hand it will be found to contain principles and purposes, entirely hostile to the existence of slavery." See Douglass, "What to the Slave Is the Fourth of July?", in *The Frederick Douglass Papers*, ed. John W. Blassingame, vol. 2: 1847–54, Frederick Douglass Papers, Series One: Speeches, Debates, and Interviews (New Haven: Yale University Press, 1982), 386.

52. Roger Taney, Dred Scott v. Sandford (U.S. Supreme Court 1857). Emphasis added.
53. Alexander H. Stephens, "Cornerstone Speech, March 21, 1861," in *The Civil War and Reconstruction: A Documentary Reader*, ed. Stanley Harrold (Malden, MA: Blackwell, 2008), 61.
54. Stephens, 62.
55. Andrew Mason, *Community, Solidarity and Belonging: Levels of Community and Their Normative Significance* (Cambridge: Cambridge University Press, 2000), 27–29; Samuel Scheffler, "Relationships and Responsibilities," in his *Boundaries and Allegiances: Problems of Justice and Responsibility in Liberal Thought* (New York: Oxford University Press, 2001), 100; Scheffler, "Families, Nations, and Strangers," in *Boundaries and Allegiances*, 51.
56. Anderson, *The Imperative of Integration*, 188. Emphasis in original.
57. For a more detailed version of the argument in this section of the chapter, see Pippenger, "Listening to Strangers, or: Three Arguments for Bounded Solidarity," *American Journal of Political Science* 67, no. 3 (July 2023): 764–75.
58. Jacob T. Levy, "Against Fraternity: Democracy Without Solidarity," in *The Strains of Commitment: The Political Sources of Solidarity in Diverse Societies*, ed. Keith Banting and Will Kymlicka (Oxford: Oxford University Press, 2017), 108.
59. Levy, 110.
60. Levy, 109–11.
61. Levy, 121.
62. Levy, 114–15.
63. Levy, 111. Emphasis in original.
64. Levy, 116.
65. Levy, 114–15.
66. Anderson, "Democracy: Instrumental vs. Non-Instrumental Value," 216. Emphasis in original.
67. Margaret Moore, "Is Patriotism an Associative Duty?," *The Journal of Ethics* 13, no. 4 (Dec. 2009): 385, 392.
68. Whitman, "Democratic Vistas," 470.
69. Whitman, 470.

Chapter 2

1. Eric Foner, *Reconstruction: America's Unfinished Revolution, 1863–1877* (New York: Harper & Row, 1988), xxvi.
2. Nelson Lichtenstein, *Walter Reuther: The Most Dangerous Man in Detroit* (Urbana and Chicago: University of Illinois Press, 1997), 383.
3. James Kloppenberg, "Aspirational Nationalism in America," *Intellectual History Newsletter*, 24 (2002): 61–62.
4. Pauline Maier, *American Scripture: Making the Declaration of Independence* (New York: Vintage, 1997), 48–49.
5. John Jay, "The Federalist No. 2," in *The Federalist with Letters of "Brutus,"* by Alexander Hamilton, James Madison, and John Jay, ed. Terence Ball (Cambridge: Cambridge University Press, 2003), 5. In my view, Jay's argument for a unified polity does not essentially rely on his considerable exaggeration of the similarity of Americans' descent, language, religion, and more. See Jay, 6.
6. James Madison, "The Federalist No. 14," in *The Federalist with Letters of "Brutus,"* 59–64. For a short explanation of how the Declaration of Independence establishes the colonists' shared political *peoplehood* (understood as a collective of individuals sharing common political institutions, in a sense subtly different from the suggestion of a distinctive nationality), see Danielle S. Allen, *Our Declaration: A Reading of the Declaration of Independence in Defense of Equality* (New York: Liveright, 2014), 115–18.
7. James M. McPherson, *Battle Cry of Freedom: The Civil War Era* (New York: Oxford University Press, 1988), 6.
8. See McPherson, 6–11, 31–32.
9. Joshua D. Rothman, "Antebellum Era," in *The Oxford Encyclopedia of American Social History*, ed. Lynn Dumenil (New York: Oxford University Press, 2012), 41. By the late 1840s, Rothman adds, these changes "had led Americans everywhere to believe in a democratic, prosperous, and nationally triumphant future" but with radically different understandings among Northerners and Southerners about whether that future would rest on, respectively, free labor or slave labor. See Rothman, 45.
10. Samuel H. Beer, *To Make a Nation: The Rediscovery of American Federalism* (Cambridge, MA: Belknap Press of Harvard University Press, 1993), 8.
11. For a sympathetic reading of Webster as a contextualist moral and political thinker, see Scott M. Reznick, "On Liberty and Union: Moral Imagination and Its Limits in Daniel Webster's Seventh of March Speech," *American Political Thought* 6, no. 3 (Summer 2017): 371–95, https://doi.org/10.1086/692572.
12. Beer, *To Make a Nation*, 12.
13. Daniel Webster, "Address delivered at the laying of the Corner Stone of the Bunker Hill Monument.—June 17, 1825.," in Daniel Webster, *Speeches and Forensic Arguments*, vol. 3, (Boston: Tappan and Dennet, 1843), 70.
14. Webster, 70.
15. Garry Wills identifies Webster as the singular contemporary politician "whose style and arguments Lincoln used as models all through his political life." See Garry Wills, *Lincoln at Gettysburg: The Words That Remade America* (New York: Simon & Schuster, 1992), 122. See also Craig R. Smith, *Daniel Webster and the Oratory of Civil Religion* (Columbia: University of Missouri Press, 2005), 267–68.

16. James Kloppenberg's evaluation of Lincoln in the context of nineteenth-century nationalism notes the romantic character of his thought but also links it to a specifically political ideal with expansive implications: "Lincoln's deep commitment to the American national project may be read as another aspect of his romanticism. From his earliest speeches to his last, he harbored hopes for his homeland as ambitious as those of any nineteenth-century romantic nationalist. For Lincoln those hopes were rooted not in blood, soil, or other *volkish* notions but in his commitments to individual autonomy and human equality, principles only democracy could safeguard." James Kloppenberg, *Toward Democracy: The Struggle for Self-Rule in European and American Thought* (New York: Oxford University Press, 2016), 636.
17. Eric Foner, "Who Is an American?," in his *Who Owns History? Rethinking the Past in a Changing World* (New York: Hill and Wang, 2002), 158.
18. Quoted in Beer, *To Make a Nation*, 8. Although Calhoun is commonly invoked as the classic antebellum defender of states' rights, Sotirios Barber has contended that, in effect, he was actually more of a "proslavery nationalist than a states' righter" whose arguments drifted over time as circumstances demanded: "Starting from an effort to defend a state's right to choose slavery, Calhoun ended by denying a state's right to oppose slavery. He left the states only with rights whose exercise either advanced or did not impede a view of the national interest in which slavery was essential." Still, as a mature thinker Calhoun "denied the existence of one national community," and he "denied that one American people ever had existed or ever would exist." See Sotirios A. Barber, *The Fallacies of States' Rights* (Cambridge, MA: Harvard University Press, 2013), 130, 133.
19. This distinctive feature has long fascinated students of American nationalism. In 1944, Hans Kohn asserted: "The American constitutional laws of 1789 have lasted because the idea for which they stand was so intimately welded with the existence of the American nation that without the idea there would have been no nation . . . With all its vigorous political and economic aspects, American nationalism nevertheless has been primarily an ideological nationalism." See Hans Kohn, *The Idea of Nationalism: A Study in Its Origins and Background* (New Brunswick, NJ: Transaction, 2005), 289. See also Susan-Mary Grant, "A Nation Before Nationalism: The Civic and Ethnic Construction of America," in *The SAGE Handbook of Nations and Nationalism*, ed. Gerard Delanty and Krishan Kumar (London: SAGE, 2006), 527. On the paradoxical speech act that forms the American people, see Jacques Derrida, "Declarations of Independence," *New Political Science* 7, no. 1 (Summer 1986): 7–15. For a wider discussion of how invocations of "the people" retrospectively authorize action within American politics, see Jason Frank, *Constituent Moments: Enacting the People in Postrevolutionary America* (Durham: Duke University Press, 2010).
20. "Interchange: Nationalism and Internationalism in the Era of the Civil War," *Journal of American History* 98, no. 2 (Sept. 2011): 478, https://doi.org/10.1093/jahist/jar330.
21. Lincoln, "Gettysburg Address," November 19, 1863, Avalon Project, Yale University, http://avalon.law.yale.edu/19th_century/gettyb.asp.
22. The exact nature of these limits is the subject of some debate. In her extensive analysis of the Declaration of Independence, Danielle Allen notes that an earlier draft contained a passage, later excised, in which Jefferson condemned British participation in the slave trade in terms markedly similar to the final draft's famous invocation of rights, nature, life, and liberty. In that excised passage, Jefferson's reference to slaves (in which he must,

Allen notes, have been referring to men, women, and children of African descent, held in bondage), Jefferson simply uses the gendered pronoun "men." Inferring that Jefferson's usage in that instance signals a broader meaning than the white male property holders who were, in practice, the beneficiaries of the Declaration's language, Allen concludes that the Declaration of Independence's reference to "all men" "must mean all people—whatever their color, sex, age, or status." Allen, *Our Declaration*, 153–54.

23. Wills, *Lincoln at Gettysburg*, 101.
24. Wills, 103.
25. Foner, *Reconstruction*, xxvi.
26. Richard White, *The Republic for Which It Stands: The United States During Reconstruction and the Gilded Age, 1865–1896*, Oxford History of the United States (New York: Oxford University Press, 2017), 56.
27. White, 56.
28. White, 59.
29. Sumner, "'Are We a Nation?' (Address Before the New York Young Men's Republican Union at the Cooper Institute, November 19, 1867)," 32, https://ia902302.us.archive.org/16/items/arewenationaddre00sumn/arewenationaddre00sumn.pdf. Emphasis in original.
30. Sumner, 3.
31. As Carrie Hyde has noted, the legal codification of citizenship was a relatively late development in U.S. history. There was no statutory definition until the 1860s, despite the appearance of the term "citizen" in the Constitution and its obvious salience to a number of antebellum debates about the acquisition of, and rights and obligations associated with, political membership. In part because no authoritative legal definition existed, Hyde argues, the term's meaning became the site of widespread cultural imagining and contestation, carried out in extralegal and extrapolitical settings that more narrowly legal-political analyses sometimes overlook. Because of its "few clearly specified boundaries, 'citizenship' was a uniquely powerful terminological cipher for a range of political ideals and agendas"; it was a not-yet "fully articulated ideological concept" that underwent "cultural development" in "the era of its legal nascence." See Carrie Hyde, *Civic Longing: The Speculative Origins of U.S. Citizenship* (Cambridge, MA: Harvard University Press, 2018), 19–24.
32. White, *The Republic for Which It Stands*, 66, 70, 84. Other studies of American democracy have overlooked the significance of these nineteenth-century nationalizing reforms, which generates a tendency to exaggerate the novelty of Progressivism and other twentieth-century reform movements. For instance, referring to the Progressives and their descendants, Michael Sandel has written: "This nationalizing project would be consummated in the New Deal, but for the democratic tradition in America, the embrace of the nation was a decisive departure. From Jefferson to the populists, the party of democracy in American political debate had been, roughly speaking, the party of the provinces, of decentralized power, of small-town and small- scale America." On my interpretation, Sandel's account locates this shift at too late a date, which partly explains why it overstates the extent to which nationalization marks a departure from democratization in American politics. See Michael J. Sandel, "The Procedural Republic and the Unencumbered Self," *Political Theory* 12, no. 1 (Feb. 1984): 92–93.
33. David W. Blight, *Race and Reunion: The Civil War in American Memory* (Cambridge, MA: Belknap Press of Harvard University Press, 2001), 2.

34. Danielle S. Allen, *Talking to Strangers: Anxieties of Citizenship Since Brown v. Board of Education* (Chicago: University of Chicago Press, 2004), 19.
35. Allen, 19.
36. Allen, 20.
37. Joseph R. Fishkin and William E. Forbath, *The Anti-Oligarchy Constitution: Reconstructing the Economic Foundations of American Democracy* (Cambridge, MA: Harvard University Press, 2022), 77.
38. Frederick Douglass, "We Are Here and Want the Ballot-Box: An Address Delivered in Philadelphia, Pennsylvania, on September 4, 1866," in *The Frederick Douglass Papers*, ed. John W. Blassingame and John R. McKivigan, vol. 4: *1864–80*, Frederick Douglass Papers, Series One: Speeches, Debates, and Interviews (New Haven: Yale University Press, 1991), 129–30.
39. Sumner, "'Are We A Nation?,'" 7.
40. This is especially true of Douglass, who in other contexts forcefully denounced the claim that Indigenous peoples stood somehow outside American civilization. In a March 1854 edition of *Frederick Douglass' Paper*, we find an article (almost certainly by Douglass) condemning the declaration of Indiana Senator John Pettit that "civilization" would arrive on the North American continent when the people "first planted here ... give way to a race of men heavier physically, and heavier mentally," and that this "doom" of Native Americans was "inevitable." Scorning this view, Douglass's editorial specifically castigates Pettit's use of the term "civilization" and responds: "With whisky, gunpowder, small-pox, bad faith and fraud, you have robbed the poor Indian of home and country ... You have communicated to the poor untaught savages all the soul and body destroying vices of civilization, and withheld from them its saving virtues—thus poisoned they die, mocked in their death by the sanctimonious whine, that their destruction is the work of the Almighty. The soul sickens over such shocking blasphemy, and the pen quivers with moral indignation, unable to write in terms suitably severe, in dealing with such a monster of wickedness.— 'The Indians have no future' says the Christian Senator from the Christian State of Indiana. Why have they not? Are they not men? Do they not propagate their species? Why have they no future? The true answer is that young America does not mean that they shall have any. It has no sympathy for this outcast people ... From the depths of our soul we protest against this pirate's plea for national murder." Frederick Douglass, "National Depravity," *Frederick Douglass' Paper*, March 3, 1854, Frederick Douglass Newspapers Collection, 1847 to 1874, Library of Congress, https://www.loc.gov/resource/sn84026366/1854-03-03/ed-1/?sp=2.
41. This is an example of what Charles Mills has critiqued as "white time, which "[helps] to constitute exclusionary gated moral communities protected by temporal, no less than spatial, walls." Charles W. Mills, "White Time: The Chronic Injustice of Ideal Theory," *Du Bois Review* 11, no. 1 (2014): 29, https://doi.org/10.1017/S1742058X14000022.
42. Duncan Ivison, *Can Liberal States Accommodate Indigenous Peoples?* (Cambridge: Polity Press, 2020), 3.
43. Ivison, 96; see also Roger Maaka and Augie Fleras, "Engaging with Indigeneity: Tino Rangatiratanga in Aotearoa," in *Political Theory and the Rights of Indigenous Peoples*, ed. Duncan Ivison, Paul Patton, and Will Sanders (Cambridge: Cambridge University Press, 2000), 108; Will Kymlicka, "American Multiculturalism and the 'Nations Within,'" in Ivison et al., *Political Theory*, 222.

44. Philip Pettit, "Minority Claims Under Two Conceptions of Democracy," in Ivison et al., *Political Theory*, 200.
45. For a fuller elaboration of this view, see Pippenger, "Contested Past, Contested Future: Identity Politics and Liberal Democracy," *Ethics & International Affairs* 37, no. 4 (Winter 2023): 391–400.
46. Ivison, *Can Liberal States Accommodate Indigenous Peoples?*, 105.
47. Ivison, 115.
48. Herbert Croly, *The Promise of American Life* (1909; repr., Princeton: Princeton University Press, 2014), 332.
49. Croly, 263.
50. Rogers M. Smith, *Civic Ideals: Conflicting Visions of Citizenship in U.S. History* (New Haven: Yale University Press, 1997), 411–20.
51. Jonathan Hansen, *The Lost Promise of Patriotism: Debating American Identity, 1890–1920* (Chicago: The University of Chicago Press, 2003), 39.
52. Randolph S. Bourne, "Trans-National America," *The Atlantic Monthly*, July 1916, 94.
53. John Dewey, "Nationalizing Education," *The Journal of Education* 84, no. 16 (Nov. 2, 1916): 425.
54. Dewey, 425.
55. Dewey, 425–26.
56. Frederick Douglass, "The Work of the Future (*Douglass' Monthly*, November 1862)," in *Frederick Douglass: Selected Speeches and Writings*, ed. Philip Sheldon Foner and Yuval Taylor (Chicago: Chicago Review Press, 1999), 521.
57. Douglass, 521–22.
58. Douglass, 522.
59. Whitman, "Democratic Vistas," in *Complete Poetry and Selected Prose*, ed. James E. Miller, Jr., Riverside Editions (Boston: Houghton Mifflin, 1959), 475.
60. Whitman, 472.
61. Whitman, 475.
62. Whitman, 491.
63. Bourne, "Trans-National America," 92.
64. James Baldwin, "Down at the Cross: Letter from a Region in My Mind," in his *The Fire Next Time*, Reissue (New York: Vintage, 1993), 105.
65. Richard Rorty, *Achieving Our Country: Leftist Thought in Twentieth-Century America* (Cambridge, MA: Harvard University Press, 1998), 22.
66. Rorty, 22.
67. Whitman, "Democratic Vistas," 456.
68. Rorty, *Achieving Our Country*, 23.
69. Gary Gerstle, *American Crucible: Race and Nation in the Twentieth Century* (Princeton: Princeton University Press, 2001), 128.
70. See Ira Katznelson, *Fear Itself: The New Deal and the Origins of Our Time* (New York: Liveright, 2013).
71. David A. Hollinger, *Postethnic America: Beyond Multiculturalism* (New York: Basic Books, 1995), 148–49. See also Gerstle, *American Crucible*, 130.
72. Rorty, *Achieving Our Country*, 55.
73. Todd Gitlin, *The Sixties: Years of Hope, Days of Rage* (New York: Bantam, 1987), 162.
74. Gerstle, *American Crucible*, 269–70.

75. Rorty, *Achieving Our Country*, 55. See also Gitlin, *The Sixties*, 162–63.
76. Michael Kazin and Joseph A. McCartin, "Introduction," in *Americanism: New Perspectives on the History of an Ideal*, ed. Michael Kazin and Joseph A. McCartin (Chapel Hill: University of North Carolina Press, 2006), 6.
77. Kloppenberg, "Aspirational Nationalism in America," 68.
78. Jefferson Cowie, "Reclaiming Patriotism for the Left," *The New York Times*, August 21, 2018, sec. Opinion, https://www.nytimes.com/2018/08/21/opinion/nationalism-patriotism-liberals-.html.
79. Gitlin, *The Sixties*, 6.
80. Smith, *Civic Ideals*, 508n5.
81. Gerstle, *American Crucible*, 345. Emphasis added. It is true that Gerstle periodizes the major period of American nationalism differently (locating its origins later), but this is not so much a disagreement as it is a decision to emphasize other factors. In any case, Gerstle's timeline is compatible with the short account I give here.
82. See, e.g., Arthur Meier Schlesinger, *The Disuniting of America: Reflections on a Multicultural Society* (New York: W. W. Norton, 1991); Todd Gitlin, *The Twilight of Common Dreams: Why America Is Wracked by Culture Wars* (New York: Metropolitan Books, 1995); Hollinger, *Postethnic America*; Michael J. Sandel, *Democracy's Discontent: America in Search of a Public Philosophy* (Cambridge, MA: Belknap Press of Harvard University Press, 1996); Robert D. Putnam, *Bowling Alone: The Collapse and Revival of American Community* (New York: Simon & Schuster, 2000); Desmond S. King and Rogers M. Smith, *Still a House Divided: Race and Politics in Obama's America* (Princeton: Princeton University Press, 2011); Doug McAdam and Karina Kloos, *Deeply Divided: Racial Politics and Social Movements in Postwar America* (New York: Oxford University Press, 2014).
83. Daniel T. Rodgers, *Age of Fracture* (Cambridge, MA: Belknap Press of Harvard University Press, 2011), 2–3. Emphasis added.
84. "What Is Americanism?," *American Journal of Sociology* 20, no. 4 (Jan. 1915): 433.
85. "What Is Americanism?," 435.
86. W. E. B. Du Bois, quoted in "What Is Americanism?," 463. Emphasis in original.
87. Du Bois, quoted in "What Is Americanism?," 463. Emphasis added.

Chapter 3

1. Nathan Pippenger, "One Family in Limbo: What Obama's Immigration Policy Looks Like in Practice," *The New Republic*, September 15, 2011, https://newrepublic.com/article/95005/pippenger-immigration-obama-deportation-ice.
2. John Morton, "Exercising Prosecutorial Discretion Consistent with the Civil Immigration Enforcement Priorities of the Agency for the Apprehension, Detention, and Removal of Aliens," U.S. Immigration and Customs Enforcement, June 17, 2011, 2.
3. "Vote of No Confidence in ICE Director John Morton and ICE ODPP Assistant Director Phyllis Coven," National Council 118—Immigration and Customs Enforcement, American Federation of Government Employees (AFL-CIO), June 25, 2010, https://www.aila.org/aila-files/2ED7DB65-55BD-4265-B0B5-7D5B031123CE/10080563.pdf.

4. Julia Preston, "Deportations Under New U.S. Policy Are Inconsistent," *The New York Times*, November 12, 2011, sec. U.S., https://www.nytimes.com/2011/11/13/us/politics/president-obamas-policy-on-deportation-is-unevenly-applied.html.
5. Julia Preston, "Romney's Plan for 'Self-Deportation' Has Conservative Support," *The Caucus* (blog), *The New York Times*, January 24, 2012, https://thecaucus.blogs.nytimes.com/2012/01/24/romneys-plan-for-self-deportation-has-conservative-support/.
6. Mark Hugo Lopez and Paul Taylor, "Latino Voters in the 2012 Election," Pew Research Center, November 7, 2012, http://www.pewhispanic.org/2012/11/07/latino-voters-in-the-2012-election/.
7. "Growth & Opportunity Project," Republican National Committee, March 18, 2013, 4, http://s3.documentcloud.org/documents/623664/republican-national-committees-growth-and.pdf.
8. "Growth & Opportunity Project," 15.
9. "Growth & Opportunity Project," 8.
10. "Growth & Opportunity Project," 8.
11. "Full Text: Donald Trump Announces a Presidential Bid," *The Washington Post*, June 6, 2015, https://www.washingtonpost.com/news/post-politics/wp/2015/06/16/full-text-donald-trump-announces-a-presidential-bid/?noredirect=on&utm_term=.71a9db7e2857.
12. Nolan D. McCaskill, "Trump Promises Wall and Massive Deportation Program," *POLITICO*, August 31, 2016, https://www.politico.com/story/2016/08/donald-trump-immigration-address-arizona-227612.
13. Robert L. Tsai, "Immigration Unilateralism and American Ethnonationalism," *Loyola University Chicago Law Journal* 51, no. 2 (Winter 2019): 524.
14. Tsai, 524–26.
15. Lyndon B. Johnson, "Remarks at the Signing of the Immigration Bill, Liberty Island, New York," October 3, 1965, American Presidency Project, UC Santa Barbara, https://www.presidency.ucsb.edu/documents/remarks-the-signing-the-immigration-bill-liberty-island-new-york.
16. Jeff Sessions, "Immigration Handbook for the New Republican Majority," January 2015, 3. https://www.aila.org/aila-files/52023919-1F93-4F98-A6F6-665B4157964C/16111436.pdf?1697589936.
17. Sessions, 3.
18. Adam Serwer, "Jeff Sessions's Unqualified Praise for a 1924 Immigration Law," *The Atlantic*, January 10, 2017, https://www.theatlantic.com/politics/archive/2017/01/jeff-sessions-1924-immigration/512591/.
19. Paul Farhi, "White House Aide Stephen Miller Held Wide Sway over Breitbart News, According to Emails," *The Washington Post*, November 19, 2019, https://www.washingtonpost.com/lifestyle/style/white-house-aide-stephen-miller-held-wide-sway-over-breitbart-news-according-to-emails/2019/11/19/23e473fa-0ae8-11ea-8397-a955cd542d00_story.html.
20. Michael Edison Hayden, "Stephen Miller's Affinity for White Nationalism Revealed in Leaked Emails," Southern Poverty Law Center, November 12, 2019, https://www.splcenter.org/hatewatch/2019/11/12/stephen-millers-affinity-white-nationalism-revealed-leaked-emails; Katie Rogers and Jason DeParle, "The White Nationalist Websites Cited

by Stephen Miller," *The New York Times*, November 18, 2019, sec. U.S., https://www.nytimes.com/2019/11/18/us/politics/stephen-miller-white-nationalism.html.
21. Michelle Hackman, "The Speechwriter Behind Donald Trump's Republican Convention Address," *The Wall Street Journal*, July 21, 2016.
22. Josh Dawsey, "Trump Derides Protections for Immigrants from 'Shithole' Countries," *The Washington Post*, January 11, 2018, https://www.washingtonpost.com/politics/trump-attacks-protections-for-immigrants-from-shithole-countries-in-oval-office-meeting/2018/01/11/bfc0725c-f711-11e7-91af-31ac729add94_story.html.
23. See Martin Ruhs and Philip Martin, "Numbers vs. Rights: Trade-Offs and Guest Worker Programs," *International Migration Review* 42, no. 1 (Mar. 2008): 254, https://doi.org/10.1111/j.1747-7379.2007.00120.x.
24. McPherson, *Battle Cry of Freedom: The Civil War Era* (New York: Oxford University Press, 1988), 136.
25. "Examiner's Questions for Admittance to the American (or Know-Nothing) Party, July 1854," July 1854, Manuscript Division, Library of Congress, https://www.loc.gov/resource/mcc.062/?sp=1.
26. Bruce Levine, "Conservatism, Nativism, and Slavery: Thomas R. Whitney and the Origins of the Know-Nothing Party," *The Journal of American History* 88, no. 2 (Sept. 2001): 463, https://doi.org/10.2307/2675102.
27. Levine, 469–70. See also Susan F. Martin, *A Nation of Immigrants* (Cambridge: Cambridge University Press, 2011), 98.
28. Levine, "Conservatism, Nativism, and Slavery," 470.
29. Thomas R. Whitney, *A Defence of the American Policy, as Opposed to the Encroachments of Foreign Influence, and Especially to the Interference of the Papacy in the Political Interests and Affairs of the United States* (New York: DeWitt & Davenport, 1856), 135, http://hdl.handle.net/2027/coo1.ark:/13960/t2g73zp37. Emphasis in original.
30. Whitney, 135.
31. Whitney, 135.
32. Whitney, 135–36.
33. Whitney, 139.
34. Whitney, 140. Emphasis in original.
35. Abraham Lincoln, "Letter to Joshua Speed, Springfield, Illinois: August 24, 1855," in *The Essential Lincoln: Speeches and Correspondence*, ed. Orville Vernon Burton (New York: Hill and Wang, 2009), 31–35. Emphasis in original.
36. As discussed in Chapter 2, and as noted by Danielle Allen, the Declaration was understood in universalist terms by at least some of Lincoln's contemporaries: the Confederates who explicitly repudiated it. It was also understood in such terms by at least some figures at the time of its adoption. See Allen, *Our Declaration: A Reading of the Declaration of Independence in Defense of Equality* (New York: Liveright, 2014), 240–42.
37. Abraham Lincoln, "Address to Germans at Cincinnati, Ohio, February 12, 1861," in *Abraham Lincoln: His Speeches and Writings*, ed. Roy P. Basler (New York: Da Capo Press, 2001), 573.
38. Charles Sumner, "Political Parties and Our Foreign-Born Population: Speech at Faneuil Hall, November 2, 1855," in *Charles Sumner: His Complete Works*, vol. 5 (Boston: Lee and Shepard, 1900), 75.
39. Sumner, 77.

40. Sumner, 77.
41. Sumner, 78. Emphases added. In this context, Sumner's distinction between religion and "priestcraft" seems calculated not to stoke anti-Catholic sentiment but to dismiss the fears underlying it—since he allows that while "priestcraft" would merit opposition if it represented a genuine danger, in practice it provides no basis for restricting "the welcome to foreigners." John McGreevy, however, has counted Sumner among "theorists of American nationalism in the 1860s and 1870s . . . [who] instinctively mistrusted Catholicism," citing an 1871 letter in which Sumner, celebrating Italian unity, "regretted the 'condition of Rome under papal power.'" Sumner did indeed celebrate the end of papal rule in Rome, and his letter makes his reasons explicit. In addition to believing that unification was a "triumph" for Italian nationality, Sumner saw "in this event two other things of surpassing importance in the history of Liberty." First, he wrote, "the union of Church and State is overthrown in its greatest example. The Pope remains the pastor of a mighty flock, but without temporal power." Sumner hoped that this precedent would be "followed everywhere, until Church and State are no longer conjoined, and all are at liberty to worship God according to conscience, without compulsion from Man." Second, Sumner wrote that the "Pope was an absolute sovereign for life. In the overthrow of his temporal power Absolutism receives a blow, and the people everywhere obtain new assurance for the future." In other words, Sumner listed three reasons to celebrate the end of papal rule in Rome: his nationalism, his secularism, and his opposition to absolute, lifelong rule. Moreover, in this 1855 speech, Sumner lists Catholics among the religious groups that settled the United States while affirming his rejection of the Know-Nothing Party on the grounds that it "interferes with religious belief." See John T. McGreevy, *Catholicism and American Freedom: A History* (New York: W. W. Norton, 2003), 100–101; Charles Sumner, "Italian Unity: Letter to a Public Meeting at the Academy of Music in New York, January 10, 1871," in *Charles Sumner: His Complete Works*, vol. 18 (Boston: Lee and Shepard, 1900), 308; Sumner, "Political Parties and Our Foreign-Born Population," 76–77, 80.
42. Frederick Douglass, "Our Composite Nationality: An Address Delivered in Boston, Massachusetts, on 7 December 1869," in *The Frederick Douglass Papers*, ed. John W. Blassingame and John R. McKivigan, vol. 4: *1864–80*, Frederick Douglass Papers, Series One: Speeches, Debates, and Interviews (New Haven: Yale University Press, 1991), 251. Emphasis in original.
43. Douglass, 256.
44. Douglass, 259.
45. Eric Foner, *The Story of American Freedom* (New York: W. W. Norton, 1998), 177.
46. Foner, 187.
47. Foner, 187.
48. Randolph Bourne, "Trans-National America," *The Atlantic Monthly*, July 1916, 94.
49. John Dewey, "Nationalizing Education," *The Journal of Education* 84, no. 16 (Nov. 2, 1916): 426.
50. Dewey, 426.
51. "The Work of the Foreign Language Information Service: A Summary and Survey," Foreign Language Information Service, 1921, 8–9, Widener Library, Harvard University, https://curiosity.lib.harvard.edu/immigration-to-the-united-states-1789-1930/catalog/39-990013685600203941.
52. "The Work of the Foreign Language Information Service of the American Red Cross," Bureau of Foreign Language Information Service, Department of Civilian Relief, June

10, 1920, Widener Library, Harvard University, https://curiosity.lib.harvard.edu/immigration-to-the-united-states-1789-1930/catalog/39-990085954750203941; "Foreign Language Information Service on Independent Basis," *The Red Cross Bulletin*, May 16, 1921.
53. Richard W. Steele, "The War on Intolerance: The Reformulation of American Nationalism, 1939–1941," *Journal of American Ethnic History* 9, no. 1 (Fall 1989): 15.
54. "Foreign Language Information Service," 5.
55. "Foreign Language Information Service," 5–6.
56. "Foreign Language Information Service," 5–6.
57. "Foreign Language Information Service," 5–6.
58. "Foreign Language Information Service," 7.
59. "Americanization vs. 'Americanization,'" *The Interpreter*, April 1923, 3.
60. "Americanization vs. 'Americanization,'" 3–4.
61. "Americanization vs. 'Americanization,'" 4.
62. Julius Drachsler, "The Immigrant and the Realities of Assimilation," *The Interpreter*, September 1924, 4. Emphases added.
63. Drachsler, 4.
64. Drachsler, 4.
65. Drachsler, 5.
66. Drachsler, 6.
67. Drachsler, 6.
68. Drachsler, 6.
69. Drachsler, 7.
70. Drachsler, 7.
71. Douglass, "The Work of the Future" (*Douglass' Monthly*, November 1862), in *Frederick Douglass: Selected Speeches and Writings*, ed. Philip Sheldon Foner and Yuval Taylor (Chicago: Chicago Review Press, 1999), 521–22.
72. Douglass, 522.
73. Gary Gerstle, *American Crucible: Race and Nation in the Twentieth Century* (Princeton: Princeton University Press, 2001), 104–13.
74. Harry H. Laughlin, "Analysis of America's Modern Melting Pot, Hearings Before the Committee on Immigration and Naturalization, House of Representatives, Sixty-Seventh Congress, Third Session, November 21, 1922, Serial 7-C" (Government Printing Office, 1923), 738; quoted in Gerstle, 108.
75. Horace M. Kallen, "Democracy Versus the Melting-Pot," *The Nation*, February 25, 1915, 220.
76. Stephen S. Wise, "What Is an American?," *The Bulletin* (Foreign Language Information Service) 1, no. 7 (Oct. 1922): 4–5. Emphasis added.
77. Drachsler, "The Immigrant and the Realities of Assimilation," 9.
78. David A. Reed, "America of the Melting Pot Comes to an End: Effects of New Immigration Legislation Described by Senate Sponsor of Bill—Chief Aim, He States, Is to Preserve Racial Type as It Exists Here Today," *The New York Times*, April 27, 1924, sec. XX.
79. "Julius Drachsler, Sociologist, Dead," *The New York Times*, July 23, 1927.
80. Whitman, "Democratic Vistas," in *Complete Poetry and Selected Prose*, ed. James E. Miller, Jr., Riverside Editions (Boston: Houghton Mifflin, 1959), 475.
81. Whitman, 477.

82. Joseph H. Carens, "Aliens and Citizens: The Case for Open Borders," *The Review of Politics* 49, no. 2 (Spring 1987): 251. In his later work on membership, Carens explained his intention to offer "an important corrective to certain tendencies in cosmopolitan thought," arguing: "If some democratic theorists focus too much on citizenship, some cosmopolitan thinkers go too far in denigrating the significance of belonging." Joseph H. Carens, *The Ethics of Immigration* (New York: Oxford University Press, 2013), 161.
83. Carens, "Aliens and Citizens," 251.
84. Carens, 268. Emphasis in original. This insistence on citizenship for guest workers marks a point of overlap between Carens and Michael Walzer, whose influential defense of border controls is one of the targets of Carens's critique. As Walzer similarly argues: "No democratic state can tolerate the establishment of a fixed status between citizen and foreigner.... Men and women are either subject to the state's authority, or they are not; and if they are subject, they must be given a say, and ultimately an equal say, in what that authority does." See Walzer, *Spheres of Justice: A Defense of Pluralism and Equality* (New York: Basic Books, 1983), 61.
85. Chandran Kukathas, "Expatriatism: The Theory and Practice of Open Borders," in *Citizenship, Borders, and Human Needs*, ed. Rogers M. Smith (Philadelphia: University of Pennsylvania Press, 2011), 332.
86. Kukathas, 334.
87. Howard F. Chang, "The Immigration Paradox: Alien Workers and Distributive Justice," in Smith, *Citizenship, Borders, and Human Needs*, 96–97.
88. Chang, 113.
89. Chang, 114.
90. In presenting this as an inadmissible exchange—one that wrongly treats political freedom as a fungible good—I draw on a similar argument from Samuel Freeman, who writes, "No liberal regime would enforce or permit enforcement of an agreement against a person who has tried to alienate one or more of her constitutionally protected basic rights. For these are the rights that define a person's status as a free agent, capable of rationally deciding her good and taking responsibility for her actions.... Being inalienable, they are secured against the wants of those who would dispossess themselves of their basic rights and abandon their freedom and independence." See Samuel Freeman, "Illiberal Libertarians: Why Libertarianism Is Not a Liberal View," in his *Liberalism and Distributive Justice* (New York: Oxford University Press, 2018), 79–80. Of course, the force of this objection depends on the exact right in question and whether it has been alienated permanently or only temporarily—and if temporarily, for how long. It may have especially limited force when the waiting period for naturalization is minimal. Thanks to Pierce Randall for raising this point with me.
91. While many theorists endorse various guest worker proposals on more-or-less consequentialist grounds, such policies have been subjected to a number of serious criticisms: that guest worker remittances worsen many economic conditions in migrants' countries of origin; that proposals to increase labor mobility distract from structural solutions to global distributive injustice; that the nature of migrant labor globalizes gendered forms of exploitation and vulnerability; that the denial of political rights to migrant workers warps electoral politics in destination countries; and that the "choice" to forgo political rights in exchange for work is not a genuinely free one, since migrants tend to make it from a position of vulnerability or even desperation. See, respectively, Peter W. Higgins, *Immigration*

Justice (Edinburgh: Edinburgh University Press, 2013), 64–70; Hein de Haas, "The Migration and Development Pendulum: A Critical View on Research and Policy," *International Migration* 50, no. 3 (June 2012): 19–22, https://doi.org/10.1111/j.1468-2435.2012.00755. x; Alison M. Jaggar, "Transnational Cycles of Gendered Vulnerability: A Prologue to a Theory of Global Gender Justice," *Philosophical Topics* 37, no. 2 (Fall 2009): 42; Christopher Bertram, "Democracy and the Representation of the Interests of Temporary Migrant Workers," *Law, Ethics and Philosophy*, no. 9 (2022): 174–75, https://doi.org/10.31009/LEAP.2022.V9.11; Anna Stilz, "Economic Migration: On What Terms?," *Perspectives on Politics* 20, no. 3 (Sept. 2022): 987, https://doi.org/10.1017/S1537592721002206. Relatedly, for a critique of distributive justice-based and rights-based arguments for open borders, see Sarah Song, *Immigration and Democracy* (New York: Oxford University Press, 2019), chaps. 5–6.

92. See Jorge M. Valadez, "Immigration, Self-Determination, and Global Justice: Towards a Holistic Normative Theory of Migration," *Journal of International Political Theory* 8, nos. 1–2 (Apr. 2012): 140, https://doi.org/10.3366/jipt.2012.0034. Emphasis in original.
93. Martin O'Neill, "What Should Egalitarians Believe?," *Philosophy & Public Affairs* 36, no. 2 (2008): 135–39.
94. For a more detailed discussion of the points raised so far in this section of the chapter, see Nathan Pippenger, "From Openness to Inclusion: Toward a Democratic Approach to Migration Policy," *Perspectives on Politics* 22, no. 4 (Dec. 2024): 975–988, https://doi.org/10.1017/S153759272400001X.
95. Arash Abizadeh, "Democratic Theory and Border Coercion: No Right to Unilaterally Control Your Own Borders," *Political Theory* 36, no. 1 (Feb. 2008): 46.
96. Abizadeh, 44. Emphasis in original.
97. Abizadeh, 47.
98. Abizadeh, 41.
99. Abizadeh, 48.
100. Abizadeh, 45.
101. Abizadeh, 41.
102. David Miller argues, for example, that territorial outsiders are not subject to coercion per se, and Sarah Song distinguishes the incidental coercion that individuals may experience if they try to cross a border from the more extensive, ongoing form of coercion experienced by people who are permanently subject to a state's authority. See David Miller, "Why Immigration Controls Are Not Coercive: A Reply to Arash Abizadeh," *Political Theory* 38, no. 1 (Feb. 2010): 111–20; Song, *Immigration and Democracy*, 70–71. The respective characterizations of coercion and of the demos are of course related, for Abizadeh defines the demos by reference to coercion and the practices of mutual justification which alone can legitimate it, according to democratic theory.
103. Abizadeh, "Democratic Theory and Border Coercion," 45.
104. Song, "The Boundary Problem in Democratic Theory: Why the Demos Should Be Bounded by the State," *International Theory* 4, no. 1 (Mar. 2012): 56, https://doi.org/10.1017/S175297191100024856. Emphasis in original.
105. Even Abizadeh's supposedly more restrictive "all-coerced" principle seems, as Song notes, "to push toward a global demos." See Song, 53. On the issue of borders, Abizadeh maintains that "Democrats are required by their own account of political legitimacy to support the formation of cosmopolitan democratic institutions that have jurisdiction either to

determine entry policy or legitimately to delegate jurisdiction over entry policy to particular states (or other institutions)." See Abizadeh, "Democratic Theory and Border Coercion," 48.
106. Charles Taylor, "Democratic Exclusion (and Its Remedies?)," in his *Dilemmas and Connections: Selected Essays* (Cambridge, MA: Belknap Press of Harvard University Press, 2011), 125.
107. Bernard Yack, *Nationalism and the Moral Psychology of Community* (Chicago: University of Chicago Press, 2012), 17.
108. Song, "The Boundary Problem in Democratic Theory," 56.
109. Robert Goodin suggests one (drastic) way to avoid this underinclusiveness: "The democratic ideal ought ideally be to enfranchise 'all affected interests.' Understood in a suitably expansive 'possibilistic' way, that would mean giving virtually everyone everywhere a vote on virtually everything decided anywhere," including many activities now considered private. See Robert E. Goodin, "Enfranchising All Affected Interests, and Its Alternatives," *Philosophy & Public Affairs* 35, no. 1 (Winter 2007): 68, https://doi.org/10.1111/j.1088-4963.2007.00098.x. For a discussion of this circularity problem and Goodin's response, see Song, "The Boundary Problem in Democratic Theory," 49–50.
110. It might be argued that *all* political problems are interpretive—that absolutely nothing in the realm of human living-together has a straightforwardly problematic character that is (or could be) evident to every single person, irrespective of individuals' differences in outlook, perception, desires, etc. This claim would obviously face its most famous opponent in Hobbes's attempt to show that violent death is precisely that problem. The point I make here, however, does not require proving this more ambitious claim.
111. Anna Stilz, *Liberal Loyalty: Freedom, Obligation, and the State* (Princeton: Princeton University Press, 2009), 81. Emphasis in original.

Chapter 4

1. C. Gerald Fraser, "J. Saunders Redding, 81, Is Dead; Pioneer Black Ivy League Teacher," *The New York Times*, March 5, 1988, sec. Obituaries, https://www.nytimes.com/1988/03/05/obituaries/j-saunders-redding-81-is-dead-pioneer-black-ivy-league-teacher.html; "Jay Saunders Redding (1906–1988) Papers," Brown University Library, accessed July 14, 2020, https://library.brown.edu/collatoz/info.php?id=253.
2. "Kenneth Clark, Haverford Discussions, Friday Afternoon Session, May 30, 1969," in *The Haverford Discussions: A Black Integrationist Manifesto for Racial Justice*, ed. Michael Lackey (Charlottesville: University of Virginia Press, 2013), 5.
3. Erica Frankenberg et al., "Harming Our Common Future: America's Segregated Schools 65 Years After *Brown*," The Civil Rights Project at UCLA, May 10, 2019, 4, https://www.civilrightsproject.ucla.edu/research/k-12-education/integration-and-diversity/harming-our-common-future-americas-segregated-schools-65-years-after-brown.
4. Nikole Hannah-Jones, "Choosing a School for My Daughter in a Segregated City," *The New York Times Magazine*, June 9, 2016, http://www.nytimes.com/2016/06/12/magazine/choosing-a-school-for-my-daughter-in-a-segregated-city.html.
5. Brown et al. vs. Board of Education of Topeka et al. (U.S. Supreme Court May 17, 1954).
6. An overview of the empirical literature can be found in Elizabeth Anderson, *The Imperative of Integration* (Princeton: Princeton University Press, 2010). See also

Douglas S. Massey and Nancy A. Denton, *American Apartheid: Segregation and the Making of the Underclass* (Cambridge, MA: Harvard University Press, 1993); Gary Orfield, "Reviving the Goal of an Integrated Society: A 21st Century Challenge," Civil Rights Project at UCLA, January 2009, http://www.racialequitytools.org/resourcefiles/orfield.pdf; Richard D. Kahlenberg and Kimberly Quick, "Attacking the Black–White Opportunity Gap That Comes from Residential Segregation," Century Foundation, June 25, 2019, https://tcf.org/content/report/attacking-black-white-opportunity-gap-comes-residential-segregation/; and "Separate and Unequal: Persistent Residential Segregation Is Sustaining Racial and Economic Injustice in the U.S," in Christopher Coes, Jennifer S. Vey, and Tracy Hadden Loh, "The Great Real Estate Reset: A Data-Driven Initiative to Remake How and What We Build" Brookings Institution, December 16, 2020, https://www.brookings.edu/essay/the-great-real-estate-reset-a-data-driven-initiative-to-remake-how-and-what-we-build/.

7. Tommie Shelby, *We Who Are Dark: The Philosophical Foundations of Black Solidarity* (Cambridge, MA: Belknap Press of Harvard University Press, 2005), xi.
8. Shelby, 3.
9. Andrew Valls, "A Liberal Defense of Black Nationalism," *The American Political Science Review* 104, no. 3 (Aug. 2010): 467–81; Andrew Valls, *Rethinking Racial Justice* (New York: Oxford University Press, 2018), chap. 4.
10. Tommie Shelby, *Dark Ghettos: Injustice, Dissent, and Reform* (Cambridge, MA: Belknap Press of Harvard University Press, 2016), 67–79.
11. Michael S. Merry, *Equality, Citizenship, and Segregation: A Defense of Separation* (New York: Palgrave Macmillan, 2013).
12. Roy L. Brooks, *Integration or Separation?: A Strategy for Racial Equality* (Cambridge, MA: Harvard University Press, 1996).
13. Shelby, *We Who Are Dark*, 4.
14. Anderson, *The Imperative of Integration*, 22.
15. Anderson, 110. Emphasis in original.
16. Anderson, 184.
17. Anderson, 184.
18. On the distinction between assimilation and mutual transformation, see Sharon Stanley, *An Impossible Dream?: Racial Integration in the United States* (Oxford, New York: Oxford University Press, 2017), 3.
19. Sean F. Reardon et al., "Brown Fades: The End of Court-Ordered School Desegregation and the Resegregation of American Public Schools," *Journal of Policy Analysis and Management* 31, no. 4 (Fall 2012): 877–78.
20. Foner and Kennedy continued: "Books continue to appear with the word in their titles, but most seem resigned to integration's failure, treating it as an ongoing 'ordeal' or seeking to allocate blame for the nation's departure from integrationist principles." See Eric Foner and Randall Kennedy, "Reclaiming Integration," *The Nation*, December 14, 1998, 11. See also Brooks, *Integration or Separation?* and Eugene F. Rivers, "Beyond the Nationalism of Fools: Toward an Agenda for Black Intellectuals," *Boston Review*, Summer 1995, http://new.bostonreview.net/BR20.3/rivers.html. On the "deepening pessimism and alienation" palpable at the turn of the century, see Lawrence D. Bobo, "Racial Attitudes and Relations at the Close of Twentieth Century," in *America Becoming: Racial Trends and Their Consequences*, vol. 1, ed. Neil J. Smelser, William Julius Wilson, and Faith Mitchell (Washington, D.C.: National Academy Press, 2001), 285–90, https://doi.org/10.17226/9599.

21. See Andrew Valls, "The Broken Promise of Racial Integration," *Nomos*, 43 (2002): 456. On the separation vs. integration debate, Valls remarked: "Perhaps what lies at the bottom of this disagreement is the level of optimism or pessimism about the prospects of eliminating racism in the United States." Valls, 470.
22. Michelle Adams, "Radical Integration," *California Law Review* 94, no. 2 (Mar. 2006): 264, https://doi.org/10.2307/20439036.
23. James T. Patterson, *Brown v. Board of Education: A Civil Rights Milestone and Its Troubled Legacy* (Oxford: Oxford University Press, 2001), 71.
24. Patterson, 71.
25. C. Vann Woodward, *The Strange Career of Jim Crow* (New York: Oxford University Press, 1955), 9–11.
26. Harold Wright Cruse, "An Afro-American's Cultural Views," *Présence Africaine*, no. 17 (Dec. 1957): 34–35.
27. Norman Podhoretz, in Nathan Glazer et al., "Liberalism & the Negro: A Round-Table Discussion," *Commentary*, March 1964, 25, https://www.commentarymagazine.com/articles/liberalism-the-negro-a-round-table-discussion/.
28. Oscar Handlin, "The Goals of Integration," *Daedalus* 95, no. 1 (Winter 1966): 268.
29. Handlin, 270.
30. Handlin, 270.
31. Touré F. Reed, "Oscar Handlin and the Problem of Ethnic Pluralism and African American Civil Rights," *Journal of American Ethnic History* 32, no. 3 (Spring 2013): 37–45, https://doi.org/10.5406/jamerethnhist.32.3.0037.
32. Handlin, "The Goals of Integration," 283.
33. Handlin, 276.
34. Handlin, 276.
35. Handlin, 271.
36. Harold Cruse, "An Afro-American's Cultural Views," in his *Rebellion or Revolution?* (Minneapolis: University of Minnesota Press, 1968), 59. Here I am quoting a later reprint, since the original 1957 essay contains a number of typographical errors. For the original, see Cruse, "An Afro-American's Cultural Views," December 1957, 38.
37. Cruse, "An Afro-American's Cultural Views," 1968, 61.
38. Charles Hamilton and Kwame Ture, *Black Power: The Politics of Liberation in America* (New York: Random House, 1967), 54.
39. Hamilton and Ture, 55.
40. Robert S. Browne, "The Case for Black Separatism," *Ramparts*, December 1967, 49, http://www.unz.org/Pub/Ramparts-1967dec-00046.
41. Browne, 49.
42. Browne, 49.
43. A primer from the NAACP Legal Defense and Educational Fund briefly summarizes the experiment: "In the 1940s, psychologists Kenneth and Mamie Clark designed and conducted a series of experiments known colloquially as 'the doll tests' to study the psychological effects of segregation on African-American children. Drs. Clark used four dolls, identical except for color, to test children's racial perceptions. Their subjects, children between the ages of three to seven, were asked to identify both the race of the dolls and which color doll they prefer. A majority of the children preferred the white doll and assigned positive characteristics to it. The Clarks concluded that 'prejudice,

discrimination, and segregation' created a feeling of inferiority among African-American children and damaged their self-esteem... The Supreme Court cited Clark's 1950 paper in its Brown decision and acknowledged it implicitly in the following passage: 'To separate [African-American children] from others of similar age and qualifications solely because of their race generates a feeling of inferiority as to their status in the community that may affect their hearts and minds in a way unlikely ever to be undone.' Dr. Kenneth Clark was dismayed that the court failed to cite two other conclusions he had reached: that racism was an inherently American institution, and that school segregation inhibited the development of white children, too." See NAACP Legal Defense and Educational Fund, "Brown at 60: The Doll Test," accessed December 7, 2016, http://www.naacpldf.org/brown-at-60-the-doll-test.

44. It is this "wrongness" that explains why the racial other must be either spatially separated from or changed to be more like the dominant racial group. See john a. powell, "Is Integration Possible?," *Race, Poverty & the Environment* 15, no. 2 (Fall 2008): 42–43.
45. Kenneth B. Clark, "Letter to Dr. Edward H. Levi, May 14, 1968," in Lackey, *The Haverford Discussions*, 141.
46. Browne, "The Case for Black Separatism," 47.
47. Danielle S. Allen, *Talking to Strangers: Anxieties of Citizenship Since Brown v. Board of Education* (Chicago: University of Chicago Press, 2004).
48. James Kloppenberg, "Life Everlasting: Tocqueville in America," in his *The Virtues of Liberalism* (New York: Oxford University Press, 1998), 77.
49. Amy Gutmann, *Democratic Education* (Princeton: Princeton University Press, 1987), 39.
50. Abraham Lincoln, "Gettysburg Address," November 19, 1863, Avalon Project, Yale University, http://avalon.law.yale.edu/19th_century/gettyb.asp; Douglass, "The Work of the Future (*Douglass' Monthly*, November 1862)," in *Frederick Douglass: Selected Speeches and Writings*, ed. Philip Sheldon Foner and Yuval Taylor (Chicago: Chicago Review Press, 1999), 521–23.
51. Browne, "The Case for Black Separatism," 50.
52. Browne, 49. Emphasis added.
53. Browne, 49.
54. Robert S. Browne, "The Case for Two Americas—One Black, One White," *The New York Times Magazine*, August 11, 1968, 56, http://query.nytimes.com/gst/abstract.html?res=9E06E0DD1F3AE03AA15752C1A96E9C946991D6CF.
55. Browne, "The Case for Black Separatism."
56. Robert S. Browne and Bayard Rustin, *Separation or Integration: Which Way for America? A Dialogue* (New York: A. Philip Randolph Educational Fund, 1968), http://digitalassets.lib.berkeley.edu/irle/ucb/text/lb001278.pdf.
57. Browne, "The Case for Two Americas," 60–61.
58. Ellison, in Lackey, *The Haverford Discussions*, 111.
59. Ellison, in Lackey, 111–12. The one bond that Ellison identified across various forms of American diversity—in region, class, ethnicity, and religion—was language. American English, influenced by African culture even before the country was founded, "owes something of its directness, its flexibility, its music, its imagery, mythology and folklore to the Negro presence; it is not, therefore, a product of 'white' culture as against 'black' culture, rather it is the product of cultural integration." See Ellison, in Lackey, 112. For more on this aspect of Ellison's thought, see Nathan Pippenger, "Reading Ellison Through Herder:

Language, Integration, and Democracy," *The Journal of Politics* 85, no. 2 (Apr. 2023): 749–59, https://doi.org/10.1086/722350.
60. Michael Lackey, "Redeeming the Post-Metaphysical Promise of J. Saunders Redding's 'America,'" *CR: The New Centennial Review* 12, no. 3 (Winter 2012): 223.
61. J. Saunders Redding, "The Black Arts Movement: A Modest Dissent," in *A Scholar's Conscience: Selected Writings of J. Saunders Redding, 1942–1977*, ed. Faith Berry (Lexington: University Press of Kentucky, 1992), 215.
62. Redding, 217.
63. Saunders Redding, "Background and Significance of 'Black Studies' Programs," in Lackey, *The Haverford Discussions*, 129.
64. Redding, 129. Emphasis in original.
65. Redding, 129.
66. Saunders Redding, "The Black Revolution in American Studies," *American Studies International* 17, no. 4 (Summer 1979): 8–14.
67. Redding, 8.
68. Redding, 12.
69. Imamu Amiri Baraka, "A Reply to Saunders Reddings' 'The Black Revolution in American Studies,'" *American Studies International* 17, no. 4 (Summer 1979): 19.
70. Lackey, "Redeeming the Post-Metaphysical Promise of J. Saunders Redding's 'America,'" 222–28, 234–35; Lackey, *The Haverford Discussions*, xxv–xxxii.
71. Lackey writes that "the Cruse victory, if we can now call it that, could only be categorized as short lived, for as it turns out, the metaphysical model of race underwriting Cruse's black cultural nationalism and the Black Arts Movement would be considered by today's standards profoundly misguided. Since the 1980s most academics have rejected the idea of race as an ontological fact of being and accepted the postmodern view of race as a sociopolitical invention." See Lackey, *The Haverford Discussions*, xxviii.
72. Another risk of such strong accounts of identity is their tendency to reinforce life scripts that constrain the individuals in whose interest the identity's defenders claim to speak. As Kwame Anthony Appiah has written: "What demanding respect for people *as blacks* or *as gays* requires is that there be some scripts that go with being an African-American or having same-sex desires. There will be proper ways of being black and gay: there will be expectations to be met; demands will be made. It is at this point that someone who takes autonomy seriously will want to ask whether we have not replaced one kind of tyranny with another. If I had to choose between Uncle Tom and Black Power, I would, of course, choose the latter. But I would like not to have to choose." See Kwame Anthony Appiah, "Race, Culture, Identity: Misunderstood Connections," in *Color Conscious: The Political Morality of Race*, ed. Kwame Anthony Appiah and Amy Gutmann (Princeton: Princeton University Press, 1996), 99. Appiah's example of Uncle Tom/Black Power as a forced choice calls to mind an incident in Ellison's life. Ellison's opposition to Black Power led to a number of tense exchanges with young radicals in the late 1960s, including an incident involving a young black man—clad in a black beret and a black leather jacket—who had traveled from Chicago to confront Ellison at a party following a panel at Grinnell College. During an argument about *Invisible Man*, the younger man shouted: "You're an Uncle Tom, man. You're a sell-out. You're a disgrace to your race." Visibly attempting to control his emotions, Ellison replied that he resented the charge. Later, after his accuser had left, Ellison broke down to a black student who had intervened, weeping into his

shoulder and repeating: "I'm not a Tom, I'm not a Tom." See Arnold Rampersad, *Ralph Ellison: A Biography* (New York: Alfred A. Knopf, 2007), 439–40.
73. Consider, e.g., Roy Brooks's defense of "limited separation," which states: "Likewise, limited separation rejects racism (black and white), Black Nationalism, ethnic nationalism, racial essentialism, racial mythmaking, and other belief systems that undermine unity. Limited separation, in short, broadens the American base without destroying it." Brooks, *Integration or Separation?*, 285.
74. Valls, *Rethinking Racial Justice*, 13.
75. Valls, 101.
76. Valls, 77.
77. Valls, 87.
78. Valls, 101.
79. Valls, "A Liberal Defense of Black Nationalism," 475.
80. Valls, *Rethinking Racial Justice*, 147.
81. Valls, 147.
82. Valls, 148.
83. Valls, 89–90, 93–96, 101, 146–48.
84. Valls, 192.
85. E.g., Valls's discussion of education emphasizes the importance of liberal education in "fostering a just, liberal, and democratic society," and he endorses the view that it rightly "inculcates the values and beliefs necessary for a liberal society to persist" and "creates a sense of common citizenship and national membership." Valls, 178.
86. Anderson, *The Imperative of Integration*, 93.
87. Anderson, 110. Emphasis in original.
88. I offer a more detailed critique of Valls's approach in Nathan Pippenger, "Agnosticism on Racial Integration: Liberal-Democratic or Libertarian?," *Political Research Quarterly* 76, no. 3 (Sept. 2023): 1196–1208, https://doi.org/10.1177/10659129221130296.
89. Merry, *Equality, Citizenship, and Segregation*, 2.
90. Merry, 2.
91. Merry, 7–8.
92. Merry, 4.
93. Merry, 9.
94. Merry, 17.
95. Merry, 61.
96. Merry, 73.
97. Merry, 61. Emphasis in original.
98. Merry, 68.
99. Merry, 74.
100. Merry, 75.
101. Merry, 73.
102. Merry, 73. Emphasis added.
103. Merry, 73. Emphasis added.
104. Merry, 73.
105. Merry, 74.
106. Merry, 74. Emphasis in original.
107. Merry, 74.

108. Merry, 61.
109. Merry, 68. Emphasis added.
110. Anderson, *The Imperative of Integration*, 188.
111. Shelby, *Dark Ghettos*, 78–79.
112. Stanley, *An Impossible Dream?*, 187. Emphasis in original.
113. Stanley, 188.
114. Stanley, 110.
115. Stanley, 112.
116. Shelby, *Dark Ghettos*, 79. Emphasis in original.
117. Stanley, *An Impossible Dream?*, 176.
118. Stanley, 117.
119. Stanley, 112.
120. Stanley, 112.
121. Stanley, 112. Emphasis in original.
122. Stanley, 112. Stanley's quotation of Hooker is from Juliet Hooker, *Race and the Politics of Solidarity* (New York: Oxford University Press, 2009), 33–34.
123. Stanley, *An Impossible Dream?*, 115.
124. Stanley, 5.
125. Stanley, 116.
126. Sharon Stanley, "Toward a Reconciliation of Integration and Racial Solidarity," *Contemporary Political Theory* 13, no. 1 (Feb. 2014): 59, https://doi.org/10.1057/cpt.2013.13.
127. For related accounts of democratic epistemology, see Elizabeth S. Anderson, "The Epistemology of Democracy," *Episteme: A Journal of Social Epistemology* 3, nos. 1–2 (June 2006): 8–22, https://doi.org/10.1353/epi.0.0000; Fabienne Peter, "Democratic Legitimacy and Proceduralist Social Epistemology," *Politics, Philosophy & Economics* 6, no. 3 (Oct. 2007): 329–53, https://doi.org/10.1177/1470594X07081303.
128. Frederick Douglass, "The Nation's Problem: An Address Delivered in Washington, D.C., on 16 April 1889," in *The Frederick Douglass Papers*, ed. John W. Blassingame and John R. McKivigan, vol. 5: *1881–95*, Frederick Douglass Papers, Series One: Speeches, Debates, and Interviews (New Haven: Yale University Press, 1992), 415.
129. John Dewey, *The Public and Its Problems: An Essay in Political Inquiry*, ed. Melvin L. Rogers (Athens, OH: Swallow Press, 2016), 224.
130. Quoted in Dewey, 224. This line may be apocryphal: As Melvin Rogers notes, it is unclear where Tilden made this remark. See note 6 on Dewey, 257.
131. This draws on Anderson, *The Imperative of Integration*, 184. See also Margaret Moore, "The Moral Value of Collective Self-Determination and the Ethics of Secession," *Journal of Social Philosophy* 50, no. 4 (Winter 2019): 622, https://doi.org/10.1111/josp.12327.
132. Allen, *Talking to Strangers*, 19.
133. Allen, 88.
134. Allen, 88.
135. Allen, 185–86.
136. As Nick Bromell argues: "If we seal ourselves off from each other, if we deny or foreclose on the possibility of relationship with each other, then we clearly are not putting ourselves

in a position to recognize and affirm each other's democratic dignity. Democratic citizenship is relational citizenship." See Nick Bromell, *The Time Is Always Now: Black Thought and the Transformation of US Democracy* (New York: Oxford University Press, 2013), 76.
137. Weaver, in Lackey, *The Haverford Discussions*, 131.
138. Weaver, in Lackey, 132.
139. Anderson, *The Imperative of Integration*, 188.
140. James Baldwin, in Glazer et al., "Liberalism & the Negro," 41. Emphasis added.
141. Hastie, in Lackey, *The Haverford Discussions*, 118. Emphasis added.
142. Quoted in Lackey, xxxv.
143. Ralph Ellison, Friday Evening Session, May 30, 1969, in Lackey, 61.
144. Ralph Ellison, *Invisible Man*, 2nd Vintage International Edition (New York: Vintage, 1995), xx.
145. Ellison, xx.
146. Ellison, Friday Evening Session, May 30, 1969, in Lackey, *The Haverford Discussions*, 45.
147. Jeffrey Stout, *Democracy and Tradition* (Princeton: Princeton University Press, 2004), 43.

Chapter 5

1. Barack Obama, "Remarks by the President on the Economy in Osawatomie, Kansas," The White House, Office of the Press Secretary, December 6, 2011, https://obamawhitehouse.archives.gov/the-press-office/2011/12/06/remarks-president-economy-osawatomie-kansas.
2. Daniel Henninger, "Obama's Godfather Speech," *Wall Street Journal*, December 8, 2011, sec. Opinion, https://www.wsj.com/articles/SB10001424052970203413304577084292119160060.
3. Mark Steyn, "Statist Delusions," *National Review*, December 10, 2011, http://www.nationalreview.com/article/285409/statist-delusions-mark-steyn.
4. The Editors, "New Nationalism, Old Liberalism," *National Review*, December 7, 2011, http://www.nationalreview.com/article/285186/new-nationalism-old-liberalism-editors.
5. Matthew Spalding, "The String-Pullers," *National Review*, December 31, 2011, https://www.nationalreview.com/nrd/articles/293976/string-pullers.
6. Obama, "Remarks by the President on the Economy in Osawatomie, Kansas."
7. Spalding, "The String-Pullers."
8. "Mr. Roosevelt's Issue," *The New York Times*, September 11, 1910.
9. "Mr. Roosevelt's Issue."
10. Spalding, for instance, concluded: "In his own Osawatomie speech, President Obama donned TR's progressive mantle ... By turning to TR's New Nationalism model, Obama has revealed once and for all that the intellectual antecedent of his administration is the progressive theory of governance. He is calling his party back to its most radical roots." Steyn wrote that "the president channeled Theodore Roosevelt in trust-busting mode." The editors of *National Review* concurred: "Color us skeptical, but we can see why TR's New Nationalism might appeal to Barack Obama." See, respectively, Spalding, "The String-Pullers"; Steyn, "Statist Delusions"; The Editors, "New Nationalism, Old Liberalism."

11. In 2014, Obama was criticized for remarking during a speech that "folks can make a lot more, potentially, with skilled manufacturing or the trades than they might with an art history degree." He later apologized. See Barack Obama, "Remarks by the President on Opportunity for All and Skills for America's Workers," The White House, Office of the Press Secretary, January 30, 2014, https://obamawhitehouse.archives.gov/the-press-office/2014/01/30/remarks-president-opportunity-all-and-skills-americas-workers; Jennifer Schuessler, "President Obama Writes Apology to Art Historian," ArtsBeat (blog), The New York Times, February 18, 2014, https://artsbeat.blogs.nytimes.com/2014/02/18/president-obama-writes-apology-to-art-historian/. Critics such as Wendy Brown have raised important questions about the broad erosion of the citizen-consumer distinction: "But what are the implications, for an ostensibly democratic people, of jettisoning a broad and deep university education in favor of job training? What kind of world will be made through conceptions and practices of postsecondary education that reduce students to future human capital, citizens to manipulable consumers, and the public to GDP?" See Wendy Brown, *Undoing the Demos: Neoliberalism's Stealth Revolution* (New York: Zone Books, 2015), 181.
12. Obama, "Remarks by the President on the Economy in Osawatomie, Kansas."
13. Obama.
14. Theodore Roosevelt, "The New Nationalism: Speech at Osawatomie, Kansas, August 31, 1910," in *Theodore Roosevelt: Letters and Speeches*, ed. Louis Auchincloss (New York: Library of America, 2004), 803.
15. Roosevelt, 812–13.
16. Fred Block, "Read Their Lips: Taxation and the Right-Wing Agenda," in *The New Fiscal Sociology: Taxation in Comparative and Historical Perspective*, ed. Isaac William Martin, Ajay K. Mehrotra, and Monica Prasad (New York: Cambridge University Press, 2009), 68.
17. Gary Gerstle argues that "Conservative Republicans have been so successful in demonizing income taxes that it is now impossible to imagine raising them to anywhere near the rates that prevailed from the 1940s through 1970s." This limitation of revenue, Gerstle argues, has undermined Congress's ability to confront such issues as immigration, climate change, and aging infrastructure; has inhibited the work of federal agencies and hastened regulatory capture; and has generally undermined governmental competence and public confidence, which in turn fuels increased pressure for (and ideological celebration of) privatization of key services. He concludes: "All these developments reflect the success of the Republican Party in making its antigovernment ideology predominant." See Gary Gerstle, *Liberty and Coercion: The Paradox of American Government from the Founding to the Present* (Princeton: Princeton University Press, 2015), 337–38.
18. Mike O'Connor, *A Commercial Republic: America's Enduring Debate over Democratic Capitalism* (Lawrence: University Press of Kansas, 2014), 203.
19. Jennifer Burns, "Liberalism and the Conservative Imagination," in *Liberalism for a New Century*, ed. Neil Jumonville and Kevin Mattson (Berkeley: University of California Press, 2007), 60. Even among the pro-market thinkers of the Mont Pèlerin Society (a group founded after World War II by Friedrich Hayek), a schism had emerged by the early 1960s, concluding in a turn toward more aggressively laissez-faire views. As Angus Burgin writes, the group became "unapologetically oriented toward technical economics, and inhospitable to those who did not subscribe to the near-universal preferability of free markets

to the alternatives." See Angus Burgin, *The Great Persuasion: Reinventing Free Markets Since the Depression* (Cambridge, MA: Harvard University Press, 2012), 125.
20. Burns, "Liberalism and the Conservative Imagination," 69.
21. Ajay K. Mehrotra, *Making the Modern American Fiscal State: Law, Politics, and the Rise of Progressive Taxation, 1877–1929* (New York: Cambridge University Press, 2013), 414.
22. Block, "Read Their Lips," 69–70.
23. This distinctive interpretation of freedom was both an earnest belief and a self-conscious political strategy. Conservative intellectuals of the 1950s were acutely aware that they could make political progress against the reigning New Deal coalition by influencing the public's understanding of freedom. See Eric Foner, *The Story of American Freedom* (New York: W. W. Norton, 1998), 308–309. On the international network of neoliberal intellectuals who helped to effect this change, see Burgin, *The Great Persuasion*; Jamie Peck, "Remaking Laissez-Faire," *Progress in Human Geography* 32, no. 1 (Feb. 2008): 3–43, https://doi.org/10.1177/0309132507084816; Philip Mirowski and Dieter Plehwe, eds., *The Road from Mont Pelerin: The Making of the Neoliberal Thought Collective* (Cambridge, MA: Harvard University Press, 2009).
24. Robin Einhorn's study of American taxation succinctly captures the irony of this development: "The antigovernment rhetoric that continues to saturate our political life is rooted in slavery rather than liberty. The American mistrust of government is not part of our democratic heritage. It comes from slaveholding elites who had no experience with democratic governments where they lived and knew only one thing about democracy: that it threatened slavery. The idea that government is the primary danger to liberty has many sources, but one of its main sources in the United States involved the 'liberty' of some people to hold others as chattel property." See Robin L. Einhorn, *American Taxation, American Slavery* (Chicago: University of Chicago Press, 2006), 7–8. On the ambivalence toward democracy felt by many postwar-era members of Hayek's Mont Pèlerin Society, see Burgin, *The Great Persuasion*, 116–20. On the long history of white supremacy's intertwinement with hostility to the federal government, see Jefferson Cowie, *Freedom's Dominion: A Saga of White Resistance to Federal Power* (New York: Basic Books, 2022).
25. Derek Parfit, *Equality or Priority?*, The Lindley Lecture, University of Kansas, 1995, 22–23.
26. Parfit, 23–26.
27. Parfit, 17.
28. Harry G. Frankfurt, *On Inequality* (Princeton: Princeton University Press, 2015), 7. Emphasis in original.
29. Parfit, *Equality or Priority?*, 23. Emphasis in original.
30. Elizabeth S. Anderson, "Equality," in *The Oxford Handbook of Political Philosophy*, ed. David Estlund (New York: Oxford University Press, 2012), 55, https://doi.org/10.1093/oxfordhb/9780195376692.013.0002. The original, and most significant, statement of Anderson's view appears in Elizabeth S. Anderson, "What Is the Point of Equality?," *Ethics* 109, no. 2 (Jan. 1999): 287–337, https://doi.org/10.1086/233897.
31. Anderson, "Equality," 46.
32. Anderson, 53.
33. T. M. Scanlon, "The Diversity of Objections to Inequality," in *The Difficulty of Tolerance: Essays in Political Philosophy* (Cambridge: Cambridge University Press, 2003), 202–7.

34. On this point, see generally Christian Schemmel, *Justice and Egalitarian Relations* (Oxford University Press, 2021), chap. 8, https://doi.org/10.1093/oso/9780190084240.001.0001.
35. David Rondel, "Egalitarians, Sufficientarians, and Mathematicians: A Critical Notice of Harry Frankfurt's 'On Inequality,'" *Canadian Journal of Philosophy* 46, no. 2 (2016): 154.
36. O'Neill, "What Should Egalitarians Believe?," 153.
37. O'Neill, 137–39.
38. Mehrotra, *Making the Modern American Fiscal State*, 414. Mehrotra extends this critique further in noting that while economists' complaints of inefficiency in the tax code demonstrate a "sharp analytical logic," they nonetheless "elide the complex historical and incremental development" of American policymaking, overlooking with their "ahistorical assessments ... how earlier conceptions of fiscal citizenship, social belonging, and collective responsibility" motivated earlier generations of tax reformers. This failure of historical memory is likewise mirrored in public debate, which is "clouded" by "anti-statist rhetoric and anti-tax ideology" that has caused Americans to lose sight "of how and why activists from earlier generations searched for a stronger source of financing for the positive state." Mehrotra, 417.
39. Block, "Read Their Lips," 69.
40. Rodgers, *Age of Fracture*, 41.
41. "It Is Not to Be in Oak Park," *The Montgomery Advertiser*, December 24, 1958.
42. Heather McGhee, *The Sum of Us: What Racism Costs Everyone and How We Can Prosper Together* (New York: One World, 2021), 25–26. On the history of efforts to integrate Montgomery's parks, and the fate of Oak Park, see Silvia Giagnoni, *Here We May Rest: Alabama Immigrants in the Age of HB 56* (Montgomery: NewSouth Books, 2017), 224–25; Wayne Greenhaw, *Fighting the Devil in Dixie: How Civil Rights Activists Took on the Ku Klux Klan in Alabama* (Chicago: Lawrence Hill Books, 2011), 61–62; and J. Mills Thornton III, *Dividing Lines: Municipal Politics and the Struggle for Civil Rights in Montgomery, Birmingham, and Selma* (Tuscaloosa: University of Alabama Press, 2002), 102.
43. Thomas Byrne Edsall and Mary D. Edsall, *Chain Reaction: The Impact of Race, Rights, and Taxes on American Politics* (New York: W. W. Norton, 1991), 11.
44. Ira Katznelson, *Fear Itself: The New Deal and the Origins of Our Time* (New York: Liveright, 2013), 159.
45. This coalition sometimes produced results that make for strange reading for Americans accustomed to the stable ideological-racial coalitions of today's parties. For example, objections to a national minimum wage were not only raised by pro-business conservatives asserting the primacy of capital, but also by a Democratic congressman from Texas who protested: "You cannot prescribe the same wage for the black man as for the white man." See Katznelson, 177.
46. Katznelson, 187–88.
47. Martin H. Wolfson, *Financial Crises: Understanding the Postwar U.S. Experience*, 2nd ed. (Armonk, NY: M.E. Sharpe, 1994), 31.
48. Edsall and Edsall, *Chain Reaction*, 7.
49. Martin Gilens, *Why Americans Hate Welfare: Race, Media, and the Politics of Antipoverty Policy* (Chicago: University of Chicago Press, 1999); Michael Tesler and David O. Sears, *Obama's Race: The 2008 Election and the Dream of a Post-Racial America*, Chicago Studies in American Politics (Chicago: University of Chicago Press, 2010); Michael Tesler,

"The Spillover of Racialization into Health Care: How President Obama Polarized Public Opinion by Racial Attitudes and Race," *American Journal of Political Science* 56, no. 3 (July 2012): 690–704, https://doi.org/10.1111/j.1540-5907.2011.00577.x.

50. Kevin M. Kruse, *White Flight: Atlanta and the Making of Modern Conservatism* (Princeton: Princeton University Press, 2005), chap. 9.
51. K. Sabeel Rahman, "Constructing Citizenship: Exclusion and Inclusion Through the Governance of Basic Necessities," *Columbia Law Review* 118, no. 8 (Dec. 2018): 2482; see also Stephen Tuck, *We Ain't What We Ought to Be: The Black Freedom Struggle from Emancipation to Obama* (Cambridge, MA: Belknap Press of Harvard University Press, 2010), 356–57.
52. Rahman, "Constructing Citizenship," 2451. Emphasis in original.
53. Kruse, *White Flight*, 258.
54. William Schambra, "Progressive Liberalism and American 'Community,'" *The Public Interest*, no. 80 (Summer 1985): 42. Emphasis in original.
55. Schambra, 33, 48.
56. Schambra, 42. Of this argument, a later commentator would astutely note: "Calhoun's theory of still separate and sovereign states is not as anachronistic as it may appear... Without mentioning Calhoun by name, a leading conservative theorist once offered a Calhounian denial of nationhood as the theoretical ground of the Reagan Revolution." See Barber, *The Fallacies of States' Rights*, 133.
57. Foner, *The Story of American Freedom*, 322, 324.
58. Joseph Crespino, *In Search of Another Country: Mississippi and the Conservative Counterrevolution* (Princeton: Princeton University Press, 2007), 1.
59. In fact, Americans not only disapprove of inequality, but they also underestimate its severity, suggesting that they would disapprove even more strongly if they understood its extent. See Michael I. Norton and Dan Ariely, "Building a Better America—One Wealth Quintile at a Time," *Perspectives on Psychological Science* 6, no. 1 (Jan. 2011): 9–12, https://doi.org/10.1177/1745691610393524.
60. As one critic has noted, the idea of a democratic state involved in what was once called the "mixed economy" has "disappear[ed] from normal conversation. The losses aren't just material, to be measured in terms of decaying infrastructure and poorly governed markets. They are ideological too, with a central function of the state disappearing from our worldview." See Mike Konczal, "The Forgotten State," *Boston Review*, August 2016, http://bostonreview.net/books-ideas/mike-konczal-yuval-levin-fractured-republic-jacob-hacker-paul-pierson-american-amnesia.
61. Jacob S. Hacker and Paul Pierson, *American Amnesia: How the War on Government Led Us to Forget What Made America Prosper* (New York: Simon & Schuster, 2016), 198.
62. Brown, *Undoing the Demos*, 153.
63. Thomas Piketty and Emmanuel Saez, "Income Inequality in the United States, 1913–1998," *The Quarterly Journal of Economics* 118, no. 1 (Feb. 2003): 11.
64. Piketty and Saez, 11.
65. Claudia Goldin and Robert A. Margo, "The Great Compression: The Wage Structure in the United States at Mid-Century," *The Quarterly Journal of Economics* 107, no. 1 (1992): 31, https://doi.org/10.2307/2118322.
66. Goldin and Margo, 2.
67. Goldin and Margo.

68. See Thomas Piketty, "Income, Wage, and Wealth Inequality in France, 1901–98," in *Top Incomes over the Twentieth Century: A Contrast Between European and English-Speaking Countries*, ed. A. B. Atkinson and Thomas Piketty (New York: Oxford University Press, 2007), 68.
69. As Alan Brinkley writes, many New Dealers had assumed in the 1930s that the U.S. was entering a new phrase of permanently low growth, which would require the government to adopt a larger fiscal role (in supplementing low levels of private investment) and regulatory role (in protecting consumers against collusion by fragile corporations). But the disappointing track record of New Deal managerialism, combined with the surprising resurgence of economic growth, "helped erode one of the mainstays of late-Depression liberalism" by "plac[ing] the concept of growth at the center of liberal hopes." The surprise of growth convinced many liberals that "social and economic advancement could proceed, therefore, without structural changes in capitalism and without continuing, intrusive state management of the economy." This seemed to justify a more optimistic pursuit of full employment, not through "state management of capitalist institutions, but [through] fiscal policies that would promote consumption and thus stimulate economic growth." See Alan Brinkley, "The New Deal and the Idea of the State," in *The Rise and Fall of the New Deal Order, 1930–1980*, ed. Gary Gerstle and Steve Fraser (Princeton: Princeton University Press, 1989), 98–99, 105–106.
70. David Grewal and Jedediah Purdy suggest this possibility: "However, during the *trente glorieuses*, Keynesian macroeconomic planning and a favorable international context reconciled the imperatives of capital accumulation and democratic legitimacy through sustained and relatively equitably shared growth ... Thus, the tensions inherent in democratic capitalism were effectively evaded in the immediate decades following World War II through what Charles Maier called 'the politics of productivity.' Rising wages and capital accumulation proved mutually compatible and even allowed for the modest redistribution that the more ambitious welfare states of the period undertook." David Grewal and Jedediah Purdy, "Law and Neoliberalism," *Law and Contemporary Problems* 77, no. 4 (2015): 21–22.
71. Daniel Rodgers identifies the macroeconomics discipline around the early 1960s, particularly after the discovery of an apparent trade-off between unemployment and inflation, as experiencing a "peak" in "confidence in economic management for full-capacity employment." Scarcely a decade later, the economic crisis of the 1970s seriously undermined this prestige and confidence, resulting in a "collapse of economic predictability" and a "crisis in ideas and intellectual authority" for left-of-center Keynesian macroeconomists. See Rodgers, *Age of Fracture*, 47–49.
72. Quoted in Theodore Lowi, "The New Public Philosophy: Interest-Group Liberalism," in *The Political Economy: Readings in the Politics and Economics of American Public Policy*, ed. Thomas Ferguson and Joel Rogers (Armonk, NY: M.E. Sharpe, 1984), 58.
73. John F. Kennedy, "Commencement Address at Yale University, June 11, 1962," John F. Kennedy Presidential Library and Museum, https://www.jfklibrary.org/Research/Research-Aids/JFK-Speeches/Yale-University_19620611.aspx.
74. Kennedy.
75. Franklin Delano Roosevelt, "Acceptance Speech for the Renomination for the Presidency, Philadelphia, Pa.," June 27, 1936, American Presidency Project, UC Santa Barbara, http://www.presidency.ucsb.edu/ws/?pid=15314. Emphasis added. Joseph Fishkin and William

Forbath identify the New Deal as the climactic moment in a clash over constitutional political economy that went back as far as the Jacksonian era, and they label Roosevelt's 1936 nomination acceptance speech as "the democracy-of-opportunity tradition—the anti-oligarchy Constitution—in its purest modern form." See Joseph R., Fishkin and William E. Forbath, *The Anti-Oligarchy Constitution: Reconstructing the Economic Foundations of American Democracy* (Cambridge, MA: Harvard University Press, 2022), 252. But as they observe, and as noted earlier in this chapter, Roosevelt's program was limited by what the Southern wing of his party regarded as the proper scope of the distributive community. See also Katznelson, *Fear Itself*.

76. Gerstle, *American Crucible: Race and Nation in the Twentieth* Century (Princeton: Princeton University Press, 2001), 267.
77. After all, it is possible to imagine technocrats empowered to self-consciously pursue a social-democratic agenda—and in fact, a combination of this sort characterized Progressive ambition in earlier decades. As Richard Adelstein has noted, Progressive thinkers were attracted, for political reasons, to "the new, empirical social sciences and techniques of control derived from them": "Once the laws that governed modern civilization were understood, humankind could turn them to the collective good . . . Politics could be separated from administration; while the former concerned itself with articulating the common good, the latter could draw upon neutral theories of management science to bring it about." Richard P. Adelstein, "'The Nation as an Economic Unit': Keynes, Roosevelt, and the Managerial Ideal," *The Journal of American History* 78, no. 1 (June 1991): 166, https://doi.org/10.2307/2078092. K. Sabeel Rahman has expressed skepticism that technocracy and left-wing politics can be combined in this way; for Rahman, managerialism is unlikely to become the servant of social democracy precisely because its rationale, for most people, is rooted in a quixotic hope to escape ideology. The appeal of technocracy, argues Rahman, "derives from an idealized vision of objective, neutral expertise motivated by ethics of professionalism and bureaucratic discipline. This technocratic impulse is also driven by a faith in the ability of such experts to determine and then pursue the common good independently of the partialities and vagaries of politics." K. Sabeel Rahman, "Conceptualizing the Economic Role of the State: Laissez-Faire, Technocracy, and the Democratic Alternative," *Polity* 43, no. 2 (Apr. 2011): 270.
78. Joseph R. Fishkin and William E. Forbath, "Wealth, Commonwealth, and the Constitution of Opportunity," in *Wealth: NOMOS LVIII*, ed. Jack Knight and Melissa Schwartzberg, Nomos: Yearbook of the American Society for Political and Legal Philosophy 58 (New York: New York University Press, 2017), 53–54.
79. Forbath and Fishkin refer to the decline of the "constitution of opportunity" tradition in the 1960s as a "great forgetting" that occurred at an "inopportune moment." The advocates of that tradition had sought to show that the Constitution makes substantive demands on the structure of the nation's political economy, but they came to abandon that argument for largely pragmatic reasons. Just as it was abandoned, the period of growth that the Johnson administration had relied on, and which midcentury liberals had come to take for granted, came to a halt. See Fishkin and Forbath, 58–59. Michael Katz offers a similar interpretation, writing that as a result of 1970s stagflation, "public psychology shifted away from its relatively relaxed attitude toward the expansion of social welfare," with significant effects: "Increasingly worried about downward mobility and their children's future, many Americans returned to an older psychology of scarcity. As they examined

the sources of their distress, looking for both villains and ways to cut public spending, ordinary Americans and their elected representatives focused on welfare and its beneficiaries, deflecting attention from the declining profits and returns on investments that, since the mid-1970s, should have alerted them to the end of unlimited growth and abundance." Michael B. Katz, *The Undeserving Poor: America's Enduring Confrontation with Poverty*, 2nd ed. (New York: Oxford University Press, 2013), 164.

80. O'Connor, *A Commercial Republic*, 200. See also Katrina Forrester, *In the Shadow of Justice: Postwar Liberalism and the Remaking of Political Philosophy* (Princeton: Princeton University Press, 2019), xi.

81. Rawls, *A Theory of Justice* (Cambridge, MA: Belknap Press of Harvard University Press, 1971), 7; Charles R. Beitz, *Political Theory and International Relations* (Princeton: Princeton University Press, 1979); Thomas W. Pogge, *Realizing Rawls* (Ithaca: Cornell University Press, 1989).

82. See, e.g., Herbert Croly, *The Promise of American Life* (1909, repr., Princeton: Princeton University Press, 2014). On FDR's deployment and radicalization of civic nationalist themes, see Gerstle, *American Crucible*, chap. 4.

83. Burns, "Liberalism and the Conservative Imagination," 64–65.

84. Jacob Hacker and Paul Pierson have argued that stagflation was not only a crisis moment for believers in the mixed economy but also a major opportunity for a well-prepared opposition ready to step into the vacuum of intellectual authority. Had these critics not been "at the ready," stagflation "would not have precipitated such a fundamental reversal" in the fortunes of the mixed-economy tradition. See Hacker and Pierson, *American Amnesia*, 171–72. Similarly, Mark Blyth argues that understanding the "crisis" of the 1970s requires attention to ideational factors, since "what constitutes an economic crisis *as a crisis* is not a self-apparent phenomenon." Ignoring such factors impoverishes our ability to understand institutional reorganizations in the post-1970s political economy: "Since structures do not come with an instruction sheet, economic ideas make such an institutional resolution possible by providing the authoritative diagnosis as to what a crisis *actually is* and when a given situation *actually constitutes* a crisis. They diagnose 'what has gone wrong' and 'what is to be done.' In short, the nature of a crisis is not simply given by its effects, dislocations, or casualties, nor are the actions of agents simply determined by their 'given' interests. Instead, the diagnosis of a situation as a 'crisis' by a particular set of ideas is a construction that makes the uncertainty that agents perceive explicable, manageable, and indeed, actionable. Therefore, in periods of *economic crisis*, it is imperative to attend to the *economic ideas* that key economic agents have." Mark Blyth, *Great Transformations: Economic Ideas and Institutional Change in the Twentieth Century* (New York: Cambridge University Press, 2002), 9, 10. Emphasis in original. Regarding liberals' failure to "produce a convincing counter-narrative," see Katz, *The Undeserving Poor*, 167. See also K. Sabeel Rahman, *Democracy Against Domination* (New York: Oxford University Press, 2017), 33.

85. Rahman, *Democracy Against Domination*, 32.

86. Rodgers, *Age of Fracture*, 76.

87. William F. Buckley Jr., "The Case for Goldwater," in *Athwart History: Half a Century of Polemics, Animadversions, and Illuminations: A William F. Buckley Jr. Omnibus*, ed. Linda Bridges and Roger Kimball (New York: Encounter Books, 2010), 69.

88. Burns, "Liberalism and the Conservative Imagination."

89. Barry M. Goldwater, *The Conscience of a Conservative*, ed. C. C. Goldwater (Princeton: Princeton University Press, 2007), 53.
90. Goldwater, 55. Emphasis in original.
91. Goldwater, 56. Emphasis in original.
92. Goldwater, 56. Emphasis in original. Later in the chapter, Goldwater lists in more detail those areas where the federal government is acting outside its constitutional authority: "The government must begin to *withdraw* from a whole series of programs that are outside its constitutional mandate—from social welfare programs, education, public power, agriculture, public housing, urban renewal and all the other activities that can be better performed by lower levels of government or by private institutions or by individuals... It is only through this kind of determined assault on the principle of unlimited government that American people will obtain relief from high taxes, and will start making progress toward regaining their freedom." See Goldwater, 61–62.
93. Goldwater, 54. Emphasis in original.
94. Goldwater, 54.
95. Goldwater, 55.
96. Goldwater, 56–57. Emphasis in original.
97. Goldwater, 57. Emphasis in original.
98. Joseph R. Fishkin and William E. Forbath, "Congress Has Broad Power to Tax," National Constitution Center, accessed March 9, 2018, https://constitutioncenter.org/interactive-constitution/amendments/amendment-xvi.
99. This remark appears in a discussion of farm subsidies: "The reason government intervention has created more problems than it has solved is quite simple. *Farm production, like any other production is best controlled by the natural operation of the free market*... If, however, the government interferes with this natural economic process, and pegs prices higher than the consumer is willing to pay, the result will be, in Hamilton's phrase, 'troublesome.'" See Goldwater, *The Conscience of a Conservative*, 36. Emphasis in original.
100. Ian Shapiro, "Resources, Capacities, and Ownership: The Workmanship Ideal and Distributive Justice," *Political Theory* 19, no. 1 (1991): 47–48. Goldwater brings these preindustrial arguments into the modern era by acknowledging that earnings are just as much a form of property as land—indeed, he writes that "in the industrial age, earnings are probably the most prevalent form of property." See Goldwater, *The Conscience of a Conservative*, 54.
101. There is a long and "vituperative debate," as Shapiro notes, over the ideal's caveat that the resources must be justly acquired. See Shapiro, "Resources, Capacities, and Ownership," 48.
102. Einhorn, *American Taxation, American Slavery*, 3.
103. In a similar vein, Fred Block notes that market fundamentalism's appeal to conservative voters can be explained in "geographic and racial" terms: "The heartland of the religious Right coincides with the states of the old Confederacy that harbor a long-standing hostility to the power of the federal government. In the aftermath of the civil rights movement, when Southern voters abandoned the Democratic Party in huge numbers, they embraced Republican politicians who echoed the traditional state's rights rhetoric of Southern Democratic politicians. Because the federal government in that period was clearly aligned with the aspirations for equality of African Americans and women, hostility to federal taxation had an obvious appeal to conservatives who resisted racial and

gender equality." Block notes that this explanation does not account for opposition to taxation at the state level, which is partly accounted for by the naturalist outlook I discuss here. See Block, "Read Their Lips," 77.
104. Brown, *Undoing the Demos*, 176.
105. Milton Friedman, *Capitalism and Freedom* (Chicago: University of Chicago Press, 1962), 13. Emphasis in original.
106. For a thorough summary, see Steven Vogel, *Marketcraft: How Governments Make Markets Work* (New York: Oxford University Press, 2018).
107. Larry M. Bartels, *Unequal Democracy: The Political Economy of the New Gilded Age*, 2nd ed. (Princeton: Princeton University Press, 2016), 23.
108. See Albert O. Hirschman, *The Rhetoric of Reaction: Perversity, Futility, Jeopardy* (Cambridge, MA: Belknap Press of Harvard University Press, 1991). Michael Katz traced the argument from perversity to "the oldest and most coherent tradition in the political economy of poverty in the United States as well as in Europe," a tradition that "views the poor as the unfortunate casualties of a dynamic, competitive economy, unable to gain a secure foothold on the ladder of opportunity and too incompetent or ill-disciplined to reap the bounty of increasing productivity." According to thinkers within this tradition, "aiding them with charity or relief only interferes with the natural working of markets, retards growth, and, in the end, does more harm than good. Often dressed with quantitative sophistication and theoretical skill, this idea has retained an amazing purchase on popular thought as well as on politics. The widowed, the sick, and a few others remain exceptions, but for the most part the poor are losers." Katz, *The Undeserving Poor*, 272.
109. Margaret Somers calls this the "binary logic of *social naturalism*," an "epistemological construct" that first divides the social world into natural and unnatural categories and then "assigns epistemological privilege and ontological superiority to those entities deemed natural, such as the market," while it "demeans all that is deemed unnatural, such as the state." Margaret R. Somers, *Genealogies of Citizenship: Markets, Statelessness, and the Right to Have Rights* (Cambridge: Cambridge University Press, 2008), 33.
110. The normative implications of this point are obviously not limited to domestic economic matters, although—following the relational approach described earlier in the chapter—I do not explore implications for transnational and global political economy here, since social relations among democratic citizens are generally thicker and thus raise distinctive demands from the perspective of egalitarianism. Moreover, since I am chiefly concerned with those frameworks of interpretation and debate through which citizens of a democracy can understand economic governance as part of their broader, ongoing project of collective self-rule, I pay special attention to the democratic *state*, whose boundaries mark, in principle, the scope of the political actor that bears ultimate responsibility for bringing the market into existence and facilitating its operation.
111. Inequality, e.g., dampens political engagement and biases political participation toward the rich, which partly explains why politicians (themselves from affluent backgrounds) enact policies that benefit the already affluent, perpetuating an oligarchic cycle that uses political power to direct more wealth and, ultimately, more political power to the wealthy. See Frederick Solt, "Economic Inequality and Democratic Political Engagement," *American Journal of Political Science* 52, no. 1 (Jan. 2008): 48–60; Kay Lehman Schlozman, Sidney Verba, and Henry E. Brady, *The Unheavenly Chorus: Unequal Political Voice and the Broken Promise of American Democracy* (Princeton: Princeton University Press,

2012); Martin Gilens, *Affluence and Influence: Economic Inequality and Political Power in America* (Princeton: Princeton University Press, 2012).
112. Spalding, "The String-Pullers."
113. Obama, "Remarks by the President on the Economy in Osawatomie, Kansas." Emphasis added.
114. Robert Rector and Rachel Sheffield, "Air Conditioning, Cable TV, and an Xbox: What Is Poverty in the United States Today?," Heritage Foundation, July 18, 2011, 2, https://www.heritage.org/poverty-and-inequality/report/air-conditioning-cable-tv-and-xbox-what-poverty-the-united-states.
115. Rector and Sheffield, 6.
116. Rector and Sheffield, 20.
117. Rector and Sheffield, 20.
118. Derek Thompson, "30 Million in Poverty Aren't as Poor as You Think, Says Heritage Foundation," *The Atlantic*, July 19, 2011, https://www.theatlantic.com/business/archive/2011/07/30-million-in-poverty-arent-as-poor-as-you-think-says-heritage-foundation/242191/; Joseph E. Stiglitz, *The Price of Inequality: How Today's Divided Society Endangers Our Future* (New York: W. W. Norton, 2012), 32–33.
119. Rector and Sheffield, "Air Conditioning, Cable TV, and an Xbox," 20. Emphasis added.
120. Joseph R. Fishkin and William E. Forbath, "The Anti-Oligarchy Constitution," *Boston University Law Review* 94, no. 3 (May 2014): 693.
121. "Ronald Reagan: Remarks to Business Leaders in Cincinnati, Ohio," October 3, 1985, American Presidency Project, UC Santa Barbara, http://www.presidency.ucsb.edu/ws/?pid=37850.
122. Blyth, *Great Transformations*, 190.
123. Friedman, *Capitalism and Freedom*, xiv.

Conclusion

1. Walt Whitman, "Democratic Vistas," in *Complete Poetry and Selected Prose*, ed. James E. Miller, Jr., Riverside Editions (Boston: Houghton Mifflin, 1959), 455.
2. Whitman, 474–75.
3. Whitman, 459.
4. Whitman, 459.
5. Whitman, 460.
6. Whitman, 460.
7. Ralph Ellison, "Roscoe Dunjee and the American Language," in *The Collected Essays of Ralph Ellison*, ed. John Callahan (New York: Modern Library, 2003), 459.
8. James Baldwin, *No Name in the Street* (New York: Vintage International, 2007), 10. Emphasis in original.
9. Sumner, "'Are We a Nation?' (Address Before the New York Young Men's Republican Union at the Cooper Institute, November 19, 1867)," 3.
10. See, e.g., Rev. Dr. William J. Barber II and Jonathan Wilson-Hartgrove, *The Third Reconstruction: Moral Mondays, Fusion Politics, and the Rise of a New Justice Movement* (Boston: Beacon Press, 2016); Robert Greene, "The Urgency of a Third Reconstruction," *Dissent*, July 9, 2018, https://www.dissentmagazine.org/online_articles/the-urgency-of-a-third-reconstruction; K. Sabeel Rahman, "Reconstructing Democracy," *Democracy*

Journal, December 6, 2018, https://democracyjournal.org/arguments/reconstructing-democracy/. In 2015, *The Nation* hosted a panel discussion entitled "Toward a Third Reconstruction" featuring Eric Foner, Darryl Pinckney, Mychal Denzel Smith, Isabel Wilkerson, and Patricia J. Williams. See The Nation, "Toward a Third Reconstruction," Schomburg Center for Research in Black Culture, March 23, 2015, https://www.thenation.com/article/toward-third-reconstruction/.

11. Sumner, "'Are We a Nation?,'" 34.
12. Harold Holzer, ed., "The Third Joint Debate at Jonesboro, September 15, 1858," in *The Lincoln-Douglas Debates: The First Complete, Unexpurgated Text* (New York: Fordham University Press, 2004), 151.
13. Hawes Spencer and Sheryl Gay Stolberg, "Virginia Town Is on Edge over Confederate Statue," *The New York Times*, August 11, 2017, sec. A; Paul Duggan, "Four Alleged Members of Hate Group Charged in 2017 'Unite the Right' Rally in Charlottesville," *The Washington Post*, October 2, 2018.
14. A. C. Thompson and Ford Fischer, "Members of Several Well-Known Hate Groups Identified at Capitol Riot," *ProPublica*, January 9, 2021, https://www.propublica.org/article/several-well-known-hate-groups-identified-at-capitol-riot?token=nKHfqzzFyex_uZ4Pu7DPxey6pD87Kv3z.
15. Anthony Michael Kreis, "The New Redeemers," *Georgia Law Review* 55, no. 4 (Summer 2021): 1483–1528.
16. Steven Levitsky and Daniel Ziblatt write that "it was only after 1965 that the United States fully democratized." See Steven Levitsky and Daniel Ziblatt, *How Democracies Die* (New York: Crown, 2018), 204. Similarly, Francisco E. González and Desmond King write that the "implementation of the (1964) Civil Rights and the (1965) Voting Rights Acts . . . made the United States a full liberal democracy." Francisco E. González and Desmond King, "The State and Democratization: The United States in Comparative Perspective," *British Journal of Political Science* 34, no. 2 (2004): 195.
17. Kermit Roosevelt, "The Voting Rights Act and the Second Redemption," *Constitution Daily* (blog), National Constitution Center, August 5, 2015, https://constitutioncenter.org/blog/the-voting-rights-act-and-the-second-redemption; Adam Serwer, "Welcome to the Second Redemption," *The Atlantic*, November 10, 2016, https://www.theatlantic.com/politics/archive/2016/11/welcome-to-the-second-redemption/507317/; Richard Primus, "Second Redemption, Third Reconstruction," *California Law Review* 106, no. 6 (Dec. 2018): 1987–2000, https://doi.org/10.15779/Z383R0PT5J.
18. Levitsky and Ziblatt, *How Democracies Die*, 1.
19. Levitsky and Ziblatt, 9.
20. Jack M. Balkin, *The Cycles of Constitutional Time* (New York: Oxford University Press, 2020), 45–46.
21. Steven Levitsky and Daniel Ziblatt, "Is Our Democracy Wobbly?," *The New York Times*, January 27, 2018, sec. Sunday Review.
22. Corey Robin, "Democracy Is Norm Erosion," *Jacobin*, January 29, 2018, https://jacobin.com/2018/01/democracy-trump-authoritarianism-levitsky-zillblatt-norms.
23. Jedediah Britton-Purdy, "Normcore," *Dissent*, Summer 2018.
24. Levitsky and Ziblatt, *How Democracies Die*, 195.
25. Ashraf Ahmed, "A Theory of Constitutional Norms," *Michigan Law Review* 120, no. 7 (May 2022): 1363, 1381, https://doi.org/10.36644/mlr.120.7.theory; Robin, "Democracy Is Norm Erosion"; Britton-Purdy, "Normcore."

26. Levitsky and Ziblatt, *How Democracies Die*, 9.
27. Smith, *Civic Ideals: Conflicting Visions of Citizenship in U.S. History* (New Haven: Yale University Press, 1997), 490.
28. Smith, 490.
29. In practice, whether this happens will not only depend on whether the United States can overcome the threat of the candidly antidemocratic far right. The threats to identification in the contemporary U.S. are more systemic and require a richer conception of how citizens might be empowered to imagine their civic community in broader and more inclusive terms. These threats include profound disruptions to the information and media ecosystem of the modern U.S., which is characterized by the decline or demise of important news outlets (including public media), the rise of oligarchic or otherwise unaccountable control, the often-manipulative role played by algorithms and tech platforms, and so on. While these problems have been widely discussed, their importance to democratic solidarity *specifically* is often understated; normally, they are framed in terms of citizens losing access to reliable information about (e.g.) the actions of their representatives, the substance of proposed laws, important events in their community, etc. But from the perspective of democratic self-rule, the ideal of an informed public refers not only to citizens' level of policy knowledge but also to their tendency to read, imagine, listen, converse, empathize, etc. in ways that intersubjectively generate the perspective of a democratic "We." Failures of political knowledge extend well beyond the most familiar forms of voter ignorance (such as the inability to identify key leaders, accurately describe basic elements of the constitutional structure, and so on). A high level of policy knowledge could be attained in solitude, without citizens either consulting or prioritizing each other's perspectives, but democratic self-determination envisions a more demanding, and more social, process—one that relies on a rich media landscape that brings citizens into contact with one another. For a longer discussion of these points, see Pippenger, "Listening to Strangers, or: Three Arguments for Bounded Solidarity," *American Journal of Political Science* 67, no. 3 (July 2023): 764–75. https://doi.org/10.1111/ajps.12671.

Bibliography

Abizadeh, Arash. "Democratic Theory and Border Coercion: No Right to Unilaterally Control Your Own Borders." *Political Theory* 36, no. 1 (Feb. 2008): 37–65.

Adams, Michelle. "Radical Integration." *California Law Review* 94, no. 2 (Mar. 2006): 261–311. https://doi.org/10.2307/20439036.

Adelstein, Richard P. "'The Nation as an Economic Unit': Keynes, Roosevelt, and the Managerial Ideal." *The Journal of American History* 78, no. 1 (June 1991): 160–87. https://doi.org/10.2307/2078092.

Ahmed, Ashraf. "A Theory of Constitutional Norms." *Michigan Law Review* 120, no. 7 (May 2022): 1361–418. https://doi.org/10.36644/mlr.120.7.theory.

Allen, Danielle S. *Our Declaration: A Reading of the Declaration of Independence in Defense of Equality*. New York: Liveright, 2014.

Allen, Danielle S. *Talking to Strangers: Anxieties of Citizenship Since Brown v. Board of Education*. Chicago: University of Chicago Press, 2004.

Anderson, Elizabeth S. "Democracy: Instrumental vs. Non-Instrumental Value." In *Contemporary Debates in Political Philosophy*, edited by Thomas Christiano and John Christman, 213–27. Chichester, West Sussex, U.K.: Wiley-Blackwell, 2009.

Anderson, Elizabeth S. "The Epistemology of Democracy." *Episteme: A Journal of Social Epistemology* 3, nos. 1–2 (June 2006): 8–22. https://doi.org/10.1353/epi.0.0000.

Anderson, Elizabeth S. "Equality." In *The Oxford Handbook of Political Philosophy*, edited by David Estlund, 40–57. New York: Oxford University Press, 2012. https://doi.org/10.1093/oxfordhb/9780195376692.013.0002.

Anderson, Elizabeth S. *The Imperative of Integration*. Princeton: Princeton University Press, 2010.

Anderson, Elizabeth S. "What Is the Point of Equality?" *Ethics* 109, no. 2 (Jan. 1999): 287–337. https://doi.org/10.1086/233897.

Appiah, Kwame Anthony. "Race, Culture, Identity: Misunderstood Connections." In *Color Conscious: The Political Morality of Race*, edited by Kwame Anthony Appiah and Amy Gutmann, 30–105. Princeton: Princeton University Press, 1996.

Baldwin, James. "Down at the Cross: Letter from a Region in My Mind." In his *The Fire Next Time*, Reissue, 11–106. New York: Vintage, 1993.

Baldwin, James. *No Name in the Street*. New York: Vintage International, 2007.

Balkin, Jack M. *The Cycles of Constitutional Time*. New York: Oxford University Press, 2020.

Baraka, Imamu Amiri. "A Reply to Saunders Reddings' 'The Black Revolution in American Studies.'" *American Studies International* 17, no. 4 (Summer 1979): 15–24.

Barber, Sotirios A. *The Fallacies of States' Rights*. Cambridge, MA: Harvard University Press, 2013.

Rev. Dr. William J. Barber, and Jonathan Wilson-Hartgrove. *The Third Reconstruction: Moral Mondays, Fusion Politics, and the Rise of a New Justice Movement*. Boston: Beacon Press, 2016.

Bartels, Larry M. *Unequal Democracy: The Political Economy of the New Gilded Age*. 2nd ed. Princeton: Princeton University Press, 2016.

Beer, Samuel H. *To Make a Nation: The Rediscovery of American Federalism*. Cambridge, MA: Belknap Press of Harvard University Press, 1993.

Beitz, Charles R. *Political Theory and International Relations*. Princeton: Princeton University Press, 1979.

Benhabib, Seyla. *Situating the Self: Gender, Community, and Postmodernism in Contemporary Ethics*. New York: Routledge, 1992.

Bertram, Christopher. "Democracy and the Representation of the Interests of Temporary Migrant Workers." *Law, Ethics and Philosophy*, no. 9 (2022): 170–79. https://doi.org/10.31009/LEAP.2022.V9.11.

Bevir, Mark, and R. A. W. Rhodes. "Interpretation and Its Others." *Australian Journal of Political Science* 40, no. 2 (June 2005): 169–87.

Blake, Michael, and Patrick Taylor Smith. "International Distributive Justice." In *The Stanford Encyclopedia of Philosophy*, edited by Edward N. Zalta, 2015. http://plato.stanford.edu/archives/spr2015/entries/international-justice/.

Blight, David W. *Race and Reunion: The Civil War in American Memory*. Cambridge, MA: Belknap Press of Harvard University Press, 2001.

Block, Fred. "Read Their Lips: Taxation and the Right-Wing Agenda." In *The New Fiscal Sociology: Taxation in Comparative and Historical Perspective*, edited by Isaac William Martin, Ajay K. Mehrotra, and Monica Prasad, 68–85. New York: Cambridge University Press, 2009.

Blyth, Mark. *Great Transformations: Economic Ideas and Institutional Change in the Twentieth Century*. New York: Cambridge University Press, 2002.

Bobo, Lawrence D. "Racial Attitudes and Relations at the Close of Twentieth Century." In *America Becoming: Racial Trends and Their Consequences*, edited by Neil J. Smelser, William Julius Wilson, and Faith Mitchell, vol. 1, 264–301. Washington, D.C.: National Academy Press, 2001. https://doi.org/10.17226/9599.

Bourne, Randolph S. "Trans-National America." *The Atlantic Monthly*, July 1916.

Brinkley, Alan. "The New Deal and the Idea of the State." In *The Rise and Fall of the New Deal Order, 1930–1980*, edited by Gary Gerstle and Steve Fraser, 85–121. Princeton: Princeton University Press, 1989.

Britton-Purdy, Jedediah. "Normcore." *Dissent*, Summer 2018.

Bromell, Nick. *The Time Is Always Now: Black Thought and the Transformation of US Democracy*. New York: Oxford University Press, 2013.

Brooks, Roy L. *Integration or Separation?: A Strategy for Racial Equality*. Cambridge, MA: Harvard University Press, 1996.

Brown et al. v. Board of Education of Topeka et al. (U.S. Supreme Court May 17, 1954).

Brown University Library. "Jay Saunders Redding (1906–1988) Papers." Accessed July 14, 2020. https://library.brown.edu/collatoz/info.php?id=253.

Brown, Wendy. "We Are All Democrats Now. . ." In *Democracy in What State?*, by Giorgio Agamben, Alain Badiou, Daniel Bensaid, Wendy Brown, Jean-Luc Nancy, Jacques Ranciere, Kristin Ross, and Slavoj Žižek, 44–57. New York: Columbia University Press, 2011.

Brown, Wendy. *Undoing the Demos: Neoliberalism's Stealth Revolution*. New York: Zone Books, 2015.

Browne, Robert S. "The Case for Black Separatism." *Ramparts*, December 1967. http://www.unz.org/Pub/Ramparts-1967dec-00046.

Browne, Robert S. "The Case for Two Americas—One Black, One White." *The New York TimesMagazine*, August 11, 1968. http://query.nytimes.com/gst/abstract.html?res=9E06E0DD1F3AE03AA15752C1A96E9C946991D6CF.

Browne, Robert S., and Bayard Rustin. *Separation or Integration: Which Way for America? A Dialogue*. New York: A. Philip Randolph Educational Fund, 1968. http://digitalassets.lib.berkeley.edu/irle/ucb/text/lb001278.pdf.

Brubaker, Rogers, and Frederick Cooper. "Beyond 'Identity.'" *Theory and Society* 29, no. 1 (Feb. 2000): 1–47.

Buckley, William F., Jr. "The Case for Goldwater." In *Athwart History: Half a Century of Polemics, Animadversions, and Illuminations: A William F. Buckley Jr. Omnibus*, edited by Linda Bridges and Roger Kimball, 68–72. New York: Encounter Books, 2010.

Burgin, Angus. *The Great Persuasion: Reinventing Free Markets Since the Depression*. Cambridge, MA: Harvard University Press, 2012.

Burns, Jennifer. "Liberalism and the Conservative Imagination." In *Liberalism for a New Century*, edited by Neil Jumonville and Kevin Mattson, 58–72. Berkeley: University of California Press, 2007.

Carens, Joseph H. "Aliens and Citizens: The Case for Open Borders." *The Review of Politics* 49, no. 2 (Spring 1987): 251–73.

Carens, Joseph H. *The Ethics of Immigration*. New York: Oxford University Press, 2013.

Chang, Howard F. "The Immigration Paradox: Alien Workers and Distributive Justice." In *Citizenship, Borders, and Human Needs*, edited by Rogers M. Smith, 92–114. Philadelphia: University of Pennsylvania Press, 2011.

Clark, Kenneth B. "Letter to Dr. Edward H. Levi, May 14, 1968." In *The Haverford Discussions: A Black Integrationist Manifesto for Racial Justice*, edited by Michael Lackey, 140–43. Charlottesville: University of Virginia Press, 2013.

Coes, Christopher, Jennifer S. Vey, and Tracy Hadden Loh. "The Great Real Estate Reset: A Data-Driven Initiative to Remake How and What We Build." Brookings Institution, December 16, 2020. https://www.brookings.edu/essay/the-great-real-estate-reset-a-data-driven-initiative-to-remake-how-and-what-we-build/.

Cowie, Jefferson. *Freedom's Dominion: A Saga of White Resistance to Federal Power*. New York: Basic Books, 2022.

Cowie, Jefferson. "Reclaiming Patriotism for the Left." *The New York Times*, August 21, 2018, sec. Opinion. https://www.nytimes.com/2018/08/21/opinion/nationalism-patriotism-liberals-.html.

Cramer, Maria. "The Confederate Flag Inside the Capitol a 'Jarring and Disheartening' Sight." *The New York Times*, January 11, 2021, sec. U.S.

Crespino, Joseph. *In Search of Another Country: Mississippi and the Conservative Counterrevolution*. Princeton: Princeton University Press, 2007.

Croly, Herbert. *The Promise of American Life*. 1909. Reprint, Princeton: Princeton University Press, 2014.

Cruse, Harold. "An Afro-American's Cultural Views." In his *Rebellion or Revolution?*, 48–67. Minneapolis: University of Minnesota Press, 1968.

Cruse, Harold Wright. "An Afro-American's Cultural Views." *Présence Africaine*, no. 17 (December 1957): 31–45.

Dawsey, Josh. "Trump Derides Protections for Immigrants from 'Shithole' Countries." *The Washington Post*, January 11, 2018. https://www.washingtonpost.com/politics/trump-attacks-protections-for-immigrants-from-shithole-countries-in-oval-office-meeting/2018/01/11/bfc0725c-f711-11e7-91af-31ac729add94_story.html.

Derrida, Jacques. "Declarations of Independence." *New Political Science* 7, no. 1 (Summer 1986): 7–15.

Dewey, John. "Nationalizing Education." *The Journal of Education* 84, no. 16 (Nov. 2, 1916): 425–28.

Dewey, John. *The Public and Its Problems: An Essay in Political Inquiry*. Edited by Melvin L. Rogers. Athens, OH: Swallow Press, 2016.

Donald, David Herbert. *Charles Sumner and the Coming of the Civil War*. Naperville, IL: Sourcebooks, 2009.

Bibliography

Douglass, Frederick. "The Nation's Problem: An Address Delivered in Washington, D.C., on 16 April 1889." In *The Frederick Douglass Papers*, edited by John W. Blassingame and John R. McKivigan, vol. 5: *1881–95*, 403–26. Frederick Douglass Papers, Series One: Speeches, Debates, and Interviews. New Haven: Yale University Press, 1992.

Douglass, Frederick. "National Depravity." *Frederick Douglass' Paper*, March 3, 1854. Frederick Douglass Newspapers Collection, 1847 to 1874, Library of Congress. https://www.loc.gov/resource/sn84026366/1854-03-03/ed-1/?sp=2.

Douglass, Frederick. "Our Composite Nationality: An Address Delivered in Boston, Massachusetts, on 7 December 1869." In *The Frederick Douglass Papers*, edited by John W. Blassingame and John R. McKivigan, vol. 4: 1864–80, 240–59. Frederick Douglass Papers, Series One: Speeches, Debates, and Interviews. New Haven: Yale University Press, 1991.

Douglass, Frederick. "We Are Here and Want the Ballot-Box: An Address Delivered in Philadelphia, Pennsylvania, on September 4, 1866." In *The Frederick Douglass Papers*, edited by John W. Blassingame and John R. McKivigan, vol. 4: 1864–80, 123–33. Frederick Douglass Papers, Series One: Speeches, Debates, and Interviews. New Haven: Yale University Press, 1991.

Douglass, Frederick. "What to the Slave Is the Fourth of July?: An Address Delivered in Rochester, New York, on 5 July, 1852." In *The Frederick Douglass Papers*, edited by John W. Blassingame, vol. 2: 1847–54, 359–88. Frederick Douglass Papers, Series One: Speeches, Debates, and Interviews. New Haven: Yale University Press, 1982.

Douglass, Frederick. "The Work of the Future (*Douglass' Monthly*, November 1862)." In *Frederick Douglass: Selected Speeches and Writings*, edited by Philip Sheldon Foner and Yuval Taylor, 521–23. Chicago: Chicago Review Press, 1999.

Drachsler, Julius. "The Immigrant and the Realities of Assimilation." *The Interpreter*, September 1924.

Duggan, Paul. "Four Alleged Members of Hate Group Charged in 2017 'Unite the Right' Rally in Charlottesville." *The Washington Post*, October 2, 2018.

Edsall, Thomas Byrne, and Mary D. Edsall. *Chain Reaction: The Impact of Race, Rights, and Taxes on American Politics*. New York: W. W. Norton, 1991.

Einhorn, Robin L. *American Taxation, American Slavery*. Chicago: University of Chicago Press, 2006.

Ellison, Ralph. *Invisible Man*. 2nd Vintage International Edition. New York: Vintage, 1995.

Ellison, Ralph. "Roscoe Dunjee and the American Language." In *The Collected Essays of Ralph Ellison*, edited by John Callahan, 453–64. New York: Modern Library, 2003.

Ellmers, Glenn. "'Conservatism' Is No Longer Enough." *The American Mind*, March 24, 2021. https://americanmind.org/salvo/why-the-claremont-institute-is-not-conservative-and-you-shouldnt-be-either/.

"Examiner's Questions for Admittance to the American (or Know-Nothing) Party, July 1854." July 1854. Manuscript Division, Library of Congress. https://www.loc.gov/resource/mcc.062/?sp=1.

Farhi, Paul. "White House Aide Stephen Miller Held Wide Sway over Breitbart News, According to Emails." *The Washington Post*, November 19, 2019. https://www.washingtonpost.com/lifestyle/style/white-house-aide-stephen-miller-held-wide-sway-over-breitbart-news-according-to-emails/2019/11/19/23e473fa-0ae8-11ea-8397-a955cd542d00_story.html.

Fishkin, Joseph R., and William E. Forbath. "The Anti-Oligarchy Constitution." *Boston University Law Review* 94, no. 3 (May 2014): 669–96.

Fishkin, Joseph R., and William E. Forbath. *The Anti-Oligarchy Constitution: Reconstructing the Economic Foundations of American Democracy*. Cambridge, MA: Harvard University Press, 2022.

Fishkin, Joseph R., and William E. Forbath. "Congress Has Broad Power to Tax." National Constitution Center. Accessed March 9, 2018. https://constitutioncenter.org/interactive-constitution/amendments/amendment-xvi.

Fishkin, Joseph R., and William E. Forbath. "Wealth, Commonwealth, and the Constitution of Opportunity." In *Wealth: NOMOS LVIII*, edited by Jack Knight and Melissa Schwartzberg, 45–124. Nomos: Yearbook of the American Society for Political and Legal Philosophy 58. New York: New York University Press, 2017.

Foner, Eric. *Reconstruction: America's Unfinished Revolution, 1863–1877*. New York: Harper & Row, 1988.

Foner, Eric. *The Story of American Freedom*. New York: W. W. Norton, 1998.

Foner, Eric. "Who Is an American?" In his *Who Owns History? Rethinking the Past in a Changing World*, 149–66. New York: Hill and Wang, 2002.

Foner, Eric, and Randall Kennedy. "Reclaiming Integration." *The Nation*, December 14, 1998.

Forrester, Katrina. *In the Shadow of Justice: Postwar Liberalism and the Remaking of Political Philosophy*. Princeton: Princeton University Press, 2019.

Frank, Jason. *Constituent Moments: Enacting the People in Postrevolutionary America*. Durham: Duke University Press, 2010.

Frankenberg, Erica, Jongyeon Ee, Jennifer B. Ayscue, and Gary Orfield. "Harming Our Common Future: America's Segregated Schools 65 Years after *Brown*." The Civil Rights Project at UCLA, May 10, 2019. https://www.civilrightsproject.ucla.edu/research/k-12-education/integration-and-diversity/harming-our-common-future-americas-segregated-schools-65-years-after-brown.

Frankfurt, Harry G. *On Inequality*. Princeton: Princeton University Press, 2015.

Fraser, C. Gerald. "J. Saunders Redding, 81, Is Dead; Pioneer Black Ivy League Teacher." *The New York Times*, March 5, 1988, sec. Obituaries. https://www.nytimes.com/1988/03/05/obituaries/j-saunders-redding-81-is-dead-pioneer-black-ivy-league-teacher.html.

Freeman, Samuel. "Illiberal Libertarians: Why Libertarianism Is Not a Liberal View." In his *Liberalism and Distributive Justice*, 62–104. New York: Oxford University Press, 2018.

Friedman, Milton. *Capitalism and Freedom*. Chicago: University of Chicago Press, 1962.

Garrison, William Lloyd. *The Letters of William Lloyd Garrison*. Vol. V: *Let the Oppressed Go Free (1861–1867)*. Edited by Walter M. Merrill. Cambridge, MA: Belknap Press of Harvard University Press, 1979.

Gerstle, Gary. *American Crucible: Race and Nation in the Twentieth Century*. Princeton: Princeton University Press, 2001.

Gerstle, Gary. *Liberty and Coercion: The Paradox of American Government from the Founding to the Present*. Princeton: Princeton University Press, 2015.

Giagnoni, Silvia. *Here We May Rest: Alabama Immigrants in the Age of HB 56*. Montgomery: NewSouth Books, 2017.

Gilens, Martin. *Affluence and Influence: Economic Inequality and Political Power in America*. Princeton: Princeton University Press, 2012.

Gilens, Martin. *Why Americans Hate Welfare: Race, Media, and the Politics of Antipoverty Policy*. Chicago: University of Chicago Press, 1999.

Gitlin, Todd. *The Sixties: Years of Hope, Days of Rage*. New York: Bantam, 1987.

Gitlin, Todd. *The Twilight of Common Dreams: Why America Is Wracked by Culture Wars*. New York: Metropolitan Books, 1995.

Glazer, Nathan, Norman Podhoretz, Gunnar Myrdal, Sidney Hook, and James Baldwin. "Liberalism & the Negro: A Round-Table Discussion." *Commentary*, March 1964. https://www.commentarymagazine.com/articles/liberalism-the-negro-a-round-table-discussion/.

Goldin, Claudia, and Robert A. Margo. "The Great Compression: The Wage Structure in the United States at Mid-Century." *The Quarterly Journal of Economics* 107, no. 1 (1992): 1–34. https://doi.org/10.2307/2118322.

Goldwater, Barry M. *The Conscience of a Conservative*. Edited by C. C. Goldwater. Princeton: Princeton University Press, 2007.

González, Francisco E., and Desmond King. "The State and Democratization: The United States in Comparative Perspective." *British Journal of Political Science* 34, no. 2 (2004): 193–210.

Goodin, Robert E. "Enfranchising All Affected Interests, and Its Alternatives." *Philosophy & Public Affairs* 35, no. 1 (Winter 2007): 40–68. https://doi.org/10.1111/j.1088-4963.2007.00098.x.

Grant, Susan-Mary. "A Nation Before Nationalism: The Civic and Ethnic Construction of America." In *The SAGE Handbook of Nations and Nationalism*, edited by Gerard Delanty and Krishan Kumar, 527–40. London: SAGE, 2006.

Greene, Robert. "The Urgency of a Third Reconstruction." *Dissent*, July 9, 2018. https://www.dissentmagazine.org/online_articles/the-urgency-of-a-third-reconstruction.

Greenhaw, Wayne. *Fighting the Devil in Dixie: How Civil Rights Activists Took on the Ku Klux Klan in Alabama*. Chicago: Lawrence Hill Books, 2011.

Grewal, David, and Jedediah Purdy. "Law and Neoliberalism." *Law and Contemporary Problems* 77, no. 4 (2015): 1–23.

"Growth & Opportunity Project." Republican National Committee, March 18, 2013. http://s3.documentcloud.org/documents/623664/republican-national-committees-growth-and.pdf.

Gutmann, Amy. *Democratic Education*. Princeton: Princeton University Press, 1987.

Haas, Hein de. "The Migration and Development Pendulum: A Critical View on Research and Policy." *International Migration* 50, no. 3 (June 2012): 8–25. https://doi.org/10.1111/j.1468-2435.2012.00755.x.

Habermas, Jürgen. "Appendix II: Citizenship and National Identity (1990)." In *Between Facts and Norms: Contributions to a Discourse Theory of Law and Democracy*, translated by William Rehg, 491–515. Cambridge, MA: MIT Press, 1996.

Habermas, Jürgen. "Three Normative Models of Democracy." *Constellations* 1, no. 1 (Dec. 1994): 1–10. https://doi.org/10.1111/j.1467-8675.1994.tb00001.x.

Habermas, Jürgen. "Why Europe Needs a Constitution." *New Left Review* 2, no. 11 (Oct. 2001): 5–26.

Hacker, Jacob S., and Paul Pierson. *American Amnesia: How the War on Government Led Us to Forget What Made America Prosper*. New York: Simon & Schuster, 2016.

Hackman, Michelle. "The Speechwriter Behind Donald Trump's Republican Convention Address." *The Wall Street Journal*, July 21, 2016.

Hamilton, Charles, and Kwame Ture. *Black Power: The Politics of Liberation in America*. New York: Random House, 1967.

Handlin, Oscar. "The Goals of Integration." *Daedalus* 95, no. 1 (Winter 1966): 268–86.

Hannah-Jones, Nikole. "Choosing a School for My Daughter in a Segregated City." *The New York Times Magazine*, June 9, 2016. http://www.nytimes.com/2016/06/12/magazine/choosing-a-school-for-my-daughter-in-a-segregated-city.html.

Hansen, Jonathan. *The Lost Promise of Patriotism: Debating American Identity, 1890–1920*. Chicago: University of Chicago Press, 2003.

Hayden, Michael Edison. "Stephen Miller's Affinity for White Nationalism Revealed in Leaked Emails." Southern Poverty Law Center, November 12, 2019. https://www.splcenter.org/hatewatch/2019/11/12/stephen-millers-affinity-white-nationalism-revealed-leaked-emails.

Henninger, Daniel. "Obama's Godfather Speech." *Wall Street Journal*, December 8, 2011, sec. Opinion. https://www.wsj.com/articles/SB10001424052970203413304577084292119160060.

Higgins, Peter W. *Immigration Justice*. Edinburgh: Edinburgh University Press, 2013.

Hirschman, Albert O. *The Rhetoric of Reaction: Perversity, Futility, Jeopardy*. Cambridge, MA: Belknap Press of Harvard University Press, 1991.

Hoffer, Williamjames Hull. *The Caning of Charles Sumner: Honor, Idealism, and the Origins of the Civil War*. Baltimore: Johns Hopkins University Press, 2010.

Hollinger, David A. *Postethnic America: Beyond Multiculturalism*. New York: Basic Books, 1995.

Holzer, Harold, ed. "The Third Joint Debate at Jonesboro, September 15, 1858." In *The Lincoln-Douglas Debates: The First Complete, Unexpurgated Text*, 136–84. New York: Fordham University Press, 2004.

Hooker, Juliet. *Race and the Politics of Solidarity*. New York: Oxford University Press, 2009.

Hugo Lopez, Mark, and Paul Taylor. "Latino Voters in the 2012 Election." Pew Research Center, November 7, 2012. http://www.pewhispanic.org/2012/11/07/latino-voters-in-the-2012-election/.

Hyde, Carrie. *Civic Longing: The Speculative Origins of U.S. Citizenship*. Cambridge, MA: Harvard University Press, 2018.

"Interchange: Nationalism and Internationalism in the Era of the Civil War." *Journal of American History* 98, no. 2 (Sept. 2011): 455–89. https://doi.org/10.1093/jahist/jar330.

Ivison, Duncan. *Can Liberal States Accommodate Indigenous Peoples?* Cambridge: Polity Press, 2020.

Jaggar, Alison M. "Transnational Cycles of Gendered Vulnerability: A Prologue to a Theory of Global Gender Justice." *Philosophical Topics* 37, no. 2 (Fall 2009): 33–52.

Jay, John. "The Federalist No. 2." In *The Federalist with Letters of "Brutus,"* by Alexander Hamilton, James Madison, and John Jay, edited by Terence Ball, 5–8. Cambridge: Cambridge University Press, 2003.

Johnson, Lyndon B. "Remarks at the Signing of the Immigration Bill, Liberty Island, New York." October 3, 1965. The American Presidency Project, UC Santa Barbara. https://www.presidency.ucsb.edu/documents/remarks-the-signing-the-immigration-bill-liberty-island-new-york.

Kahlenberg, Richard D., and Kimberly Quick. "Attacking the Black–White Opportunity Gap That Comes from Residential Segregation." The Century Foundation, June 25, 2019. https://tcf.org/content/report/attacking-black-white-opportunity-gap-comes-residential-segregation/.

Kallen, Horace M. "Democracy Versus the Melting-Pot." *The Nation*, February 25, 1915.

Katz, Michael B. *The Undeserving Poor: America's Enduring Confrontation with Poverty*. 2nd ed. New York: Oxford University Press, 2013.

Katznelson, Ira. *Fear Itself: The New Deal and the Origins of Our Time*. New York: Liveright, 2013.

Kazin, Michael, and Joseph A. McCartin. "Introduction." In *Americanism: New Perspectives on the History of an Ideal*, edited by Michael Kazin and Joseph A. McCartin, 1–21. Chapel Hill: University of North Carolina Press, 2006.

Kennedy, John F. "Commencement Address at Yale University, June 11, 1962." John F. Kennedy Presidential Library and Museum. Accessed Sept. 25, 2018. https://www.jfklibrary.org/Research/Research-Aids/JFK-Speeches/Yale-University_19620611.aspx.

King, Desmond S., and Rogers M. Smith. *Still a House Divided: Race and Politics in Obama's America*. Princeton: Princeton University Press, 2011.

Kloppenberg, James. "Aspirational Nationalism in America." *Intellectual History Newsletter*, 24 (2002): 60–71.

Kloppenberg, James. "Life Everlasting: Tocqueville in America." In his *The Virtues of Liberalism*, 71–81. New York: Oxford University Press, 1998.

Kloppenberg, James. *Toward Democracy: The Struggle for Self-Rule in European and American Thought*. New York: Oxford University Press, 2016.

Kohn, Hans. *The Idea of Nationalism: A Study in Its Origins and Background*. New Brunswick, NJ: Transaction, 2005.

Konczal, Mike. "The Forgotten State." *Boston Review*, August 2016. http://bostonreview.net/books-ideas/mike-konczal-yuval-levin-fractured-republic-jacob-hacker-paul-pierson-american-amnesia.

Kreis, Anthony Michael. "The New Redeemers." *Georgia Law Review* 55, no. 4 (Summer 2021): 1483–528.

Kruse, Kevin M. *White Flight: Atlanta and the Making of Modern Conservatism*. Princeton: Princeton University Press, 2005.

Kukathas, Chandran. "Expatriatism: The Theory and Practice of Open Borders." In *Citizenship, Borders, and Human Needs*, edited by Rogers M. Smith, 324–42. Philadelphia: University of Pennsylvania Press, 2011.

Kymlicka, Will. "American Multiculturalism and the 'Nations Within.'" In *Political Theory and the Rights of Indigenous Peoples*, edited by Duncan Ivison, Paul Patton, and Will Sanders, 216–36. Cambridge: Cambridge University Press, 2000.

Lackey, Michael, ed. *The Haverford Discussions: A Black Integrationist Manifesto for Racial Justice*. Charlottesville: University of Virginia Press, 2013.

Lackey, Michael. "Redeeming the Post-Metaphysical Promise of J. Saunders Redding's 'America.'" *CR: The New Centennial Review* 12, no. 3 (Winter 2012): 217–43.

Laughlin, Harry H. "Analysis of America's Modern Melting Pot, Hearings Before the Committee on Immigration and Naturalization, House of Representatives, Sixty-Seventh Congress, Third Session, November 21, 1922, Serial 7-C." Government Printing Office, 1923.

Levine, Bruce. "Conservatism, Nativism, and Slavery: Thomas R. Whitney and the Origins of the Know-Nothing Party." *The Journal of American History* 88, no. 2 (Sept. 2001): 455–88. https://doi.org/10.2307/2675102.

Levitsky, Steven, and Daniel Ziblatt. *How Democracies Die*. New York: Crown, 2018.

Levitsky, Steven, and Daniel Ziblatt. "Is Our Democracy Wobbly?" *The New York Times*, January 27, 2018, sec. Sunday Review.

Levy, Jacob T. "Against Fraternity: Democracy Without Solidarity." In *The Strains of Commitment: The Political Sources of Solidarity in Diverse Societies*, edited by Keith Banting and Will Kymlicka, 107–24. Oxford: Oxford University Press, 2017.

Lichtenstein, Nelson. *Walter Reuther: The Most Dangerous Man in Detroit*. Urbana, Chicago: University of Illinois Press, 1997.

Lincoln, Abraham. "Address to Germans at Cincinnati, Ohio, February 12, 1861." In *Abraham Lincoln: His Speeches and Writings*, edited by Roy P. Basler, 572–74. New York: Da Capo Press, 2001.

Lincoln, Abraham. "Gettysburg Address," November 19, 1863. The Avalon Project, Yale University. http://avalon.law.yale.edu/19th_century/gettyb.asp.

Lincoln, Abraham. "Letter to Joshua Speed, Springfield, Illinois: August 24, 1855." In *The Essential Lincoln: Speeches and Correspondence*, edited by Orville Vernon Burton, 31–35. New York: Hill and Wang, 2009.

Lowi, Theodore. "The New Public Philosophy: Interest-Group Liberalism." In *The Political Economy: Readings in the Politics and Economics of American Public Policy*, edited by Thomas Ferguson and Joel Rogers, 49–66. Armonk, NY: M.E. Sharpe, 1984.

Maaka, Roger, and Augie Fleras. "Engaging with Indigeneity: Tino Rangatiratanga in Aotearoa." In *Political Theory and the Rights of Indigenous Peoples*, edited by Duncan Ivison, Paul Patton, and Will Sanders, 89–109. Cambridge: Cambridge University Press, 2000.

Madison, James. "The Federalist No. 14." In *The Federalist with Letters of "Brutus,"* by Alexander Hamilton, James Madison, and John Jay, edited by Terence Ball, 59–64. Cambridge: Cambridge University Press, 2003.

Maier, Pauline. *American Scripture: Making the Declaration of Independence*. New York: Vintage, 1997.

Martin, Susan F. *A Nation of Immigrants*. Cambridge: Cambridge University Press, 2011.

Mason, Andrew. *Community, Solidarity and Belonging: Levels of Community and Their Normative Significance*. Cambridge: Cambridge University Press, 2000.

Massey, Douglas S., and Nancy A. Denton. *American Apartheid: Segregation and the Making of the Underclass*. Cambridge, MA: Harvard University Press, 1993.

McAdam, Doug, and Karina Kloos. *Deeply Divided: Racial Politics and Social Movements in Postwar America*. New York: Oxford University Press, 2014.

McCaskill, Nolan D. "Trump Promises Wall and Massive Deportation Program." *POLITICO*, August 31, 2016. https://www.politico.com/story/2016/08/donald-trump-immigration-address-arizona-227612.

McGhee, Heather. *The Sum of Us: What Racism Costs Everyone and How We Can Prosper Together*. New York: One World, 2021.

McGreevy, John T. *Catholicism and American Freedom: A History*. New York: W. W. Norton, 2003.

McPherson, James M. *Battle Cry of Freedom: The Civil War Era*. New York: Oxford University Press, 1988.

Mehrotra, Ajay K. *Making the Modern American Fiscal State: Law, Politics, and the Rise of Progressive Taxation, 1877–1929*. New York: Cambridge University Press, 2013.

Merry, Michael S. *Equality, Citizenship, and Segregation: A Defense of Separation*. New York: Palgrave Macmillan, 2013.

Miller, David. *On Nationality*. Oxford: Oxford University Press, 1995.

Miller, David. "Why Immigration Controls Are Not Coercive: A Reply to Arash Abizadeh." *Political Theory* 38, no. 1 (Feb. 2010): 111–20.

Mills, Charles W. "White Time: The Chronic Injustice of Ideal Theory." *Du Bois Review* 11, no. 1 (2014): 27–42. https://doi.org/10.1017/S1742058X14000022.

Mills Thornton III, J. *Dividing Lines: Municipal Politics and the Struggle for Civil Rights in Montgomery, Birmingham, and Selma*. Tuscaloosa: University of Alabama Press, 2002.

Mirowski, Philip, and Dieter Plehwe, eds. *The Road from Mont Pelerin: The Making of the Neoliberal Thought Collective*. Cambridge, MA: Harvard University Press, 2009.

Moore, Margaret. "Is Patriotism an Associative Duty?" *The Journal of Ethics* 13, no. 4 (Dec. 2009): 383–99.

Moore, Margaret. "The Moral Value of Collective Self-Determination and the Ethics of Secession." *Journal of Social Philosophy* 50, no. 4 (Winter 2019): 620–41. https://doi.org/10.1111/josp.12327.

Morton, John. "Exercising Prosecutorial Discretion Consistent with the Civil Immigration Enforcement Priorities of the Agency for the Apprehension, Detention, and Removal of Aliens." U.S. Immigration and Customs Enforcement, June 17, 2011.

Müller, Jan-Werner. *Constitutional Patriotism*. Princeton: Princeton University Press, 2007.

NAACP Legal Defense and Educational Fund. "Brown at 60: The Doll Test." Accessed December 7, 2016. http://www.naacpldf.org/brown-at-60-the-doll-test.

Norton, Michael I., and Dan Ariely. "Building a Better America—One Wealth Quintile at a Time." *Perspectives on Psychological Science* 6, no. 1 (Jan. 2011): 9–12. https://doi.org/10.1177/1745691610393524.

Obama, Barack. "Remarks by the President on Opportunity for All and Skills for America's Workers." The White House, Office of the Press Secretary, January 30, 2014. https://obamawhitehouse.archives.gov/the-press-office/2014/01/30/remarks-president-opportunity-all-and-skills-americas-workers.

Obama, Barack. "Remarks by the President on the Economy in Osawatomie, Kansas." The White House, Office of the Press Secretary, December 6, 2011. https://obamawhitehouse.archives.gov/the-press-office/2011/12/06/remarks-president-economy-osawatomie-kansas.

O'Connor, Mike. *A Commercial Republic: America's Enduring Debate over Democratic Capitalism.* Lawrence: University Press of Kansas, 2014.

O'Neill, Martin. "What Should Egalitarians Believe?" *Philosophy & Public Affairs* 36, no. 2 (2008): 119–56.

Orfield, Gary. "Reviving the Goal of an Integrated Society: A 21st Century Challenge." The Civil Rights Project at UCLA, January 2009. http://www.racialequitytools.org/resourcefiles/orfield.pdf.

Parfit, Derek. *Equality or Priority?* The Lindley Lecture, University of Kansas, 1995.

Patterson, James T. *Brown v. Board of Education: A Civil Rights Milestone and Its Troubled Legacy.* Oxford: Oxford University Press, 2001.

Peck, Jamie. "Remaking Laissez-Faire." *Progress in Human Geography* 32, no. 1 (Feb. 2008): 3–43. https://doi.org/10.1177/0309132507084816.

Peter, Fabienne. "Democratic Legitimacy and Proceduralist Social Epistemology." *Politics, Philosophy & Economics* 6, no. 3 (Oct. 2007): 329–53. https://doi.org/10.1177/1470594X07081303.

Pettit, Philip. "Minority Claims Under Two Conceptions of Democracy." In *Political Theory and the Rights of Indigenous Peoples*, edited by Duncan Ivison, Paul Patton, and Will Sanders, 199–215. Cambridge: Cambridge University Press, 2000.

Phillips, Wendell. *The Constitution a Pro-Slavery Compact; or, Extracts from the Madison Papers, Etc.* 2nd ed. New York: American Anti-Slavery Society, 1845.

Piketty, Thomas. "Income, Wage, and Wealth Inequality in France, 1901–98." In *Top Incomes over the Twentieth Century: A Contrast Between European and English-Speaking Countries*, edited by A. B. Atkinson and Thomas Piketty, 43–81. New York: Oxford University Press, 2007.

Piketty, Thomas, and Emmanuel Saez. "Income Inequality in the United States, 1913–1998." *The Quarterly Journal of Economics* 118, no. 1 (Feb. 2003): 1–39.

Pippenger, Nathan. "Agnosticism on Racial Integration: Liberal-Democratic or Libertarian?" *Political Research Quarterly* 76, no. 3 (Sept. 2023): 1196–208. https://doi.org/10.1177/10659129221130296.

Pippenger, Nathan. "Contested Past, Contested Future: Identity Politics and Liberal Democracy." *Ethics & International Affairs* 37, no. 4 (Winter 2023): 391–400. https://doi.org/10.1017/S0892679423000382.

Pippenger, Nathan. "From Openness to Inclusion: Toward a Democratic Approach to Migration Policy." *Perspectives on Politics* 22, no. 4 (Dec. 2024): 975–988. https://doi.org/10.1017/S153759272400001X.

Pippenger, Nathan. "Listening to Strangers, or: Three Arguments for Bounded Solidarity." *American Journal of Political Science* 67, no. 3 (July 2023): 764–75. https://doi.org/10.1111/ajps.12671.

Pippenger, Nathan. "One Family in Limbo: What Obama's Immigration Policy Looks Like in Practice." *The New Republic*, September 15, 2011. https://newrepublic.com/article/95005/pippenger-immigration-obama-deportation-ice.

Pippenger, Nathan. "Reading Ellison Through Herder: Language, Integration, and Democracy." *The Journal of Politics* 85, no. 2 (Apr. 2023): 749–59. https://doi.org/10.1086/722350.

Pitkin, Hanna. "The Idea of a Constitution." *Journal of Legal Education* 37, no. 2 (1987): 167–69.

Pogge, Thomas W. *Realizing Rawls*. Ithaca: Cornell University Press, 1989.

powell, john a. "Is Integration Possible?" *Race, Poverty & the Environment* 15, no. 2 (Fall 2008): 42–44.

Preston, Julia. "Deportations Under New U.S. Policy Are Inconsistent." *The New York Times*, November 12, 2011, sec. U.S. https://www.nytimes.com/2011/11/13/us/politics/president-obamas-policy-on-deportation-is-unevenly-applied.html.

Preston, Julia. "Romney's Plan for 'Self-Deportation' Has Conservative Support." *The Caucus* (blog), *The New York Times*, January 24, 2012. https://thecaucus.blogs.nytimes.com/2012/01/24/romneys-plan-for-self-deportation-has-conservative-support/.

Primus, Richard. "Second Redemption, Third Reconstruction." *California Law Review* 106, no. 6 (Dec. 2018): 1987–2000. https://doi.org/10.15779/Z383R0PT5J.

Putnam, Robert D. *Bowling Alone: The Collapse and Revival of American Community*. New York: Simon & Schuster, 2000.

Rahman, K. Sabeel. "Conceptualizing the Economic Role of the State: Laissez-Faire, Technocracy, and the Democratic Alternative." *Polity* 43, no. 2 (Apr. 2011): 264–86.

Rahman, K. Sabeel. "Constructing Citizenship: Exclusion and Inclusion Through the Governance of Basic Necessities." *Columbia Law Review* 118, no. 8 (Dec. 2018): 2447–503.

Rahman, K. Sabeel. *Democracy Against Domination*. New York: Oxford University Press, 2017.

Rahman, K. Sabeel. "Reconstructing Democracy." *Democracy Journal*, December 6, 2018. https://democracyjournal.org/arguments/reconstructing-democracy/.

Rampersad, Arnold. *Ralph Ellison: A Biography*. New York: Alfred A. Knopf, 2007.

Rawls, John. *A Theory of Justice*. Cambridge, MA: Belknap Press of Harvard University Press, 1971.

Reagan, Ronald. "Remarks to Business Leaders in Cincinnati, Ohio." October 3, 1985. The American Presidency Project, UC Santa Barbara. http://www.presidency.ucsb.edu/ws/?pid=37850.

Reardon, Sean F., Elena Tej Grewal, Demetra Kalogrides, and Erica Greenberg. "Brown Fades: The End of Court-Ordered School Desegregation and the Resegregation of American Public Schools." *Journal of Policy Analysis and Management* 31, no. 4 (Fall 2012): 876–904.

Rector, Robert, and Rachel Sheffield. "Air Conditioning, Cable TV, and an Xbox: What Is Poverty in the United States Today?" The Heritage Foundation, July 18, 2011. https://www.heritage.org/poverty-and-inequality/report/air-conditioning-cable-tv-and-xbox-what-poverty-the-united-states.

Redding, Saunders. "Background and Significance of 'Black Studies' Programs." In *The Haverford Discussions: A Black Integrationist Manifesto for Racial Justice*, edited by Michael Lackey, 125–30. Charlottesville: University of Virginia Press, 2013.

Redding, Saunders. "The Black Revolution in American Studies." *American Studies International* 17, no. 4 (Summer 1979): 8–14.

Redding, J. Saunders. "The Black Arts Movement: A Modest Dissent." In *A Scholar's Conscience: Selected Writings of J. Saunders Redding, 1942–1977*, edited by Faith Berry, 212–18. Lexington: University Press of Kentucky, 1992.

Reed, David A. "America of the Melting Pot Comes to an End; Effects of New Immigration Legislation Described by Senate Sponsor of Bill—Chief Aim, He States, Is to Preserve Racial Type as It Exists Here Today." *The New York Times*, April 27, 1924, sec. XX.

Reed, Touré F. "Oscar Handlin and the Problem of Ethnic Pluralism and African American Civil Rights." *Journal of American Ethnic History* 32, no. 3 (Spring 2013): 37–45. https://doi.org/10.5406/jamerethnhist.32.3.0037.

Reznick, Scott M. "On Liberty and Union: Moral Imagination and Its Limits in Daniel Webster's Seventh of March Speech." *American Political Thought* 6, no. 3 (Summer 2017): 371–95. https://doi.org/10.1086/692572.

Rivers, Eugene F. "Beyond the Nationalism of Fools: Toward an Agenda for Black Intellectuals." *Boston Review*, Summer 1995. http://new.bostonreview.net/BR20.3/rivers.html.

Robin, Corey. "Democracy Is Norm Erosion." *Jacobin*, January 29, 2018. https://jacobin.com/2018/01/democracy-trump-authoritarianism-levitsky-zillblatt-norms.

Rodgers, Daniel T. *Age of Fracture*. Cambridge, MA: Belknap Press of Harvard University Press, 2011.

Rogers, Katie, and Jason DeParle. "The White Nationalist Websites Cited by Stephen Miller." *The New York Times*, November 18, 2019, sec. U.S. https://www.nytimes.com/2019/11/18/us/politics/stephen-miller-white-nationalism.html.

Rondel, David. "Egalitarians, Sufficientarians, and Mathematicians: A Critical Notice of Harry Frankfurt's 'On Inequality.'" *Canadian Journal of Philosophy* 46, no. 2 (2016): 145–62.

Roosevelt, Franklin Delano. "Acceptance Speech for the Renomination for the Presidency, Philadelphia, Pa." June 27, 1936. The American Presidency Project, UC Santa Barbara. http://www.presidency.ucsb.edu/ws/?pid=15314.

Roosevelt, Kermit. "The Voting Rights Act and the Second Redemption." *Constitution Daily* (blog), National Constitution Center, August 5, 2015. https://constitutioncenter.org/blog/the-voting-rights-act-and-the-second-redemption.

Roosevelt, Theodore. "The New Nationalism: Speech at Osawatomie, Kansas, August 31, 1910." In *Theodore Roosevelt: Letters and Speeches*, edited by Louis Auchincloss, 799–814. New York: Library of America, 2004.

Rorty, Richard. *Achieving Our Country: Leftist Thought in Twentieth-Century America*. Cambridge, MA: Harvard University Press, 1998.

Rothman, Joshua D. "Antebellum Era." In *The Oxford Encyclopedia of American Social History*, edited by Lynn Dumenil, 41–45. New York: Oxford University Press, 2012.

Ruhs, Martin, and Philip Martin. "Numbers vs. Rights: Trade-Offs and Guest Worker Programs." *International Migration Review* 42, no. 1 (Mar. 2008): 249–65. https://doi.org/10.1111/j.1747-7379.2007.00120.x.

Sandel, Michael J. *Democracy's Discontent: America in Search of a Public Philosophy*. Cambridge, MA: Belknap Press of Harvard University Press, 1996.

Sandel, Michael J. "The Procedural Republic and the Unencumbered Self." *Political Theory* 12, no. 1 (Feb. 1984): 81–96.

Scanlon, T. M. "The Diversity of Objections to Inequality." In his *The Difficulty of Tolerance: Essays in Political Philosophy*, 202–18. Cambridge: Cambridge University Press, 2003.

Schambra, William. "Progressive Liberalism and American 'Community.'" *The Public Interest*, no. 80 (Summer 1985): 31–48.

Scheffler, Samuel. "Families, Nations, and Strangers." In his *Boundaries and Allegiances: Problems of Justice and Responsibility in Liberal Thought*, 48–65. New York: Oxford University Press, 2001.

Scheffler, Samuel. "Relationships and Responsibilities." In his *Boundaries and Allegiances: Problems of Justice and Responsibility in Liberal Thought*, 97–110. New York: Oxford University Press, 2001.

Schemmel, Christian. *Justice and Egalitarian Relations*. Oxford University Press, 2021. https://doi.org/10.1093/oso/9780190084240.001.0001.

Schlesinger, Arthur Meier. *The Disuniting of America: Reflections on a Multicultural Society*. New York: W. W. Norton, 1991.

Schlozman, Kay Lehman, Sidney Verba, and Henry E. Brady. *The Unheavenly Chorus: Unequal Political Voice and the Broken Promise of American Democracy*. Princeton: Princeton University Press, 2012.

Schuessler, Jennifer. "President Obama Writes Apology to Art Historian." *The New York Times*. ArtsBeat (blog), February 18, 2014. https://artsbeat.blogs.nytimes.com/2014/02/18/president-obama-writes-apology-to-art-historian/.

Serwer, Adam. "Jeff Sessions's Unqualified Praise for a 1924 Immigration Law." *The Atlantic*, January 10, 2017. https://www.theatlantic.com/politics/archive/2017/01/jeff-sessions-1924-immigration/512591/.

Serwer, Adam. "Welcome to the Second Redemption." *The Atlantic*, November 10, 2016. https://www.theatlantic.com/politics/archive/2016/11/welcome-to-the-second-redemption/507317/.

Sessions, Jeff. "Immigration Handbook for the New Republican Majority," January 2015. https://www.aila.org/aila-files/52023919-1F93-4F98-A6F6-665B4157964C/16111436.pdf?1697589936.

Shapiro, Ian. "Resources, Capacities, and Ownership: The Workmanship Ideal and Distributive Justice." *Political Theory* 19, no. 1 (1991): 47–72.

Shelby, Tommie. *Dark Ghettos: Injustice, Dissent, and Reform*. Cambridge, MA: Belknap Press of Harvard University Press, 2016.

Shelby, Tommie. *We Who Are Dark: The Philosophical Foundations of Black Solidarity*. Cambridge, MA: Belknap Press of Harvard University Press, 2005.

Smith, Craig R. *Daniel Webster and the Oratory of Civil Religion*. Columbia: University of Missouri Press, 2005.

Smith, Rogers M. *Civic Ideals: Conflicting Visions of Citizenship in U.S. History*. New Haven: Yale University Press, 1997.

Solt, Frederick. "Economic Inequality and Democratic Political Engagement." *American Journal of Political Science* 52, no. 1 (Jan. 2008): 48–60.

Somers, Margaret R. *Genealogies of Citizenship: Markets, Statelessness, and the Right to Have Rights*. Cambridge: Cambridge University Press, 2008.

Song, Sarah. *Immigration and Democracy*. New York: Oxford University Press, 2019.

Song, Sarah. "The Boundary Problem in Democratic Theory: Why the Demos Should Be Bounded by the State." *International Theory* 4, no. 1 (Mar. 2012): 39–68. https://doi.org/10.1017/S1752971911000248.

Song, Sarah. "Three Models of Civic Solidarity." In *Citizenship, Borders, and Human Needs*, edited by Rogers M. Smith, 192–207. Philadelphia: University of Pennsylvania Press, 2011.

Spalding, Matthew. "The String-Pullers." *National Review*, December 31, 2011. https://www.nationalreview.com/nrd/articles/293976/string-pullers.

Spencer, Hawes, and Sheryl Gay Stolberg. "Virginia Town Is on Edge over Confederate Statue." *The New York Times*, August 11, 2017, sec. A.

Stanley, Sharon. *An Impossible Dream?: Racial Integration in the United States*. New York: Oxford University Press, 2017.

Stanley, Sharon. "Toward a Reconciliation of Integration and Racial Solidarity." *Contemporary Political Theory* 13, no. 1 (Feb. 2014): 46–63. https://doi.org/10.1057/cpt.2013.13.

Steele, Richard W. "The War on Intolerance: The Reformulation of American Nationalism, 1939–1941." *Journal of American Ethnic History* 9, no. 1 (Fall 1989): 9–35.

Stephens, Alexander H. "Cornerstone Speech, March 21, 1861." In *The Civil War and Reconstruction: A Documentary Reader*, edited by Stanley Harrold, 59–64. Malden, MA: Blackwell, 2008.

Steyn, Mark. "Statist Delusions." *National Review*, December 10, 2011. http://www.nationalreview.com/article/285409/statist-delusions-mark-steyn.

Stiglitz, Joseph E. *The Price of Inequality: How Today's Divided Society Endangers Our Future*. New York: W. W. Norton, 2012.

Stilz, Anna. "Economic Migration: On What Terms?" *Perspectives on Politics* 20, no. 3 (Sept. 2022): 983–98. https://doi.org/10.1017/S1537592721002206.

Stilz, Anna. *Liberal Loyalty: Freedom, Obligation, and the State*. Princeton: Princeton University Press, 2009.

Stout, Jeffrey. *Democracy and Tradition*. Princeton: Princeton University Press, 2004.

Sumner, Charles. "Admission of Mississippi to Representation in Congress. Speech in the Senate, February 17, 1870." In *The Works of Charles Sumner*, vol. 13, 331–35. Boston: Lee and Shepard, 1880.

Sumner, Charles. "'Are We a Nation?' (Address Before the New York Young Men's Republican Union at the Cooper Institute, November 19, 1867)." https://ia902302.us.archive.org/16/items/arewenationaddre00sumn/arewenationaddre00sumn.pdf.

Sumner, Charles. "The Equal Rights of All: The Great Guaranty and Present Necessity, for the Sake of Security, and to Maintain a Republican Government. Speech in the Senate, on the Proposed Amendment of the Constitution Fixing the Basis of Representation, February 5 and 6, 1866." In *The Works of Charles Sumner*, vol. 10, 115–269. Boston: Lee and Shepard, 1876.

Sumner, Charles. "Guaranty of Republican Governments in the Rebel States. Resolutions in the Senate, February 25, 1865." In *The Works of Charles Sumner*, vol. 9, 329–32. Boston: Lee and Shepard, 1874.

Sumner, Charles. "Italian Unity: Letter to a Public Meeting at the Academy of Music in New York, January 10, 1871." In *Charles Sumner: His Complete Works*, vol. 18, 307–309. Boston: Lee and Shepard, 1900.

Sumner, Charles. "Political Parties and Our Foreign-Born Population: Speech at Faneuil Hall, November 2, 1855." In *Charles Sumner: His Complete Works*, vol. 5, 62–82. Boston: Lee and Shepard, 1900.

Sumner, Charles. "Promises of the Declaration of Independence, and Abraham Lincoln. Eulogy on Abraham Lincoln, Before the Municipal Authorities of the City of Boston, June 1, 1865." In *The Works of Charles Sumner*, vol. 9, 367–428. Boston: Lee and Shepard, 1874.

Sumner, Charles. "The True Principles of Reconstruction. Illegality of Existing Governments in the Rebel States. Resolutions and Remarks in the Senate, December 5, 1866." In *The Works of Charles Sumner*, vol. 11, 44–47. Boston: Lee and Shepard, 1875.

Taney, Roger. Dred Scott v. Sandford (U.S. Supreme Court 1857).

Taylor, Charles. "Democratic Exclusion (and Its Remedies?)." In his *Dilemmas and Connections: Selected Essays*, 124–45. Cambridge, MA: Belknap Press of Harvard University Press, 2011.

Tesler, Michael. "The Spillover of Racialization into Health Care: How President Obama Polarized Public Opinion by Racial Attitudes and Race." *American Journal of Political Science* 56, no. 3 (July 2012): 690–704. https://doi.org/10.1111/j.1540-5907.2011.00577.x.

Tesler, Michael, and David O. Sears. *Obama's Race: The 2008 Election and the Dream of a Post-Racial America*. Chicago Studies in American Politics. Chicago: University of Chicago Press, 2010.

The Editors. "New Nationalism, Old Liberalism." *National Review*, December 7, 2011. http://www.nationalreview.com/article/285186/new-nationalism-old-liberalism-editors.

The Interpreter. "Americanization vs. 'Americanization.'" April 1923.
The Nation. "Toward a Third Reconstruction." Schomburg Center for Research in Black Culture, March 23, 2015. https://www.thenation.com/article/toward-third-reconstruction/.
The Montgomery Advertiser. "It Is Not to Be in Oak Park." December 24, 1958.
The New York Times. "Julius Drachsler, Sociologist, Dead." July 23, 1927.
The New York Times. "Mr. Roosevelt's Issue." September 11, 1910.
The Red Cross Bulletin. "Foreign Language Information Service on Independent Basis." May 16, 1921.
The Washington Post. "Full Text: Donald Trump Announces a Presidential Bid," June 6, 2015. https://www.washingtonpost.com/news/post-politics/wp/2015/06/16/full-text-donald-trump-announces-a-presidential-bid/?noredirect=on&utm_term=.71a9db7e2857.
"The Work of the Foreign Language Information Service: A Summary and Survey." Foreign Language Information Service, 1921. Widener Library, Harvard University. https://curiosity.lib.harvard.edu/immigration-to-the-united-states-1789-1930/catalog/39-990013685600203941.
"The Work of the Foreign Language Information Service of the American Red Cross." Bureau of Foreign Language Information Service, Department of Civilian Relief, June 10, 1920. Widener Library, Harvard University. https://curiosity.lib.harvard.edu/immigration-to-the-united-states-1789-1930/catalog/39-990085954750203941.
Thompson, A. C., and Ford Fischer. "Members of Several Well-Known Hate Groups Identified at Capitol Riot." *ProPublica*, January 9, 2021. https://www.propublica.org/article/several-well-known-hate-groups-identified-at-capitol-riot?token=nKHfqzzFyex_uZ4Pu7DPxey6pD87Kv3z.
Thompson, Derek. "30 Million in Poverty Aren't as Poor as You Think, Says Heritage Foundation." *The Atlantic*, July 19, 2011. https://www.theatlantic.com/business/archive/2011/07/30-million-in-poverty-arent-as-poor-as-you-think-says-heritage-foundation/242191/.
Tsai, Robert L. "Immigration Unilateralism and American Ethnonationalism." *Loyola University Chicago Law Journal* 51, no. 2 (Winter 2019): 523–54.
Tuck, Stephen. *We Ain't What We Ought to Be: The Black Freedom Struggle from Emancipation to Obama*. Cambridge, MA: Belknap Press of Harvard University Press, 2010.
Valadez, Jorge M. "Immigration, Self-Determination, and Global Justice: Towards a Holistic Normative Theory of Migration." *Journal of International Political Theory* 8, nos. 1–2 (Apr. 2012): 135–46. https://doi.org/10.3366/jipt.2012.0034.
Valls, Andrew. "A Liberal Defense of Black Nationalism." *The American Political Science Review* 104, no. 3 (Aug. 2010): 467–81.
Valls, Andrew. "The Broken Promise of Racial Integration." *Nomos* 43 (2002): 456–74.
Valls, Andrew. *Rethinking Racial Justice*. New York: Oxford University Press, 2018.
Vogel, Steven. *Marketcraft: How Governments Make Markets Work*. New York: Oxford University Press, 2018.
"Vote of No Confidence in ICE Director John Morton and ICE ODPP Assistant Director Phyllis Coven." National Council 118—Immigration and Customs Enforcement, American Federation of Government Employees (AFL-CIO), June 25, 2010. https://iceunion.org/download/259-259-vote-no-confidence.pdf.
Walzer, Michael. *Spheres of Justice: A Defense of Pluralism and Equality*. New York: Basic Books, 1983.
Webster, Daniel. "Address delivered at the laying of the Corner Stone of the Bunker Hill Monument.—June 17, 1825." In *Speeches and Forensic Arguments*, vol. 3: 57-71. Boston: Tappan and Dennet, 1843.

Weiner, Rachel. "Man Carrying Confederate Flag in Capitol on Jan. 6 Sentenced to 3 Years." *The Washington Post*, February 10, 2023. https://www.washingtonpost.com/dc-md-va/2023/02/09/kevin-seefried-confederate-capitol/.

"What Is Americanism?" *American Journal of Sociology* 20, no. 4 (Jan. 1915): 433–86.

White, Richard. *The Republic for Which It Stands: The United States During Reconstruction and the Gilded Age, 1865–1896.* Oxford History of the United States. New York: Oxford University Press, 2017.

Whitman, Walt. "Democratic Vistas." In *Complete Poetry and Selected Prose*, edited by James E. Miller, Jr., Riverside Editions, 455–501. Boston: Houghton Mifflin, 1959.

Whitney, Thomas R. *A Defence of the American Policy, as Opposed to the Encroachments of Foreign Influence, and Especially to the Interference of the Papacy in the Political Interests and Affairs of the United States.* New York: DeWitt & Davenport, 1856. http://hdl.handle.net/2027/coo1.ark:/13960/t2g73zp37.

Wills, Garry. *Lincoln at Gettysburg: The Words That Remade America.* New York: Simon & Schuster, 1992.

Wise, Stephen S. "What Is an American?" *The Bulletin*, Foreign Language Information Service, 1, no. 7 (Oct. 1922): 4–5.

Wolfson, Martin H. *Financial Crises: Understanding the Postwar U.S. Experience.* 2nd ed. Armonk, NY: M.E. Sharpe, 1994.

Woodward, C. Vann. *The Strange Career of Jim Crow.* New York: Oxford University Press, 1955.

Yack, Bernard. *Nationalism and the Moral Psychology of Community.* Chicago: University of Chicago Press, 2012.

Index

For the benefit of digital users, indexed terms that span two pages (e.g., 52–53) may, on occasion, appear on only one of those pages.

Abizadeh, Arash, 77–79, 160 n.102
Adams, Michelle, 86
Addams, Jane, 47
Adelstein, Richard, 174 n.77
affiliation, 65–67, 109
African Americans: assimilation pressure, 83, 95
   cultural estrangement of, 90–91
   debates on citizenship of, 44, 110
   doll tests, 89, 163 n.43
   enclave separatism of, 92
   identity of, 26–27, 93–94
   integration into white institutions, 95, 110
   political ideology of, 107, 109
Afro-American studies, 93–94
all-coerced principle, 78–80
Allen, Danielle, 22–23, 43–44, 107–108, 150 n.22
Alsop, Joseph, 128
American citizenship, 4–5, 9, 26–27, 43, 51–52, 68, 123
American democracy: crisis of, 54, 139–140, 141–142
   importance of norms, 141–142
   optimism about, 138–139
   prioritization of the local over the national in, 85
Americanism: cultivation of inclusive, 70–71
   debates over, 53
   ideal of, 49–50, 73–74
   transformation of, 51
American studies, 93–94
"America of the Melting Pot Comes to an End" (article), 74
Anderson, Elizabeth: call for solidarity, 101–102
   on democracy, 6–7, 16, 18, 34–35, 85, 96–97
   on equality, 118
   The Imperative of Integration, 84–85
   on integration, 84, 100–101, 110
   on mutual identification, 32–33
anti-egalitarianism, 6
anti-tax activism, 115–116, 171 n.38
Appiah, Kwame Anthony, 165 n.72
Armitage, David, 39–40

Baldwin, James, 50, 87, 110, 139–140
Balkin, Jack, 141–142
Bannon, Steve, 61
Baraka, Amiri, 93–94
Barber, Sotirios, 150 n.18
Bartels, Larry, 133
Beer, Samuel, 39
Black Americans. *See* African Americans
black institutions, 96
blackness, 110
Blake, Michael, 20–21
Blight, David, 42–43
Block, Fred, 115–116
Blyth, Mark, 136–137, 175 n.84
border control, 75–78
boundaries: of the demos, 20, 28, 44–45
   political, 20–21, 23–24
   of the state, 20, 29–30, 37
bounded solidarity, 33–34
Bourne, Randolph, 48–49, 69
Bozell, L. Brent, Jr., 129
Brinkley, Alan, 173 n.69
Britton-Purdy, Jedediah, 141–142, 189 n.70
Brooks, Preston, 1
Brooks, Roy, 166 n.73
Brown, Wendy, 13–14, 123, 131–132, 169 n.11
Browne, Robert, 89–92
Brown v. Board of Education, 82–83, 87–88
Brubaker, Rogers, 146 n.13
Buckley, William F., Jr., 128–129
Bunker Hill, Battle of, 39
Burns, Jennifer, 116, 127

Calhoun, John, 39–40
Carens, Joseph, 75–76, 159 n.84
Catholic immigrants, 66–67
Chang, Howard F., 76
Chinese Exclusion Act of 1882, 50–51, 60–61, 68
Chinese immigration, 68
citizenship: benefits of, 76
  birthright, 4–5
  civil society and, 96–97
  conservative vision of, 132
  construction of, 121–122
  democratic, 8–10, 15, 35–36, 96–97, 99, 105, 136–137, 167 n.136
  distributive justice and, 117
  elements of, 14–15
  formation of, 110–111
  for guest workers, 159 n.84
  happenstance quality of, 35
  idea of homogeneous, 41–42
  identification and, 20, 80
  immigrants' aspiration for, 65–66, 72, 80–81
  individualistic view of, 116–117
  institutional ties, 108
  legal codification of, 151 n.31
  localist understanding of, 94, 99–100
  market naturalism and, 119
  "pluralist" account of, 98
  psychology of, 7–8
  responsibilities of, 25–26, 104–105, 107
  solidarity and, 102–103, 105
  taxation and, 116–117
  theories of, 9
civic nationalism, 27–28
civic relations: vs. neighborly relations, 108
civic virtue, 98–100
civic "wholeness," 107–108
Civil Rights Act of 1866, 4–5, 60–61
civil rights movement, 5, 87–88, 139–141
civil society, 16, 96–97
Civil War: Lincoln's interpretation of, 40–41
  outcome of, 41–42, 49
  reconciliation after, 42–43
Clark, Kenneth, 82, 89
Clark, Mamie Phipps, 82, 89
coercion, 78–80, 96, 160 n.102
collective self-rule: as conception of political freedom, 116–117
  democracy and, 3

effects of inequality on, 119
identification and, 9, 16–17, 24, 80
informed citizens and, 180 n.29
justice and, 34–35
solidarity and, 6–7, 34–35, 63
temporal continuity of, 22–23
Committee on Public Information, 69–71
communal virtues, 99
competitive capitalism, 132–133
co-national obligations, 24–25
Confederate battle flag, 5–6
Conscience of a Conservative, The (Goldwater), 129–131
conservative movement, 116, 129
"constitution": two senses of, 19
constitutional patriotism: definition of, 28–29
  feasibility of, 29–30
  issues with, 29–30
  view of solidarity, 24
"constitution of opportunity" tradition, 174 n.79
Cooper, Frederick, 146 n.13
Cowie, Jefferson, 51–52
Croly, Herbert, 47
  The Promise of American Life, 46–47
Crow, Jim, 42–43
Cruse, Harold, 88–89, 92–93, 165 n.71

Debs, Eugene V., 47
Declaration of Independence (1776):
  contemporary meaning and status of, 31–32
  egalitarianism of, 66
  establishment of shared political peoplehood, 149 n.6
  interpretations of, 30–32, 150 n.22
  legitimacy of, 2–3
  main ideas of, 2–3, 6
  as nation's founding, 40–41
  principles of equality and consent, 144 n.5
  universalism of, 30–31
democracy: civilizational symphony and, 73–74
  collective self-consciousness and, 19–20
  as collective self-rule, 3, 13–14
  constitutional structure and, 32
  crisis of, 5, 9, 53–54
  definitions of, 6–7, 16, 46–47, 106–107
  expansion of, 4–5

freedom and, 13–14
free elections and, 106–107
goal of, 110–111
ideal of, 161 n.109
identification and, 18–19, 35–36, 107
inclusion and, 7–8
institutional structure and, 34–35
key virtues of, 90
localism and, 46–47
moral equality and, 6–7
participation in, 23
Progressive-era debate over, 47
psychological pressure of, 22–23
reconstitution of, 10
relationship between global justice and, 21
rights and, 14
solidarity and, 6–7, 9, 33
stability vs., 142
states and, 6
transformation in Americans' understanding of, 3–4, 14, 49
voting and, 18
See also American democracy
democratic decision-making process, 13–15, 17, 23, 79–80
demos, 20, 78–79
denizenship policies, 76
deportations, 59–60, 61–62
desegregation, 87–88
Dewey, John, 18, 48–49, 69, 106–107
distributive justice, 21–22, 34–35, 117–118
doll tests, 89, 163 n.43
Douglas, Stephen A., 40–41, 140
Douglass, Frederick: on black Americans, 26–27, 44
 on citizenship, 72
 on Civil War, 49
 on Constitution, 147 n.51
 on democratic self-rule, 90
 on immigration policy, 68, 72
 on Indigenous peoples, 43, 152 n.40
 on inheritance of slavery, 8–9
 on separatism, 105–106
 vision of "composite nationality," 68
Drachsler, Julius: approach to immigration, 71–72
 death, 74
 on national unity, 71
 on policy of harmonization, 71–74
Drake, St. Clair, 82

Dred Scott v. Sandford, 4–5
DuBois, W. E. B., 47, 53

economic crisis: definition of, 175 n.84
economic development, 123–125, 136, 173 n.69
economic inequality, 54, 132–133, 177 n.108
economic liberalism, 127–128
Edsall, Mary, 121
Edsall, Thomas, 121
egalitarianism, 6, 117–120
Einhorn, Robin, 131–132
Ellison, Ralph, 82, 92, 105–106, 110–111, 139
 Invisible Man, 110–111
equality: cosmopolitan affirmation of, 8
 as element of democracy, 14
 integration and, 112
 moral commitment to, 6–7
 "relational" approach to, 118
 of rights, 2–3
 sufficientarian approach to, 117–118
ethnic nationalism, 27–28
European citizenship, 28
European state-building, 147 n.45

15th Amendment, 41–42
Fishkin, Joseph, 43, 126, 130–131, 136, 174 n.79
Foner, Eric, 37, 68–69, 86, 122–123
Forbath, William, 43, 126, 130–131, 136, 174 n.79
Foreign Language Information Service (FLIS), 69, 70–71, 73–74
14th Amendment, 1, 4–5, 26–27, 41–42
Frankfurt, Harry, 117
Franklin, John Hope, 82, 110
free market, 131, 176 n.99
Friedman, Milton, 132–133, 136–137

Gerstle, Gary, 50–52, 125–126, 169 n.17
Gitlin, Todd, 51–52
Glazer, Nathan, 87
Goldwater, Barry: *The Conscience of a Conservative*, 129–131
 market naturalism of, 131, 136
 political economy of, 129–130
 presidential nomination, 128–129
 taxation scheme, 129–132

government: American mistrust of, 170 n.24
  constitutional authority and, 176 n.92
"Great Compression," 124
Grewal, David, 173 n.70
guest worker programs, 76–77
Gutmann, Amy, 90

Habermas, Jürgen, 17, 24, 28–30, 147 n.45
Hacker, Jacob, 123, 175 n.84
Hamilton, Charles, 88–89
Handlin, Oscar, 87–88
Hansen, Jonathan, 47
Hastie, William, 82, 110
Haverford Group, 82–83, 92, 109–112
Heritage Foundation report on poverty, 135
Herrenvolk democracy, 43, 63
Hispanic Americans, 60
Hook, Sidney, 87
Hooker, Juliet, 101–102
How Democracies Die (Levitsky and Ziblatt), 141
Human rights, 2–3
Hume, David, 34

identification: citizenship and, 20, 80
  conditions for, 95
  decision-making and, 105–106
  dismissals of, 20, 35–36
  as element of democracy, 15–17, 18–19, 32–33, 35–36, 54–55
  vs. identity, 85
  inclusive forms of, 143
  integration and, 85
  knowledge generating, 105–106
  meaning and practices of, 7–8, 15, 18–19, 32–33, 146 n.13
  necessity of, 108
  promotion of, 9
  scope of, 20, 95
  solidarity and, 32–36, 105–106
  stability and legibility problems, 78–80
identity: contextual aspects of, 94, 165 n.72
  vs. identification, 85
  "inegalitarian ascriptive" tradition of, 52
  racial, 83–84, 94
  separatist accounts of, 92
  shared, 7, 18–19, 96–97
immigrants: aspiration for citizenship, 65–66, 72, 80–81
  assimilation policy, 70–71
  harmonization policy, 71–74
  ideal of membership and, 62–63
  incorporation strategies, 62–63, 71
  laissez-faire approach to, 71–72
  rights and obligations, 70
  utilitarian approach to, 62
immigration: illegal, 61
  open policy, 72
  political debates over, 60
  reasons for, 62
  regulation of, 60–61, 76–77
  as threat to solidarity, 80
  before World War I, 68–69
Immigration Act of 1924, 60–61, 74
Immigration Act of 1965, 60–62
income tax, 130–131, 169 n.17
Indigenous peoples: claims of, 44–46
  common values and, 45–46
  democratic inclusion of, 44–45
  prejudices against, 43–44
  secession and, 45
inequality: debates over, 134, 136–137
  industrialization and, 124
  as political problem, 120, 134, 177 n.111
  project of combating, 136
  social relations and, 118–119
  as state of deprivation, 135
  theory of, 124
integration: assimilation and, 85, 89
  benefits of, 101–102
  choice-based approach to, 95–97
  critics of, 84–86, 88–89, 90–91, 94–95, 100–101
  debates over role of, 87–88
  definition of, 86, 88
  democracy and, 84–85
  identification and, 85
  identity and, 84–85, 88–89, 92
  philosophical defense of, 84–85
  as plausible democratic future, 92
  racial justice and, 94–95, 110
  as route to equality, 86, 112
  shift from desegregation to, 87–88
  strategies for, 86
  temporal paradox, 101–102
  See also racial integration
integration/separation debate, 95–96
Interpreter, The, 70–71
Ivison, Duncan, 46

January 6, 2021 U.S. Capitol attack, 140
Jay, John, 38
Jefferson, Thomas, 31, 40–41, 47, 150 n.22
Jim Crow era, 50–51
Johnson, Lyndon, 60–61, 121
Johnson-Reed Immigration Act of 1924. *See* Immigration Act of 1924
justice: citizens' obligation to pursue, 34
   core elements of, 34–35
   democracy and, 21
   distributive schemes of, 21–22
   scope of, 21
   theory of, 20–21

Kallen, Horace: "Democracy Versus the Melting-Pot," 73
Katz, Michael, 174 n.79, 177 n.108
Katznelson, Ira, 121
Kazin, Michael, 51
Kempton, Murray, 128
Kennedy, John F.: economic policy, 124–125
Kennedy, Randall, 86
Keynesian macroeconomics, 173 n.70, n.71
King, Martin Luther, Jr., 142–143
Kloppenberg, James, 37–38, 51–52
Know-Nothings (American Party):
   conception of American peoplehood, 66
   criticism of, 66–67
   exclusionary policy, 65
   formation of, 64–65
Kruse, Kevin, 121–122
Kukathas, Chandran, 75–76
Kuznets, Simon, 124

Lackey, Michael, 92–94
Lasswell, Harold, 126
Laughlin, Harry H., 72–73
leftist reformism, 51
Levine, Bruce, 65
Levitsky, Steven, 141–142
Levy, Jacob, 33–34
liberal education, 166 n.85
liberal nationalism, 24, 26, 30, 32–33
Lichtenstein, Nelson, 37
limited separation, 166 n.73
Lincoln, Abraham: American national project of, 39, 41, 150 n.16
   on Declaration of Independence, 26–27, 30–31, 41, 142–143
   on democracy, 90
   Gettysburg Address, 40–41, 49
   on immigration, 72
   interpretation of the Civil War, 40–41
   opposition to nativism, 66
   "proposition" of equality, 40–41
   romantic character of, 150 n.16
Lippmann, Walter, 128
Little Rock's Central High School: desegregation of, 120
local communities, 99

macroeconomics discipline, 173 n.71
Madison, James, 38
Maier, Charles, 173 n.70
majority rule, 106–107
market fundamentalism, 123
market naturalism, 120, 131, 132–133, 135–136, 176 n.99
Marshall, Thurgood, 87
McCartin, Joseph, 51
McGhee, Heather, 121
McGreevy, John, 157 n.41
McPherson, James, 38–39, 64–65
Mehrotra, Ajay, 119
membership: arguments for minimizing, 75, 81
   bounded forms of political, 77
   claim of, 59–60
   democracy and, 4, 63–64
   immigration and, 62–63, 76, 81
   interpretations of the meaning of, 62, 80
   problems of, 54
   realization of, 72
   regulation of, 76–77
   restrictions on, 76
   taxation and, 120
   vision of shared, 4
Merry, Michael, 95, 97–100
migrant labor, 159 n.84, n.91
Miller, David, 24–25
Miller, Stephen, 61–62
Montgomery's public parks: closure of, 120–121
Moore, Margaret, 34–35
Müller, Jan-Werner, 24, 28
Myrdal, Gunnar, 87

national community: idea of, 8–9, 47, 52, 119, 122–123

nationalism, 27–28, 48, 52
National Review, 113–114, 129, 134–135
national unity: *vs.* democratic solidarity, 43
nationhood, 26–27
Native Americans, 152 n.40
nativism, 5, 9, 54, 63, 64–65, 67
naturalization, 65–66
neighborly relations: *vs.* civic relations, 108
New Deal, 50–51, 121, 123–124, 173 n.69, n.75
New Left, 51–52
New Nationalism, 113–115
New York Times, 114
norms, 141–142

Obama, Barack: criticism of, 113–114, 134–135, 169 n.11
  on economic inequality, 114–115
  Osawatomie speech, 113–114, 123, 134–135, 168 n.10
  support from Hispanic voters, 60
obligations of citizenship: *vs.* obligations of nationality, 25
oligarchy: ascendance of, 54
  power of, 5
  as replacement of democracy, 9, 53–54, 120
  threat of, 136
O'Neill, Martin, 118–119

Parfit, Derek, 117–118
participation: as element of democracy, 14–15
patriotism, 24, 28
  See also constitutional patriotism
peoplehood, 10, 37–38, 39–40, 47–48, 136
  See also shared peoplehood
Pettit, John, 152 n.40
Pettit, Philip, 45
Pierson, Paul, 123, 175 n.84
Pitkin, Hanna, 19–20, 31–32
Podhoretz, Norman, 87
political economy, 115, 177 n.108
political problems, 16–17, 20, 34–35, 80
political unity, 72–73
political values, 32, 84–85, 94
politics of productivity, 173 n.70
popular sovereignty, 39–40
prioritarianism, 117–119

Progressive thinkers, 50–51, 151 n.32, 174 n.77
public reasoning, 46
Purdy, Jedediah, 189 n.70

racial clustering, 94–96
racial hierarchy, 120–121
racial integration: critiques of, 83–84
  stalled progress of, 54
  See also integration
racial justice theory, 94–96, 112
racial segregation, 89
  See also segregation
Rahman, K. Sabeel, 121–122, 127–128
Rawls, John: *A Theory of Justice*, 20–21, 126–127
Reagan, Ronald, 121–123, 136
Reconstruction, 3, 5–6, 8–9, 26–27, 42–43, 140
Redding, J. Saunders, 82, 92–94
redistributionist liberalism, 126–127
redistributive schemes, 133
Reed, David, 74
Republican National Committee (RNC), 60
Republican Party: conservative shift within, 120–121
Robin, Corey, 141–142
Rodgers, Daniel, 53, 119, 128, 173 n.71
Romney, Mitt, 60
Rondel, David, 118–119
Roosevelt, Franklin D., 125–126, 173 n.75
Roosevelt, Theodore: criticism of, 114
  economic policy of, 114
  endorsement of practical equality, 115
  Osawatomie speech, 113–115
  program of New Nationalism, 113–115
Rorty, Richard, 50–51
Rossiter, Clinton, 129
Rustin, Bayard, 91

Sandel, Michael, 151 n.32
Scanlon, T. M., 118–119
Schambra, William, 122–123
Schlesinger, Arthur, 124
school segregation, 83, 87
Second Reconstruction, 5–6, 9, 87, 139–140
segregation, 83, 97–98
  See also racial segregation
  school segregation
self-deportation policy, 60

self-government, 3
separatism: critique of, 110
　as defensive strategy, 105–106
　pervasive, 97
　in political thought, 91–92
　See also voluntary separation
Sessions, Jeff, 61
Shapiro, Ian, 131
shared culture, 18–19
shared obligations, 25–26
shared peoplehood: establishment of, 149 n.6
　globalization and vision of, 8
　ideal of, 69, 74, 142–143
　notion of, 8–9
　politics of, 52
　public understanding of, 52
Shelby, Tommie, 83–84, 95, 100–101, 105–106
16th Amendment, 130–131
slavery, 1, 8–9, 31, 64–65, 141–142, 150 n.18
Smith, Patrick, 20–21
Smith, Rogers, 52, 142–143
social movements, 51–52
social naturalism, 177 n.109
solidarity: call for multiracial national, 101–102
　defense of, 142
　definition of, 32–33
　democracy and, 6–7, 33, 102–103, 180 n.29
　denied, 35
　diversity and, 53
　erosion of, 9
　fluctuating, 105
　function of, 33
　ideal of good neighborliness and, 103
　identification and, 103, 105–106
　justice and, 34–35
　multiple, 102–103
　political, 104–105
　as precondition to equality, 101–102
　regional, 104
　self-rule and, 34–35
　spatial, 103–105
　theories of, 9, 24, 101–102
　vs. unity, 44
Somers, Margaret, 177 n.109
Song, Sarah, 78–79
sovereignty of American people, 2–3

stagflation, 174 n.79, 175 n.84
Stanley, Sharon, 95, 100–104
state rights, 6, 44, 150 n.18
Stephens, Alexander, 31
Stilz, Anna, 25, 80–81
Stout, Jeffrey, 111
suburban secession, 121–122
Sumner, Charles: anti-Catholic sentiment, 157 n.41
　"Are We a Nation?" speech, 1–3
　criticism of Know-Nothings, 66–67
　on Declaration of Independence, 2, 30–31
　on democracy, 4
　on determining "qualification' of a voter" based on color, 140
　on homogeneity of the United States, 41–42
　on immigration, 72
　on Indigenous policies, 43
　on local self-government, 3
　on nationhood, 26–27, 139–140
　on reception of migrants, 67
　response to nativism, 67
　on State Rights, 2, 44

Taney, Roger, 30–31
taxation: constitutional provision on, 129–131
　democracy and, 131–132
　idea of progressive, 134
　individual freedom and, 129–130, 131–132
　opposition to, 115–117, 120
　politics of, 120
　progressive, 129–130
　public attitude to, 135–136
　racialized perceptions and, 121
Taylor, Charles, 14–15, 79–80
technocracy, 127–128, 174 n.77
temporal continuity of democratic association, 22–23
"Third Reconstruction," 140
13th Amendment, 1, 41–42
Tilden, Samuel, 106–107
Tonkin Gulf Resolution, 51
Trump, Donald, 60–62
Tsai, Robert, 60–61
Ture, Kwame, 88–89
tyranny of the majority, 17

unemployment, 134–135, 173 n.71
United States: boundary-drawing, 26
  crisis of the union, 39
  debates over poverty, 135
  declarations of independence, 37–38
  democratization of, 4, 37, 50–51, 64–65
  descent into "constitutional rot," 141–142
  disaggregation of society, 119
  diversity, 53, 164 n.59
  divides over slavery, 64–65
  economic development, 38–39, 124–125, 175 n. 84
  far right movement, 180 n.29
  financial crisis, 121
  immigration policy, 61–62, 79–80
  myths about, 50
  nationalist movement, 4, 52
  nation-building, 26–27, 38–39
  political development, 64
  population growth, 38–39
  prediction of the future of, 74
  progressive movements, 51–52
  proposal of partitioning of, 91
  racial composition, 74
  radical left, 51–52
  reactionary years, 50–51
  rivalry between nation and states, 41–42
  shared prosperity, 126
  strategies of incorporation, 71
  territory, 38–39
  top decile's share of income, 123–124
  "Unite the Right" rally in Charlottesville, Virginia, 140
unity: *vs.* solidarity, 44
U.S. Constitution: amendments, 1, 4–5, 26–27, 41–43, 130–131
  debates over, 29–30, 38
  on equality of men, 40–41
  as liberty document, 147 n.51
  ratification of, 37–38
U.S. Immigration and Customs Enforcement (ICE), 59–60
U.S. Supreme Court: *Dred Scott v. Sandford* ruling, 4–5
  ruling on desegregation of public schools, 86

Valadez, Jorge, 76–77
Valls, Andrew, 86, 94–96
Viereck, Peter, 129
voluntary separation, 97–98, 99–100
  See also separatism
Voting Rights Act, 60–61

wage equality, 124
Wallace, Phyllis A., 82
Wall Street Journal, 113–114
Walzer, Michael, 21–22, 145 n.25, 159 n.84
War on Poverty, 126
Warren, Justice, 83
Weaver, Robert C., 82, 109
Webster, Daniel, 39
Whig Party, 64–65
White, Richard, 41–42
white supremacists, 87
Whitman, Walt, 29, 35, 49, 74, 138–139
Whitney, Thomas R., 67
  A Defence of the American Policy, 65–66
Wills, Garry, 40–41
Wise, Stephen S., 73–74
Woodward, C. Vann, 87
workmanship ideal, 131

Yack, Bernard, 79–80

Ziblatt, Daniel, 141–142